S0-BMA-473

MAKING CRIME COUNT

Official statistics are one of the most important sources of knowledge about crime and the criminal-justice system. Yet little is known about the inner workings of the institutions that produce these numbers. In this groundbreaking study, Kevin D. Haggerty sheds light on the processes involved in the gathering and disseminating of crime statistics through an empirical examination of the Canadian Centre for Justice Statistics (CCJS), the branch of Statistics Canada responsible for producing data on the criminal-justice system.

Making Crime Count details how the availability of criminal-justice statistics has fostered a distinctive approach to the governance of crime and criminal justice. What has emerged is a form of actuarial justice whereby crime is increasingly understood as a statistical probability, rather than a moral failing. At the same time, statistics render criminal-justice organizations amenable to governmental strategies that aim to manage the system itself.

Using contemporary work in the sociology of science as a frame, Haggerty explores the means by which the CCJS has been able to produce its statistics. The emphasis is on the extra-scientific factors involved in this process, the complex knowledge networks that must be aligned between assorted elements and institutions, and, specifically, the continual negotiations between CCJS employees and the police over how to secure data for the 'uniform crime report' survey. The book's conclusions accentuate the need for anyone studying governance to consider the politics and processes of governmental knowledge production.

KEVIN D. HAGGERTY is Professor of Sociology at the University of Alberta.

AUGUSTANA UNIVERSITY COLLEGE
LIBRARY

KEVIN D. HAGGERTY

Making Crime Count

UNIVERSITY OF TORONTO PRESS
Toronto Buffalo London

© University of Toronto Press Incorporated 2001
Toronto Buffalo London
Printed in Canada

ISBN 0-8020-4809-9 (cloth)
ISBN 0-8020-8348-X (paper)

Printed on acid-free paper

Canadian Cataloguing in Publication Data

Haggerty, Kevin D.
  Making crime count

  Includes bibliographical references and index.
  ISBN 0-8020-4809-9 (bound)   ISBN 0-8020-8348-X (pbk.)

  1. Canadian Centre for Justice Statistics.   2. Criminal statistics – Canada.
  I. Title.

HV6806.H33 2000   353.43   C00-932097-0

This book has been published with the help of a grant from the Humanities
and Social Sciences Federation of Canada, using funds provided by the Social
Sciences and Humanities Research Council of Canada.

The University of Toronto Press acknowledges the financial assistance to its
publishing program of the Canada Council for the Arts and the Ontario Arts
Council.

University of Toronto Press acknowledges the financial support for its publishing activities of the Government of Canada through the Book Publishing
Industry Development Program (BPIDP).

Contents

AUGUSTANA UNIVERSITY COLLEGE
LIBRARY

Acknowledgments

This book uses the concept of a 'knowledge network' to examine how the Canadian Centre for Justice Statistics produces its numbers on crime and criminal justice. In conducting this research and writing the book I have relied upon my own form of 'knowledge network.' My only regret is that I am restricted to a small space in which to acknowledge the many people who made this work possible.

I would immediately like to thank the staff at the Canadian Centre for Justice Statistics. Individuals affiliated with the Centre went out of their way to make my research both productive and enjoyable. Those I interviewed were generous with their time and perceptive in their insights.

This research was financially assisted by the Social Sciences and Humanities Research Council of Canada, Award #752-94-1861, and by a University of British Columbia Graduate Scholarship. When funds were tight, the 'Bank of Haggerty' generously assisted and, as always, provided me with their love and support.

I owe a deep debt of gratitude to Brenda Began, Mirelle Cohen, Anthony Doob, Sara Eliesen, Rosemary Gartner, Joy Horan, Chantelle Marlor, Céline Q. Mauboulès, and Lili Yee, who commented on chapter drafts or provided other forms of assistance.

Other individuals deserve special mention. The comments, criticisms, and encouragement from Paul Rock, Tom Kemple, and Neil Guppy have made my arguments tighter and more comprehensible. Aaron Doyle's quiet confidence in my scholarly abilities has been tremendously empowering. Dean Barry has been unbelievably patient and generous with his assistance, particularly in matters related to computers. I have been both enlightened and reinvigorated by the many hours I have spent with Mike Pollex talking about the power and importance of ideas. Over the past decade Richard Ericson has become my great friend and mentor. If there is any merit to the arguments in this study, they can be attributed to his influence on my life and my work.

Despite her initial reservations about my distinctively Torontonian attitude, Margaret Baskette was a kind and patient guide through the complexities of the University of British Columbia's administrative apparatus. The staff at the inter-library loans offices at both the University of British Columbia and the University of Toronto were invaluable in filling my idiosyncratic requests for material.

It was again a pleasure to work with the University of Toronto Press. Virgil Duff continues to be a superb editor, and John St James's copy-editing transformed a text that starkly revealed my grammatical inadequacies into something that I am proud to exhibit.

Finally, I dedicate this work to Karen Lavoie. To the bewilderment of everyone but she and I, Karen continues to be the cornerstone of my life.

MAKING CRIME COUNT

Introduction

When you can measure what you are speaking about and express it in numbers you know something about it, but when you cannot express it in numbers, your knowledge is of a meagre and unsatisfactory kind; it may be the beginning of knowledge, but you have scarcely in your thoughts, advanced to the state of *science*, whatever the matter may be.

Sir William Thomson, Lord Kelvin (1889: 73)

To 'make crime count' involves transforming crime and the criminal-justice system into something that can be counted. Discussions about criminal justice frequently involve an exchange of statistical trends, rates, and indices. These often draw us into apparently irresolvable debates over the meaning of these indicators. This crush of numbers neglects the fact that the statistics are themselves a social accomplishment, a product of institutional regimes and processes. To date, the organizations that make crime count have not been greatly scrutinized by sociologists or criminologists. Such neglect is especially striking given how important such statistics are to public discourse, academic inquiry, and governmental practice.

Certainly, official criminal-justice statistics have not been completely ignored. Nothing could be further from the truth: official crime statistics, exemplified by those indicators on crime and justice produced by Statistics Canada, the British Home Office, and the U.S. Department of Justice, are a mainstay of several sociological and criminological enterprises. Analysts routinely dissect the statistical trends documented by these agencies. For such authors, the numbers serve as approximations of events in the real world. Still others have called the representativeness of official statistics into question, emphasizing diverse methodological and theoretical reasons why the positivist trust in the veracity of official statistics is unwarranted.

A third approach to the study of official crime statistics follows from Sir Leon Radzinowicz's pithy observation that 'crime statistics are like French bathing suits: what they reveal is highly suggestive but what they hide is vital.' Both the positivist and critical approaches to official statistics fail to appreciate the organizational routines that make these statistics possible. The constructionist approach employed in this study focuses on the extra-scientific processes involved in the production of official criminal-justice statistics and the social processes employed to ensure their truth or accuracy.

What follows is a constructionist examination of some of the background processes involved in producing official numbers on crime and deviance. While others have proclaimed that official criminal-justice statistics are 'social constructions,' this is often a shorthand dismissal of the value of a particular set of numbers with which an individual disagrees. In contrast, I take it to be the point of social-constructionist analysis to explore in detail the social and historically specific *means* by which truths are produced, rather than being a simple rhetorical device to slight the value or utility of a particular form of knowledge. To accomplish this goal I studied the Canadian Centre for Justice Statistics (CCJS), which is the sub-component of Statistics Canada responsible for producing Canada's national numbers on crime and criminal justice.

Philosopher Ian Hacking suggests that his historical studies of nineteenth-century European population statistics constitute the 'dullest of subjects' (1986: 222). If we grant them this dubious distinction, surely a study of a contemporary statistical institution would come a close second. Readers accustomed to the 'nuts, sluts, and perverts' of traditional criminology and the sociology of deviance are not likely to find much immediate visceral appeal in a study of statistical institutions. Such an aversion ignores both the sociological significance and peculiar attractions of such institutions. Much of what we know about the police, courts, and correctional institutions is a result of the work of official statistical agencies. Any effort that sheds light on how official criminal-justice statistics are produced will inevitably have repercussions on how we understand these more conventional components of the criminal-justice system. The CCJS and comparable organizations are also engaging objects of study in their own right. Statistical institutions occasionally become embroiled in public controversies and are permeated by their own politics of truth. Studying them allows us to reflect upon a constellation of theoretical concerns, including the nature of power, the production of authorized truths, the creation of subjectivities, the authority of official classifications, and techniques of governance.

This study is informed by the theorizing prompted by Michel Foucault's (1991) suggestive observations on 'governmentality' (see Rose and Miller 1992; Burchell, Gordon, and Miller 1991; Barry, Osborne, and Rose 1996). Statistical knowledges play a prominent role in practices of liberal governance. Before any particular object can be governed, its distinctive form, inclinations, and tendencies must first be known. Aggregate statistics of the population are one of the most useful ways to understand the population, and, as a result, statistical knowledges are now a key condition of possibility for governance. A massive statistical enterprise has therefore been established to monitor social change and chart transformations brought about through reform initiatives.

Despite the fact that many authors acknowledge the importance of statistics to practices of governance (Rose 1999; Hunt and Wickham 1994; Rose and Miller 1992), little attention has been directed at their institutional production. The Centre has been routinely overlooked by academics. Canada's leading introductory textbook on criminal justice (Griffiths and Verdun-Jones 1994) only mentions the Centre in one footnote as a source for data about crime trends – this despite the fact that the text frequently refers to the Centre's numbers to describe the contours of the criminal-justice system. This neglect is indicative of the general academic inclination to view statistical institutions more as sources of data than as objects deserving investigation.

National statistics are the closest thing to a set of official facts in criminal justice. As the author of these facts for Canada, the Centre implicitly assumes the mantle of science. This study was partially animated by a curiosity about this quasi-scientific status of official statistics. Consequently, the CCJS is approached as being akin to a scientific institution or laboratory involved in the production of statistical truths. Acknowledging this 'family resemblance' allows us to examine the Centre through the lens(es) offered by the sociology of science. Authors writing in this tradition have argued that the universal truths of science are actually highly localized accomplishments, achieved through the use of a host of stereotypically scientific as well as extra-scientific resources and procedures. The following pages concentrate on extra-scientific facets of the production of statistical knowledge. In particular, I draw from actor-network theory, as exemplified by the work of Latour (1999, 1987), Callon (1986), and Law (1987), to document how the Centre's production of statistical truths is related to its ability to fashion a complex knowledge network comprising a heterogeneous mixture of component parts. A series of contingent alliances between individuals, technologies, and institutions have been established in and around the Centre, and it is these linkages that allow for the collection and dissemination of numbers on crime and criminal justice. Several specific practices from within the Centre's broader knowledge network are singled out for attention. These include the development of classifications of people, events, and processes, political negotiations, standardization, and rhetoric, which all play a part in the construction of the Centre's truths.

Studying Statistical Institutions

The quote from Lord Kelvin at the head of this chapter is one of the most famous pronouncements on the role of quantification in science. His admonition to quantify has a peculiar relationship to this study. On the one hand, the importance of quantification to both the physical and social sciences is undeniable. Numbers are a powerful technology of objectification, providing a common language to communicate about vastly different phenomena. It is this power that makes reflection on the way that statistics are produced all the more essential. That said, I do not follow Lord Kelvin's admonition to quantify, but employ a methodological mix of focused interviews, participant observation, and document analysis to understand the operations of the CCJS. Consequently, if we are to apply Lord Kelvin's restricted vision of knowledge production to the study at hand, we can only conclude that the knowledge produced here is of a 'meagre and unsatisfactory kind.' It is a 'beginning of knowledge,' and a beginning that is rife with curious paradoxes. Qualitative methods are used to explore how crime and criminal justice are quantified. The following pages are strikingly devoid of statistics, concentrating instead on the human and organizational elements involved in the production of such numbers. Finally, this study is curious by virtue of the fact that it is subject to all of the ironic and reflexive paradoxes inherent in an enterprise that purports to produce knowledge about knowledge production.

Interviews were conducted from June to October of 1996. During that time I conducted full-time research out of an office provided to me by the CCJS. Many of the events, classifications, and surveys mentioned in this book are specific to that period or occurred in the Centre's recent past. As a result, respondents at times discuss surveys that may have subsequently been abandoned, classifications that have been significantly revised, and organizational structures that have mutated. While the specifics of such changes are important to understand the Centre and the knowledge it produces, they do not detract from the larger picture being painted by this study, as the emphasis here is on the general *processes* at work in the production of criminal-justice statistics. While some of the specifics may change, the processes studied remain consistent.

Readers will find that the most immediately apparent data source is the verbatim quotes taken from taped interviews with individuals associated with the Centre. Seventy-nine interviews were conducted with a total of sixty-three individuals. As table 1 indicates, the majority of interviewees were employees of the CCJS, and the largest grouping of 'analysts and other personnel' consists of an array of program managers, statistical officers, heads of operations, program chiefs, technical officers, survey managers, and systems analysts, to name a few job designations. Respondents were assured of their confidentiality and are not personally identified in the text. Some respondents also requested that I not specifically name certain organizations or jurisdictions, and these requests have been honoured.

Working at the Centre allowed me to augment interviews with informal conversations. It also provided the opportunity to observe participants, and to appreciate the formal and informal hierarchy within the Centre, its work routines, and the personalities of many of its staff. However, the specifics of some of the tasks accomplished by Centre personnel occasionally made traditional approaches to participant observation difficult. Much of an analyst's work, for example, is not conducive to participant observation, as it often involves telephone conversations or solitary work in front of a computer screen.

The third methodological prong of this analysis involved accumulating and analysing a host of Centre documents. These included official publications as well as various manuals, reviews, organizational charts, internal evaluations, minutes of meetings, newspaper-clipping files, and formal and informal correspondence. One of the most beneficial resources was the detailed summaries of the meetings of the

TABLE 1
Individuals interviewed by occupation

	N	%
Canadian Centre for Justice Statistics		
Executive director	1	1.6
Chiefs of program areas	4	6.3
Senior analysts	7	11.1
Analysts & other personnel	19	30.2
Information officers	3	4.8
Marketing officer	1	1.6
Technical assistance personnel	4	6.3
Statistics Canada		
Senior administrator	1	1.6
Senior methodologist	1	1.6
Program evaluator	1	1.6
Justice Initiative		
Deputy ministers	3	4.8
Liaison officers	4	6.3
Federal Department of Justice	4	6.3
Police statistical personnel	3	4.8
Journalists	2	3.2
Academics	3	4.8
Private software developers	2	3.2
Total	63	100

two committees that oversee the Centre: the Justice Information Council and the Liaison Officers Committee. Given that all such documents are organizational accomplishments that can mask as much as they reveal, respondents were frequently asked to comment on, and provide background to, these publications.

Any study of a single organization will face the question whether its findings can be generalized to other settings. Because there has been somewhat of a sociological neglect of these institutions, this remains an empirical question to be addressed in the due course of time. However, I anticipate that the general processes documented in this study are common to other statistical institutions. Organizations that employ a similar 'hunting and gathering' methodology to accumulate their data from the operational systems of other organizations must build networks that include standardized classifications, inscriptions, and micro-politics as documented in the following pages. Such processes are apt to be at work irrespective of whether the organization in question is another component of Statistics Canada, the United Nations, or the registrar's office of your local university.

This research focuses on the Centre's knowledge-production regime and, consequently, it produces an image that is biased towards how Centre staff conceive of how they accomplish their mandate. They ascribe interests and agendas to various individuals and institutions who might question or resent these imputations. However, for the purposes of this study, the question of whether such groups were 'really' trying to accomplish X, or were 'truly' motivated by Y, is of no great methodological significance. Such beliefs become real by virtue of their consequences, as Centre staff work to negate or capitalize on how they understand the desires, inclinations, and agendas of others.

The Centre produces numerous surveys and studies. Although many of these studies are mentioned in this inquiry, I refer most frequently to their 'uniform crime reports' (UCR). This emphasis was perhaps unavoidable given the fact that this is the Centre's flagship survey. Consequently, many of respondents who worked in a variety of different program areas tended to provide examples and anecdotes drawn from the uniform crime reports. Again, while the specifics may differ, many of the same processes documented in relation to the UCR pertain to the Centre's other surveys.

While official statistics about crime and criminal justice are a mainstay of both sociology and criminology, Dorothy Smith (1990: 54) correctly emphasizes that 'the social facts with which we work are constituted prior to our examination by processes of which we know little.' Consequently, this inquiry is partially intended to prompt reflection on the extra-scientific means by which some of our most rudimentary sociological and criminological facts arrive on our desks pre-constructed. In so doing, it emphasizes that such facts exist not because of their academic importance, but because they hold out the promise of more rational and effective governmental programming. Authors writing on governmentality have accentuated the distinct ways in which the art of governance has been conceived across different historical periods. This investigation augments such accounts by exploring the social processes involved in the production and legitimization of an important form of governmental knowledge.

Chapter Outline

The Canadian Centre for Justice Statistics is introduced in chapter 1, which commences with a discussion of its early history and overview of its current organizational structure. As the ensuing chapters demonstrate, to understand the Centre's knowledge production regime we must appreciate how it intersects with other organizations. Particular attention is paid to the Centre's relationship with its jurisdictional partners, as they are the main source for most of the Centre's data, and play a key role in shaping the distinctive form of politics at the Centre.

In the 1960s and 1970s official statistics were the topic of serious sociological discussion, prompting a number of heated exchanges. These debates pitted positivists against the then ascendant interpretive sociologists. Crime statistics played a central role in these discussions, which often focused on the methodological limitations and philosophical presumptions of official data. The second half of chapter 1 examines these debates, suggesting that some of the issues raised continue to be theoretically salient. The chapter concludes with an overview of some of the continuing methodological questions about the accuracy of official crime statistics.

Chapter 2 provides the theoretical backdrop to the study. It explores the role that the Centre and comparable organizations play in practices of governance. The role of classifications in producing official statistics is highlighted, as these establish the demarcations on which liberal rationalities of governance rest. These reflections on governance, statistics, and classification then turn to contemporary developments in criminal justice. This involves a discussion of how statistical knowledge has fostered distinctive rationalities and technologies of governance that increasingly employ actuarial techniques to manage both individuals and systems. In order for the Centre's knowledge to be of use for governmental practice, it must be accepted as true by relevant audiences. The second half of chapter 2 concentrates on the question of truth, arguing that truth is a social accomplishment, one that involves efforts to persuade relevant audiences of the veracity of different claims through a host of scientific and extra-scientific strategies. Such processes are most clearly articulated in the work of authors working under the heading of 'actor-network theory.' This theory accentuates how scientific claims are made stronger (and hence more truthful) to the degree that they successfully link together a host of 'actants' into a larger whole. Operating from a centre of calculation, scientists must structure how a host of human, technological, and organizational elements operate to ensure the routine production of scientific knowledge.

The insights of actor-network theorists run throughout this study, with the most explicit attempt to apply their approach to the CCJS occurring in chapter 3. There the Centre's efforts to construct a knowledge network specific to the uniform crime reports are examined in detail. Particular attention is paid to the Centre's ongoing efforts to impute preferred identities to police officers and organizations and to subsequently control the faithful execution of these roles. The police are a particularly appropriate focus for such an inquiry because their adoption of the Centre's preferred identities has at times proved to be problematic. Concentrating on the police, therefore, allows us to emphasize the fact that the production of a knowledge network is an ongoing process, one that is always contingent on the behaviour of myriad component parts.

Chapter 4 is a study of classificatory politics in action. It concentrates on one of the most pervasive, but nonetheless contentious, ways of classifying people: by their race or ethnicity. Such classificatory systems are connected to racialized forms of governance, as it is on the basis of the identity categories established in myriad surveys and studies that governmental strategies will ultimately operate. The chapter charts the evolution of the Centre's controversial 1990 proposal to collect data on the race or ethnicity of an accused. The arguments for and against such an endeavour are explored, with the understanding that the decision about whether to collect such data was related to how different groups conceived of the pragmatic utility or dangers represented by racial numbers. The latter half of the chapter documents a transition in the Centre's efforts to collect racialized data away from a universal attempt to document 'race' towards an attempt to collect data on a specific racial subset: Canadian Aboriginals. The emphasis here is on detailing the negotiated and political character of official identity categories. This section includes an overview of some of the difficulties Centre personnel had in discerning which representatives to consult in developing such classifications, and of their efforts to convince often unreceptive audiences of the importance of this type of data. The chapter thereby details how what are often comparatively private scientific/bureaucratic decisions about the specifics of classification can become politicized.

Politics is a recurrent theme in this study, from the micro-politics of network building to the public controversies over race/crime classifications. Chapter 5 takes up this topic in greater detail in order to document how, despite the Centre's well-founded desire to foster public trust by remaining apolitical, its enterprise is inevitably imbued with political consequences and considerations. In the Centre's day-to-day routines, politics often assumes the form of subtle (and sometimes less subtle) attempts to further the interests of particular organizations and jurisdictions. This process has involved the occasional attempt to suppress some of the Centre's studies as well as struggles over the ownership of the Centre's data and the determination of how measurement devices should be standardized. If they are to produce valid and useful knowledge, Centre staff must navigate their way through such micro-politics while maintaining the impression that they stand above partisan politics. The chapter concludes with a discussion of some of the broader political consequences of the public availability of the Centre's data – in particular, how aggregate crime data has been instrumental in fostering distinctive forms of criminal-justice discourse.

In order for the Centre's knowledge to influence public discourse, it must move outside the halls of government into the public domain. Chapter 6 examines some of the processes involved in disseminating the Centre's knowledge. It concentrates on its main publication, the *Juristat*, in order to document how institutional routines and interests can shape the form and content of Centre publications. The final form assumed by these publications is influenced by a desire not just to communicate knowledge, but to do so in a manner that ensures the Centre's claims will be accepted. This aim invests the style of presentation with epistemological importance. One of the main audiences for this knowledge, and a vital conduit to wider public audiences, is the media. The chapter examines the relations between the Centre and the media, specifically focusing on the question of whether the Centre has been able to prospectively control the media, tying them into the Centre's extended knowledge network and making them the passive reproducers of the Centre's truths.

A brief concluding chapter suggests how this study revises the dominant approaches to the study of governance. It calls for a renewed emphasis on the state, particularly on the state's abilities to produce governmental knowledge. This emphasis on knowledge production leads us to the necessity of considering more explicitly political factors as background elements to governance, a focus that will itself entail overcoming a residual hostility to more realist forms of analysis that pervades the governmentality literature.

The final comments of the study move beyond the confines of the Centre in order to speculate on the potential future uses of official statistical knowledge about crime and criminal justice. This question arises in the context of a generalized society-wide knowledge explosion, and of the political embrace of more sensational forms of criminal-justice policy. Such developments raise the spectre that the idealized rational use of official statistics may increasingly be supplanted by their use in predominantly rhetorical and symbolic displays.

1

The Canadian Centre for Justice Statistics: The Organization and Critique of Crime Statistics

Nothing is more anonymous than the bureaucracy of the statisticians.

Ian Hacking (1991: 193)

Outside of a small circle of individuals, very few people are aware of how the Canadian Centre for Justice Statistics (CCJS) operates. That said, the type of knowledge it produces has been subjected to intense sociological scrutiny. This chapter introduces the CCJS and outlines some of the limitations that have been identified with official crime statistics. The Centre's organizational structure, personnel, and early history are first outlined, as these play an important part in structuring the types of knowledge that the Centre produces and inform its political dynamics. The specifics of its main reporting vehicle, the Uniform Crime Reports (UCR), is then detailed. This survey is singled out because it is the Centre's flagship, and thus many interviewees drew examples and anecdotes from the crime reports. Furthermore, crime statistics of the type produced by the UCR have been the subject of considerable sociological reflection. Some of these debates on the value of 'official statistics' are therefore analysed here. The chapter concludes with an extended discussion of some of the potential non-crime factors that can shape official crime statistics. Cumulatively, this overview of the theoretical critiques of crime statistics, and of the practical limitations of such numbers, provides insights into the epistemological environment in which Centre employees work. Chapter 3 details some of the network-building processes that they employ in the hope of placating or silencing their critics.

The Canadian Centre for Justice Statistics

The CCJS was created in response to demands by criminal-justice practitioners and politicians in the 1970s for more reliable and comprehensive criminal-justice statistics. Before the Centre's formation in 1981
some criminal-justice statistics were collected out of the Justice Statistics Division of the Dominion Bureau of Statistics (now Statistics
Canada). However, these statistics were not comprehensive and were
often incompatible across different jurisdictions. In 1971 the federal
departments responsible for justice policy and administration met to
discuss possible ways to improve this data. While the initial goal of
this endeavour was to meet the federal government's expanding demand for statistics, it quickly became apparent that the provinces had
comparable needs.

In 1974 a Federal/Provincial Advisory Committee on Justice Information and Statistics was formed to identify and help resolve common statistical problems in criminal justice. While it was widely believed that a new organizational framework was needed to collect
such statistics, agreement on the precise composition and structure of
such an agency proved difficult. Eight years of meetings and political
discussion ensued before a consensus was ultimately reached. The
National Project on Resource Co-ordination (NPRC 1980) investigated
this issue, and recommended that a new agency be established as a
'satellite' of Statistics Canada. The specifics of how this would work in
practice were set out by the Implementation Work Group (IWG 1981),
which defined the proposed centre's structure, mandate, and funding.
Many saw this proposal as a compromise solution that struck a middle
ground between those who wanted an independent agency and those
who thought it best to have an agency entirely under the mantle of
Statistics Canada.

To appreciate the operational dynamics of the CCJS and its importance to the governance of the criminal-justice system, some knowledge of its legal, political, and geographical context is required. The
Centre produces criminal-justice statistics for a nation with a relatively small population spread across a massive land mass and represented by a federation of provinces. Approximately 28 million individuals populate Canada's 10 million square kilometres, making it the
second largest country in the world by area. By way of comparison,
the United States has 258 million individuals in its 9.5 million square

kilometres and Great Britain (including England, Scotland, and Wales) has a population of approximately 56 million people contained in only 229,000 square km. One can appreciate the sheer enormity of Canada when we realize that all of Scotland could fit into Lake Superior's 82,000-km^2 surface area.

Canada is a federation of ten provinces and three territories, with the seat of national government residing in Ottawa. As in any federation, there is a legal separation of powers between the provinces and the federal government. In relation to criminal justice, these divisions are quite complex. The Constitution Act of 1867 gives the federal parliament exclusive authority to enact criminal laws and procedures. Parliament is also responsible for offenders sentenced to serve more than two years in custody. The provinces have jurisdiction over the administration of justice within their territory and must maintain a system of provincial courts. Local policing is also a provincial responsibility, but most provinces contract with the federal Royal Canadian Mounted Police (RCMP) for their provincial policing service. Each province maintains a department dedicated to its criminal-justice responsibilities. Despite the extensive involvement of the federal government in formulating criminal legislation, policing, and corrections, no single coordinating agency has the mandate to establish uniform operating guidelines and procedures for criminal-justice agencies and personnel. As a result, the Canadian criminal-justice system is characterized by considerable diversity and variability, rather than uniformity, in its operations.

The power of taxation is primarily vested in the federal government. The provinces therefore rely on funds from the federal government in the form of transfer payments or cost-sharing agreements in order to execute their criminal-justice responsibilities. This funding arrangement has fostered ongoing tensions between the two levels of government. In fact, federal/provincial relations are often a sensitive political area, exacerbated by secessionist aspirations in the province of Québec and repeated complaints by other provinces that they are alienated from federal politics. Aspects of this federal/provincial division are reproduced in the organizational structure of the CCJS, and several parts of this study detail how tensions between these two levels of government inform the day-to-day routines of producing justice statistics.

The nation's large size, combined with program diversity across provincial boundaries and within provincial ministries, makes it difficult for individuals to have detailed first-hand knowledge of how different criminal-justice program areas operate across the country. This geographical factor heightens the importance of national statistics. Given this deterrent for researchers of spending lengthy periods of time in the provinces to gain an understanding of provincial criminal-justice programs, official statistics effectively bring these dispersed areas to the nation's capital, or to other far-flung locations. The statistics produced by the CCJS allow local organizational routines and procedures to be scrutinized in sites far from their source of origin.

The Centre exists in a broader criminal-justice context. However, any attempt to detail the specifics of this context immediately introduces a considerable degree of organizational self-referentiality into the discussion. This is because much of what we know about the nuts and bolts of the nation's criminal-justice system is itself derived from the work of the CCJS. Any competent reference librarian will tell you that the primary source for information about the dimensions and operation of the Canadian criminal-justice system is the Centre's various publications. Among the many indicators found in its reports are the provincial incarceration rate, the distribution of cases heard in youth court, the rate of persons charged with impaired driving, and the homicide rate. Hence, the Centre operates in a criminal-justice context that is largely of its own creation, a feat it accomplishes by fostering common national data definitions and standardized accounting procedures. Through such efforts, the Centre helps create the quantitative universe of national criminal-justice statistics.

The Centre began operations in 1981 as the primary component of the broader 'Justice Initiative' that comprises the federal and provincial departments with justice responsibility. The responsibility for Canada's system of justice statistics is shared between twenty-four federal, provincial, and territorial government departments, with Statistics Canada having lead responsibility. The Justice Information Council (JIC), chaired by Canada's Deputy Minister of Justice, is the governing body of the Initiative. The JIC consists of the Chief Statistician of Canada and all federal, provincial, and territorial deputy ministers with justice responsibilities. It is the Centre's senior policy body responsible for budget reviews, work-plan approval, and the establishment of programs and priorities. The Liaison Officers Committee (LOC), chaired by a member of the JIC, is the Centre's other major governing body. The LOC consists of one departmental official appointed by each member of the JIC and a representative of the Canadian Association of

Chiefs of Police. This group monitors the Centre's operations, approves its plans, and identifies problem areas. The LOC has tended to have a more hands-on relationship with the Centre than the JIC.

The Centre is jointly funded by Statistics Canada, the Department of Justice and the federal Solicitor General. In 1997/98, it had a budget of $5.7 million. Although it is funded from federal sources, the Centre's jurisdictional partners provide its policy direction and supervision. Affiliation with Statistics Canada not only provides the Centre with financial resources, but also allows it to benefit from that agency's infrastructure, training, and internation reputation. It also means that the CCJS is subject to many of the rules and procedures concerning privacy and data handling instituted by the parent organization. While it occupies an entire floor of a Statistics Canada building in Ottawa, the Centre has tentacles that run throughout Canada's justice system.

Organizational charts are notoriously dry fare. They schematically depict relations between people and institutions that invariably have a more informal and ad hoc quality. The following chapters attach flesh to the skeletal connections depicted in figure 1, but at this juncture it is worth taking a moment to reflect on the broad contours of the Justice Initiative and the Centre as displayed in this diagram. Particularly worth reiterating is the fact that the Centre, though operated out of a federal institution, is overseen by representatives from the provinces and draws much of its data from provincial jurisdictions. The following chapters accentuate the implications of these relations for the types of knowledge the Centre does and does not produce.

The CCJS is managed by an executive director who is responsible for ensuring that the Centre meets its mandate to (1) collect and present national justice statistics; (2) conduct special in-depth studies to inform the public on high-priority national justice issues; and (3) assist local jurisdictions in implementing information systems that contribute to the development of national justice statistics. The Centre is divided into three program branches that work to help fulfil these goals. The Technical Assistance Directorate (TAD) encourages local agencies to develop information systems by providing them with financial resources and technical expertise. Integration and Analysis is responsible for special in-depth studies, and Statistics and Information is primarily involved in developing and maintaining a number of programs of core national statistics.

The Statistics and Information Directorate is further divided into focused program areas for policing, courts, and corrections. Each area

Figure 1 Justice Initiative and Canadian Centre for Justice Statistics (CCJS)

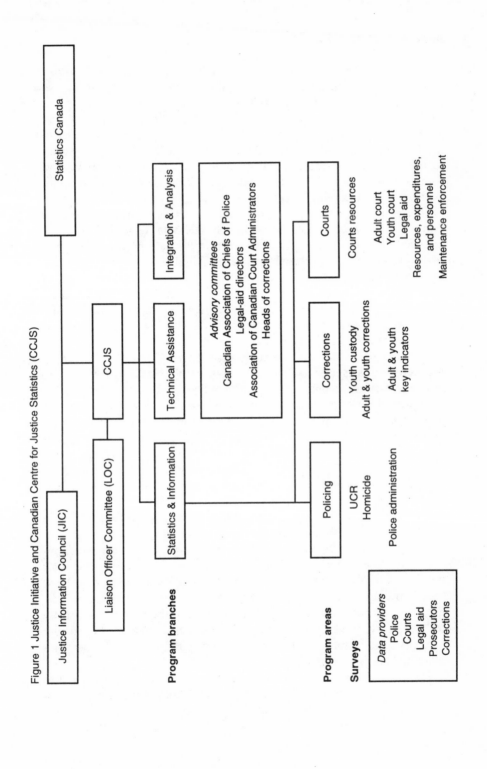

is responsible for a special set of statistical products. The Centre's main surveys include the uniform crime reporting (UCR) survey; revised uniform crime reporting (UCRII) survey; homicide survey; prosecutions survey; legal-aid survey; adult criminal-court survey (ACCS); youth-court survey (YCS); courts resources, expenditures, and personnel (REP) survey; adult corrections survey (ACS); adult and youth corrections key indicator report (A-KIR) survey; youth custody and community services (YCCS) survey; and adult-corrections resources, expenditures, and personnel (REP) survey.

These surveys are augmented by special studies conducted by the Centre's Integration and Analysis branch. The data collected from these different sources are roughly divided into (1) data on the number of cases processed, (2) personal and case-related data, (3) resource, expenditure, and personnel data, and (4) qualitative descriptions of policies and program delivery. While the Centre's mandate includes collecting data on matters of civil law as well as undertaking qualitative studies, its efforts have focused on developing quantitative surveys of matters related to criminal justice.

Two important terminological clarifications are in order. First, while the Centre is a 'statistical' organization, its statistical operations are quite distinctive. Statisticians typically approach the term 'statistics' as a numerical description of a set of numbers. Statistical operations are usually performed on numbers derived from a sample of a larger population. By contrast, the Centre does not employ a traditional sampling methodology, but instead works to acquire total coverage for its different surveys. It also does not perform statistical analysis of its data, but simply sums and reports changes pertaining to various criminal-justice processes.

The second terminological clarification concerns the Centre's habit of referring to its products as 'surveys,' which might cause some confusion given that 'surveys' are popularly associated with questionnaires aimed at individuals. The Centre's surveys, however, draw their data from different administrative systems in the jurisdictions. How they acquire these data varies across program areas and provinces. For example, most provincial police forces send their statistics directly to the Centre, but in some provinces a statistical clearing house first receives data from all of the local agencies, then forwards the combined numbers to the Centre.

The Centre's close relationship with the jurisdictions is apparent in the institutionalized place of advisory committees that comprise jurisdictional representatives who provide operational advice to the Centre's program managers. These include representatives from the Association of Canadian Court Administrators, the Canadian Association of Chiefs of Police, the heads of corrections, and the directors of legal aid.

Approximately 70 people work out of the Centre, and at times this number has been as high as 130. While these individuals have assorted educational backgrounds, most have university degrees in the social sciences or, in the Technical Assistance Directorate, computer sciences. One striking characteristic of the staff is that although many are well trained in procedures for handling and manipulating data, they are *not* statisticians. Rather than employ in-house statistical experts, the Centre draws from the methodological and statistical expertise available through Statistics Canada. Most Centre staff members have little experience working 'on the ground' with police, the courts, or corrections. While the Centre has occasionally acquired staff who have been transferred from the jurisdictions, this procedure is restricted by several factors. There are financial disincentives to the Centre to initiate such transfers, and individuals whom they might want to acquire have not always been eager to uproot and relocate in Ottawa. Most important, all of the Centre's hirings come through the general Statistics Canada recruitment program, which seeks out 'generalists' who are suited to moving through the different topic areas within Statistics Canada, rather than recruiting individuals with a specific substantive expertise.

The Uniform Crime Report

The Uniform Crime Report is the main survey on crime in Canada. It produces the CCJS's most prominent statistical indicator – the annual crime rate. While other CCJS surveys may be of greater day-to-day utility for administrators of the criminal-justice system, the UCR is unquestionably the Centre's flagship survey. This status is at least partially related to the fact that the crime rate tends to receive considerable media attention. The original UCR became operational in Canada in 1961 as the result of a joint venture between Statistics Canada and Canada's national police representative body, the Canadian Association of Chiefs of Police (CACP). It was initially a paper-and-pencil data collection regime that produced national crime statistics and standardized measures of police workload.

The police are a vital component in the operation of the UCR. When an officer attends an incident, she must first determine whether a crime has been committed. If so, she fills out an occurrence report, which is specific to her particular police organization. The officer, or an individual in a special data-entry section, then classifies the crime(s) according to the UCR criteria. This involves choosing from a list of 108 official classificatory options. Importantly, there is not necessarily a one-to-one correspondence between the Criminal Code violation and how the event is coded for the UCR. Some crimes, such as homicide, have their own UCR violation code, while other codes can subsume a host of vastly different crimes. For example, the violation code for 'offenses against public order' includes treason, assisting a deserter, duelling, unlawful drilling, piracy, and forcible confinement. The maximum penalties for this diverse amalgamation of crimes range from summary conviction to life imprisonment. Because of this structure, the Centre cannot disaggregate its final numbers to statistically scrutinize specific crimes for some of the violation codes that subsume a large number of Criminal Code offences, such as 'offences against the person or reputation.' While local reporting units generally have the ability to disaggregate their own data, the Centre must work with the larger catch-all categories.

The basic unit of count for the UCR is the 'criminal incident.' The rules specifying what counts as an incident demonstrates how the classificatory rules employed by statistical agencies are constitutive of the objects they purport to describe. A single 'incident' on the revised UCR may involve several victims, several accused, and several legal violations. Such behaviours are grouped together as a single incident if (1) they are part of a simultaneous or sequential action that occurs at the same place, (2) they are part of interrelated actions over a short period of time, or (3) when the same violent action is repeated over a long period of time against the same victim(s) but only comes to the attention of the police at one point in time (Revised UCR Documentation 1991: 5). Thus, if two people break into an apartment and rob it, this counts as one incident, but if they break into three adjoining apartments it is three separate incidents. However, if a man is arrested for committing multiple acts of incest against his daughter during the past two years, it counts as one incident. I will not try to clarify any further the specifics of what types of criminal behaviours will count as an 'incident.' Specific applications of these rules can confuse even seasoned police officers. Suffice it to say that the basic unit of count for the UCR is considerably more idiosyncratic than the public might envision when they think about measuring crime.

For each incident, the police record up to ten data elements, consisting of the type of offence, clearance type (how they have officially processed the incident, by charge or otherwise), and persons charged (adults and young offenders). These elements are then divided into three sets of variables: number of incidents, number of incidents cleared (or solved), and number of persons charged in relation to the cleared incidents.

Except for those crimes committed by military personnel, which are processed by the Department of National Defence, the UCR is a full census of all of the recorded crime in Canada. Approximately 400 police forces send UCR data to the CCJS on a monthly basis. This includes municipal forces as well as detachments from the RCMP, Ontario Provincial Police, and the Sûreté du Québec. The CCJS also receives reports from customs officials and the railway police. Such a large number of respondents distinguishes the UCR from the other CCJS surveys, which have considerably fewer reporting units. Most only receive one monthly report from each provincial and territorial representative. Other survey units have also had considerably less success than the UCR in securing data from all of the potential reporting units.

Another noteworthy attribute of the UCR is that, owing to its aggregate nature, analysts cannot statistically isolate a single incident. The Centre receives monthly aggregate tallies of the number of incidents, incidents cleared, and so on, from the different reporting units. Consequently, it can only produce numbers related to the volume of cases processed by the police and cannot develop a more detailed appreciation for the connections between the crime, the accused, and the victim. It was partially this limitation that in the 1980s prompted Centre staff, in consultation with the police community, to begin investigating the prospect of revising and updating the UCR. They sought to (1) increase the utility of the survey by expanding the number of data elements, (2) improve data quality without (3) increasing respondent burden, and (4) maintain the historical continuity of crime statistics (CCJS 1990a: 3). Protracted consultations ultimately resulted in the development of the 'revised UCR' (UCRII), which released its first preliminary findings in 1990. The new survey contains more detail about the victim, accused, and circumstances of the incident than was previously possible. Thus, there are in fact now *two* UCR surveys operating in the Centre. The original paper-and-pencil survey of aggregate crimes remains the primary reporting vehicle for many Canadian police forces, while the new UCRII incident-based survey has respondents supply data entirely in machine-readable format. Both UCR systems were expected to operate concurrently for a number of years as the original UCR was phased out.

The most important aspect of the new survey is the move to an incident-based structure, which means that each criminal incident now has its own statistical record. Analysts can now manipulate several variables potentially associated with an incident. With this greater flexibility also came new data variables. The specifics of what new information should be collected were discussed extensively during lead-up consultations. Ultimately, the survey came to include new variables related to the accused's sex, age, alcohol/drug consumption, and race, although some of these variables have subsequently been revised or abandoned (see chapter 4). Victims of violent crimes would have their age, sex, racial origin, relationship to the accused, alcohol/drug consumption, and level of injury recorded, along with an indication of the type of weapon used. Other new data elements include an indication for the 'dollar value of drugs seized,' and 'vehicle type' for traffic violations.

It is unlikely that the Centre would, or could, have embarked on these reforms were it not for the greater storage, computational, and communications abilities provided by computers. The volume of data that now courses through the Centre for this survey alone is massive. In 1996 I was informed that within a few years the UCRII would actually constitute a larger data holding than Canada's national census. At that time, approximately one and a half million annual UCRII transaction records were being processed. Roughly 1.5 million victim records and 300,000 accused records can be added to this annual total. These numbers are all the more impressive given that Canada only has a population of 28 million. A person involved in the production of the UCR observed that 'right now the *overall* data store for UCRII is about six million records. That is data going from 1988 to processing for 1996 ... [W]hen you have six million incidents with 600,000 related victims and 1.8 million related accused, it is a lot all in one chunk of space.' Even this volume does not approach the eventual size anticipated for the UCRII data holdings. In 1994 approximately eighty police departments from across the country were supplying data to the UCRII. These forces accounted for only about 30 per cent of the total reported crime in Canada (Grainger 1996: 27). As more forces adopt the UCRII conventions, the data holdings will increase correspondingly.

A final terminological clarification is in order. The name 'uniform crime reports' is used by both Canada and the United States for their official crime statistics. This is because Canada initially modelled its national crime survey on the UCR in the United States, which became operational in the early 1930s. Despite this similarity, there are significant differences in the ways that the two countries organize their criminal-statistics systems. Different laws, legislative responsibilities, organizational structures, and statistical counting rules immediately complicate cross-border comparisons of crime rates.

Early Critiques of Official Statistics

Crime statistics have been prominent in debates about the accuracy and utility of official statistics. Much of this discussion took place in the 1960s and 1970s, and was a lightning rod for fundamental methodological and epistemological debates within sociology. In part, the discussion was symptomatic of a wider reaction against the hegemony of American-style sociological empiricism, as authors who were aligned with the rise of more interpretational sociologies engaged in a fundamental critique of official statistics. These critiques, in turn, prompted a defence of such statistics and calls for broader reflections about the power of the state and the institutions that produce these numbers. In sketching some of the key elements in these arguments, this section is more than a history of the discipline or rehashing of obsolete debates. Variations on issues addressed in the 1960s and 1970s continue to be points of contention in contemporary theoretical debates, and are a launching point for this study.

The 1960s saw the ascendancy of interpretational types of sociological analysis such as ethnomethodology and phenomenology. These approaches emphasize the means by which individuals solve problems and make sense of their world. A strong part of interpretational programs involved a critique of the use of official statistics for sociological research. Some of the main advocates of such a position included Douglas (1967, 1970), Sudnow (1964) and Cicourel, writing both alone (1965, 1968) and with Kitsuse (Kitsuse and Cicourel 1963). While these critiques were multi-pronged, they often revolved around the referentiality of official statistics – that is, the degree to which the statistics correspond with the objects and events they purport to describe.

Kitsuse and Cicourel wrote one of the most influential of these early pieces (1963), wherein they start with a broad sketch of Robert Merton's theory on anomie and deviant behaviour. Specifically, they focus on Merton's claim that a discontinuity between culturally prescribed aspirations, such as wealth and commodities, and the socially structured avenues for realizing such goals can explain deviance. Merton proposes that such a social situation produces in individuals a strain that can lead to differential involvement in criminal behaviour among groups who are differentially located in the social structure. More important for the issue at hand, he also believes that sociologists can measure these processes by studying the differential criminal involvement of social groups as represented in official statistics. Kitsuse and Cicourel suggest a fundamental problem with such a methodology: it fails to deal with the schism between the social processes that produce *deviant behaviour* and the organizational activity that produces the *rates of deviant behaviour*. A host of intermediary factors peculiar to the rate-producing agencies, such as the police and probation officers, can influence the production of crime rates. Consequently, these authors suggest that official crime statistics be 'viewed as indices of organizational processes rather than as indices of the incidence of certain forms of behavior' (Kitsuse and Cicourel 1963: 137). This position was more than a methodological caveat. It signalled a fundamentally different focus for sociologists interested in deviance, a move from the study of deviant behaviour itself to the study of the processes involved in categorizing, processing, and recording deviance.

While Kitsuse and Cicourel's article directed attention towards the role of social organizations in producing deviance rates, it was a brief programmatic statement and lacked empirical detail about these processes. Cicourel's subsequent book (1968) on juvenile delinquency documented some of the ways that the social organizations of criminal-justice agencies can influence the day-to-day processes of labelling and processing youths, which ultimately affect juvenile-delinquency rates. He reiterates that there is a questionable relationship between deviant behaviour and deviance rates, observing that '[t]he ready-made "variables," provided by official bureaucratic organizations charged with certain bookkeeping operations, have no "obvious" correspondence with the daily events and practical reasoning that led to the production of rates' (1968: 28). Numbers, consequently, must be situated in a broader context to understand 'how men, resources, policies, and strategies of the police, for example, cover a given community, interpret incoming calls, assign men, screen complaints, and routinize reports' (ibid.). A major factor that accounts for variability in deviance statistics, argues Cicourel, are the background assumptions and tacit knowledge of rate-producing agents. Background assumptions transform an ambiguous environment into intelligible phenomena. Varying from individual to individual, these assumptions lead different enforcement agents to label and process some behaviours as deviant and ignore others. Cicourel paints a picture of criminal-justice operatives employing a highly discretionary set of classificatory practices, such that the law is not strictly applied, but mediated through the interpretations and tacit knowledge of officials.

Other studies at this time came to similar conclusions. Douglas's (1967) work on suicide details how there is a wide scope for variability in classifying suicides. He demonstrates that the designation of 'suicide' is not something to be unambiguously read off a corpse or death scene, but is a classificatory outcome shaped by a host of personal factors and institutional routines, and that these elements differ across time, nation, culture, and geography. Both Cicourel and Douglas conclude their critique of official statistics by urging sociologists to conduct studies that unpack the lived realities of individuals, focusing on the meaning that events have for individuals in their daily lives.

Not all sociologists were convinced by this call for a new sociological program, however, and Barry Hindess's (1973) book *The Use of Official Statistics in Sociology* was a cutting response to the phenomenological challenge. Hindess was particularly disturbed by the general threat that he thought phenomenology's epistemological base posed for rational thought. His conclusion was brutal, proposing that phenomenology's arguments are 'theoretically useless' and that '[a] manuscript produced by a monkey at a typewriter would be no less valuable' (26).

Acknowledging that background expectancies can produce statistical variations, Hindess suggests that the proper scientific response is to try and discern the degree of error such variations introduce to each particular data-collection regime, rather than abandon the enterprise entirely. In some cases, classificatory ambiguity could result in serious errors; in others, it could be so minimal that it would be of no concern. However, Hindess directs his harshest criticism at the plea by Cicourel and Douglas that sociologists should turn their attention to research that seeks to provide accurate descriptions of real-world events. He accentuates a contradiction in such a position: that such studies would not escape the very problems that Cicourel and Douglas identify in relation to statistics. If background expectancies shape how individuals record statistical data, sociologists who purport to describe real-world events would also have their observations structured by their own tacit knowledge, which operates to transform the world of objects into intelligible phenomena. Hindess concludes: 'Unless the sociologist is to be accorded the capacity, denied to ordinary mortals, to describe objects and events without the intervention of background expectancies or of tacit knowledge, then his account must be subject to precisely the same type of limitation as those of other observers' (11). He accuses phenomenology of a profound relativism, as he believes their emphasis on the role played by background assumptions in structuring knowledge production would ultimately lead to a denial of the possibility of any objective and rational knowledge whatsoever.

Hindess proposes that producing official statistics involves both conceptual and technical instruments. Conceptual instruments are those systems of categories that govern the assignment of cases into classes, as accentuated by the phenomenologists. The technical instruments are the actual surveys or recording devices used by enumerators. Hindess argues that an enumerator's background expectancies are structured by the technical instruments that they must employ, in contrast to the almost infinite classificatory latitude that he sees in Cicourel's position. Using the example of the 1951 census of India, he suggests that any space for the role of subjective experience in assigning cases 'is determined by the structure of the system of categories and not by any structure of the "consciousness" concerned' (Hindess 1973: 44). These categories not only direct an individual's tacit assumptions in certain predefined directions, they also contain an implicit theory of how the world operates. The choice of what variables to collect is related to how the designers of these instruments conceive of the world, and accentuate certain events and processes while ignoring or misrepresenting others. Hindess again uses the example of the census of India to document this point; in particular, to show how the agricultural statistics in the census of India were derived from a capitalist vision of the world that ignored or mis-recognized the agrarian elements of Indian agriculture.

Subsequent authors have continued to call attention to the issue of which theories and interests underlie data-collection regimes. In light of this recognition, Miles and Irvine (1979), for example, encourage sociologists to pay more attention to the institutional processes of the state's statistical agencies and their employees, as their interests and actions also shape the production of official statistics.

While these early exchanges often used crime and deviance statistics as an example, the debate was about the value and utility of official statistics in general. This study continues two lines of inquiry that can be traced back to these early debates. First, it explores the role played by standardized technical instruments in structuring knowledge production. Second, it moves inside of statistical agencies to detail some of the institutional processes and micro-politics that can shape how governmental knowledge is produced and communicated. At this juncture we explore in greater detail some of the ways in which tacit knowledge, organizational processes, classifications, and technical instruments have been implicated in shaping official crime statistics such as the CCJS Uniform Crime Reports.

Continuing Questions about Crime Data

The range of non-crime factors singled out as potentially influencing crime rates has expanded considerably since the 1960s. Hindess's question about whether these factors introduce enough error to invalidate the statistics remains one that must be evaluated on a case-by-case basis. That said, some Centre employees are quite concerned about how some of the following processes might be affecting their data.

The textbook metaphor that illustrates the production of crime statistics is the 'crime filter,' which screens out certain acts from the official record. This is a particularly apt metaphor, as it accentuates how not everything in the universe of harmful acts is officially registered as a crime. Many of the social harms produced by the wealthy and powerful are dealt with in non-criminal tribunals or administrative bodies, or are not dealt with at all. Nor are all of those behaviours that could receive the official designation of 'crime' reported to the police. Criminal Code definitions to the contrary, many individuals simply do not recognize trifling matters or interpersonal disputes as crimes. Indeed, 'everyone' seems to be engaged in some level of routine criminal behaviour (Gabor 1994). Fear of the authorities by illegal immigrants or people who are themselves involved in crime can make them reluctant to report their victimization, while still others, such as abused spouses, fear reprisals if they contact the police.

Nor is calling the police a guarantee that an incident will enter the official record. Police dispatchers may not view the incident as a serious criminal matter or may divert it to another organization. Manning (1992: 386) suggests that approximately 75 per cent of calls to the police are 'screened, referred or terminated without being forwarded to officers.' Although officers must operate within the scope of organizationally recognized options for taking action and recording events, they have considerable discretion in the first instance as to how to document events. Decisions about what type of, and how many, charges to lay are made with an eye towards the ultimate organizational consequences of such decisions. Included in such considerations is the practice of 'charging up,' whereby many, or more serious, charges are laid in order to produce a position of strength for the Crown for potential plea negotiations (Ericson 1981). Laying a charge is a key decision point, where personal and institutional prejudice can be manifest. All manner of biases can come into play in relation to what types of people are singled out for scrutiny and arrest, and what types of charges they face. Even though a crime has occurred, police officers may be reluctant to lay charges. Such hesitancy can be related to an officer's belief that the matter is trivial, that the victim was complicit in the crime, or that a conviction is unlikely. Indeed, uncertainty about the role of the police as accurate, faithful, and disinterested recorders of statistical data has long been recognized as one of the major failings of official crime statistics. As Sir Josiah Stamp proclaimed in 1929: 'The government are very keen on amassing statistics. They collect them, raise them to the nth power, take the cube root and prepare wonderful diagrams. But you must never forget that every one of their figures comes in the first instance from the village watchman, who just puts down what he damn pleases' (quoted in Nettler 1974: 43).

Police organizational routines can also influence crime rates. Organizational dictates related to a desire to improve a force's statistical profile can inform how particular cases are documented. Burnham (1997: 113) recounts how in the 1950s and 1960s, faced with pressures to reduce the crime rate, police departments in several large U.S. cities employed a series of informal policies whereby certain criminal behaviours were reclassified so they would not appear on the official crime count. Similar processes have been documented more recently in Britain, where the police have been encouraged to improve their 'clear-up rate,' which is essentially a measure of the number of cases they have solved. Officers have been known to encourage criminals to admit to committing a range of additional crimes, which are then officially 'taken into consideration.' In exchange, the offender is promised favourable treatment, and the police's clear-up rate is improved (Ackroyd et al. 1992; Kinsey, Lee, and Young 1986: 21).

One of the few detailed studies by the CCJS that examines police reporting practices documents how formal and informal police organizational routines can influence the crime rate. In a comparative study of the police forces in Calgary and Edmonton – two cities in the same province and viewed as being roughly comparable for the purposes of crime data – different levels of police reporting were found across the two forces, particularly in relation to minor crimes. This variation was partially attributed to Edmonton's policy of fuller reporting, but the authors still cautioned that in Edmonton 'over 10% of the data is either lost or in error. This should be kept in mind when examining UCR data' (CCJS 1990b: 50). The situation was even more troubling in Calgary, where a considerable number of cases went missing between the initial call for service and the final official documentation, a loss that was attributed to 'the failure of patrol officers to complete occurrence reports for incidents to which they have been dispatched' (49). A more recent evaluation of the quality of UCRII data reiterates such concerns. It found significant variability in response patterns across different police organizations. The author cautions that this 'lack of accurate and consistent respondent data was very much a data quality concern' (Coull 1995: 3).

Victimization studies give us a glimpse of the 'dark figure' of unreported crime (Mayhew et al. 1994; Violence Against Women Survey 1993). Such studies ask groups of randomly sampled individuals to detail instances where they have been criminally victimized, usually during the past year. Respondents are encouraged to detail their criminal victimization, irrespective of whether they reported it to the police or even viewed the incident(s) as trivial. While such methodologies have their own limitations, including the fact that they underrepresent corporate and environmental crimes as well as 'victimless' crimes such as prostitution, they do provide insight into the degree to which certain crimes go unreported. For example, the 1993 Statistics Canada General Social Survey estimated that 90 per cent of sexual assaults, 68 per cent of other assaults, and 53 per cent of robberies for that year were not reported to the police (H. Johnson 1996: 3).

Filters that depress the level of officially documented crime exist alongside processes that can augment crime rates or introduce other uncertainties into the crime data. For example, media attention to particular social problems can influence crime rates (Gusfield 1989; Hilgartner and Bosk 1988). Public crusades against specific crimes encourage a collective vigilance that can increase the reporting levels for those crimes and prompt police efforts to target such behaviour – actions that can, in turn, inflate the official numbers. Laws against impaired driving, prostitution, gambling, and the sale and possession of narcotics provide an apparently limitless resource for police charging practices. Police enforcement strategies are also related to changing social attitudes. For example, modifications in public attitudes towards, and tolerance of, violence can be reflected in the official numbers. Legislative change also plays a role in this process. One of the most important recent Canadian legal reforms in this respect concerns the 1983 modifications to the rape and indecent assault legislation, which introduced a tripartite hierarchy of seriousness for sexual assaults. Increased levels of police-recorded violence have been partially attributed to this reform (Kingsley 1996).

The above observations by no means constitute a full array of arguments levelled against the accuracy of official crime reports. Instead, they provide a sense of the Centre's epistemological environment, an atmosphere where the work is continually open to diverse deconstructive strategies. In this, the Centre's personnel are not even immune from criticism from their Initiative partners. One respondent recalled how a former liaison officer from the Department of Justice was particularly aggressive in this regard: 'We used to say that he had more people in Justice working to pull our reports apart than we had working on them. He had a staff that seemed to work constantly to critique our reports.'

Centre staff are intimately aware of the above criticisms of the UCR data, having highlighted some of the limitations themselves. Individuals deal with this situation in a variety of ways. Some narrowly concentrate on the production of crime numbers and set aside questions about the referentiality of their data. As a senior analyst at the Centre observed, 'A large part of our work is not having to do with the reality. We just work with our numbers.' Another member commented how for most staff at the Centre the relationship between the official 'crime rate' and the 'real' level of crime is 'a black hole.' Still another confided: 'If anybody got into a statistical analysis of the UCR data, which is supposed to be our flagship, I think they would have a heart attack. My own personal opinion is that the data are crap. For all of these reasons. Nobody knows who is putting what in. The question is what can you do? To a certain extent you are stuck.'

Such resigned or critical stances are not, however, the norm. Some maintain that the UCR is a wonderful approximation of the level of reported crime. Others are more pragmatic, believing there is a relationship between the level of reported crime and the 'true' level of crime, but recognize that it is difficult to ascertain the degree of fit between the representation and the reality. Still others take the critiques of their numbers very seriously and worry about the validity of the UCR data, particularly in light of the difficulties introduced by the unknown levels of variability in police reporting practices.

All of this makes it difficult to characterize the dominant view that Centre staff take towards the validity of their data. Perhaps the best approach is to recognize that Centre staff, like many scientists, are 'Janus-faced' in their belief about the validity of their data (Latour 1987, 96–9). They alternately assume more realist or constructionist positions depending upon the situation. Speaking from the realist face of the Janus head, they claim that their numbers are dictated by the level of reported crime. Adopting the more constructionist face, they accentuate the various organizational, social, and legal factors that can affect the crime rate. The choice of which voice to adopt is contextual. For example, when publicly presenting their statistics they speak of how the numbers reflect, or approximate, the amount of reported crime in Canada. During the more day-to-day routines of producing the data, frequent comment is made about the various organizational, social, and technological factors that shape or skew the data. Both of these voices speak the truth, as the Centre's knowledge is both constructed and real; it is the processes of construction that allows the reality to emerge and solidify.

Some Centre personnel have developed arguments and rationalizations to provide them with greater confidence that the trends they report are accurate or indicative of what is occurring in the 'real world' of crime. One of the most important of these claims involves the purported relationship between violent crime and non-violent crime. It is argued, or assumed, that many of the above-noted phenomena that can influence crime data are primarily related to less serious offences. When it comes to serious assaults or homicide, the crime filter is not so much in effect, as people are more apt to report serious offences and the police more likely to record them accurately. At the extreme, to put the matter bluntly, a corpse provides homicide data with an objectivity that transcends organizational discretion, reporting criteria, and classification. A continuum of ontological certainty emerges whereby, as one respondent phrased it, 'the more serious [an offence] is, the more likely it is to be real.' The realist end of this continuum is exemplified by homicide data where, as another respondent observed, 'you have to have a body. If anything is reliable, homicide is.' Yet a third interviewee reiterated this common view: 'The thing about the homicide [data] is that ... we can never be accused of it being subject to reporting criteria or numbers. A dead body is a dead body. We can't really count that wrong. So the reporting criteria by police or to police really don't impact it. It is a finite measurement.'

I want to continue to explore the criticisms levelled against official crime statistics by confronting this 'hard case.' While I too believe that these numbers are less influenced by reporting criteria than are less serious offences, I use this example to extend the argument that the Centre's truth claims exist within a hostile epistemological environment, where they are always potentially subject to deconstructive strategies. Even their hardest and most reliable numbers are shaped by reporting criteria, changing social attitudes, and institutional processes.

Every year a percentage of Canadian citizens go missing and are never seen again. Marginalized street people and prostitutes are particularly at risk of urban disappearances. We can assume that some of these people are the victims of undiscovered homicides. Even when the police find a corpse, this does not necessarily mean that a cause of death can be determined. Lundsgaarde's (1977) classic study of homicide patterns in Houston documents how interpretative and organizational factors in the coroner's office play a role in cause-of-death determinations. The grey areas associated with the classification of suicides (Douglas 1967, chap. 12), and with burned or decomposed corpses, and the differential degrees of official attention accorded to different types of death can contribute to such ambiguity. In a study of coroners' cause-of-death determinations, Leadbeater (1996: 442) concludes that the absence of evidence of a cause of death does not exclude the possibility that a homicide has occurred, and that 'where there are pathological findings which may be considered sufficient to be a cause of death, the exclusion of another party having brought about the death by a means which leaves no evidence – such as suffocation with a pillow – is, again, impossible.' What this means is that in some instances it is simply impossible to determine whether the death was the result of foul play. This situation is further complicated by the fact that if a serious crime is not suspected, the post-mortem examination can be cursory. Smith (1989: 61) reports that in the United Kingdom a post-mortem may take as little as thirteen minutes, with mortuary assistants performing much of the work. Official diagnostic routines can also be abandoned when coroners are confronted with a mortality that is 'clearly' not a homicide. A senior police officer provides a sense of the degree of classificatory latitude involved in such processes:

> You would have the situation where it's July and the coroner arrives at the scene where the corpse of a seventy-year-old male has been found. Now, it's hot and the body is up on the third floor. The coroner would ask the officer if there was any indication of violence or anything out of the ordinary. The officer would say, 'No, it just appears that the guy died.' The coroner would take the death certificate and write in 'coronary thrombosis' and leave. Not even bothering to go up and look at the body. Now this information is used by Statistics Canada and by health professionals. Ultimately it impacts on all kinds of things. For all we know heart attacks aren't the leading cause of death ... [W]e all develop our own prejudices and habits. (Ericson and Haggerty 1997: 243)

As in any other medical examination, coroners can misdiagnose. Outside of those instances where a body is found with a knife protruding from its back, there is room for interpretation in determining the role of foul play in a person's death. Coroners have the advantage, however, that they need not deal with the prospect that their 'patient' will seek a second opinion or develop symptoms that dramatically contradict the original diagnosis. Theirs is largely the final word in cause-of-death determinations. A senior police analyst tells a perhaps apocryphal tale from his secondment to a Caribbean island, where he had routine dealings with the coroner's office. This coroner was kept busy by a steady stream of suicide victims, suicide apparently being a not uncommon response of jilted lovers. In one instance the officer recounted how, after conducting an extremely cursory examination of a corpse that still had a noose around its neck, the coroner pronounced the cause of death to be yet another suicide. Purely by happenstance this officer then examined the body and found that the man's hands were tied together.

Social and institutional change can also affect homicide rates. During the research period for this study, public discussion was taking place in Ontario about 'shaken baby syndrome,' a 'syndrome' that consists of a caregiver shaking a child so hard that it is seriously injured or even dies. Such actions are typically attributed to a caregiver's exasperated attempts to stop a child from crying. In the mid-1990s 'shaken baby syndrome' was close to becoming a new social problem. An immediately evocative issue, it had already received some media attention and had a respected public champion in the Chief Coroner of Ontario. The Chief Coroner had proclaimed that such behaviour was much more frequent than had previously been imagined and publicly suggested that the previously inexplicable phenomenon of Sudden Infant Death Syndrome (SIDS, a.k.a. 'crib death') in many instances resulted from a parent or guardian shaking a baby. Here an analyst at the Centre recounts his discussion with the Chief Coroner in relation to this matter:

> I spoke to the coroner, the Coroner's Office of Ontario, and they are quite sure that there are a lot of what are classified as SIDS deaths, so that number they think is a gross undercount ... And then two months ago ... he was on TV stating his opinion about that and how infant deaths are going to be more thoroughly investigated in the future. And they had backed off in the past because of the strength of the SIDS organization and because it is such an emotional thing and such a hard thing for families so they completely backed off if it looked at all like it could be SIDS death. So they are going to be much more aggressive.

The 'more aggressive' investigative stance of the Coroner's Office was evident in new rules and regulations. A person in the Centre responsible for collecting homicide data mentioned that the Ontario Coroner's Office had recently declared that the death of any infant under two years of age would automatically be investigated and that this was being expanded to include the death of any child under the age of five.

The Centre has also recently institutionalized this phenomenon on its homicide survey by adding the option 'trauma, i.e. shaken baby syndrome' under the categories available for 'cause of death.' Given this new emphasis and institutionalization of procedures for investigating such deaths, it would be fair to estimate that the official numbers for homicides of children will increase as cases that might previously have been neglected will now receive critical scrutiny. Here a member of the Centre anticipates just such an outcome: 'It is hard to predict, but it is quite possible that a lot of deaths could have been attributed to accident or Sudden Infant Death Syndrome when in fact they could have been homicides ... What in the past could have been decided as being the result of Sudden Infant Death Syndrome or accidental, now because of the coroner's involvement in investigating these types of deaths we would uncover more.'

It is important to accentuate such qualifications, as the Uniform Crime Report is the main source of official knowledge about reported crime in Canada. It is also the flagship survey of the CCJS. However, as we have seen, the knowledge produced by this and other Centre surveys is always amenable to critique. A host of criticisms of official statistics shape the epistemological environment inhabited by Centre employees. While many of these critiques have been directed specifically at crime statistics, their broad conclusions apply to other official statistics. All such numbers are conditioned as much by the organizational routines they emerge from as by the objects they purport to describe.

The validity of the Centre's facts depend on their ability to counter, incorporate, or silence these diverse criticisms, which involves efforts to fashion a series of complex and heterogeneous knowledge networks. The ensuing chapters demonstrate that statistical facts are not merely the result of science and proper methodology. They are also a human, bureaucratic, organizational, and political achievement.

2

Numerical Governance and Knowledge Networks

Aggregate forms of knowledge foster a distinctive conception of governance and provide the tools to accomplish governmental agendas. The past few decades have witnessed transformations in governmental rationalities and techniques for governing criminal justice, and the statistical knowledges about crime trends and criminal-justice processes produced by agencies such as the Canadian Centre for Justice Statistics have contributed to these changes. Knowledge about aggregate crime trends fosters a distinctive approach towards dealing with crime and criminals, one that has been characterized as 'actuarial justice' (Feeley and Simon 1994). At the same time, the availability of statistical indicators about the operations of criminal-justice institutions encourages us to conceive of these tenuously connected organizations as an interconnected and potentially manageable system.

To accentuate the importance of these processes, this chapter situates the Centre in the context of a burgeoning literature inspired by Michel Foucault's work on governmentality. It stresses the need to understand the constitutive role of official classifications in producing the objects of governmental knowledge, which, in turn, shape popular understandings of the world and ourselves. Whether they distinguish among people, places, or events, such classifications establish the objects towards which governmental strategies are directed.

Such knowledge is itself a social and institutional accomplishment. The production of something as apparently simple as a national indicator for 'incarceration' relies on a massive effort to align a host of heterogeneous elements, including people, technologies, information, and institutions. The latter half of the chapter draws from work in the sociology of science, specifically Actor Network Theory (ANT), to detail some of the processes that must be put in place to produce this type of knowledge. These include efforts to interest various elements in the knowledge network and then impute identities to these elements that must subsequently be monitored and controlled. These processes are coordinated from a central locale into which information flows and from which a host of techniques for 'control at a distance' are fostered and coordinated. While it is these networks that ultimately allow for the production of truths, these truths are always contingent, and rely on the ongoing maintenance of networks.

Governance

The previous chapter outlined the broad contours of the Canadian Centre for Justice Statistics and the Justice Initiative. Beyond the mere fact that little critical attention has been paid to this institution, there are important pragmatic and theoretical reason why the CCJS warrants detailed study. These revolve around the unique epistemological resources that such organizations provide to governmental institutions, and the means deployed to produce such knowledge. This section situates the Centre in the context of theoretical reflections on 'governmentality,' emphasizing the role that statistical institutions play in fostering a particular style of liberal governance. However, this should not be seen as a comprehensive review of the literature on governmentality (see Burchell, Gordon, and Miller 1991; Rose 1999; Dean 1990; Barry, Osborne, and Rose 1996). Instead, it concentrates on detailing the relationship between liberal and neo-liberal forms of governance and statistical knowledge.

The later works of Michel Foucault (1991) offer a distinctive approach to the topic of 'government.' In these writings, government is not confined to the formal trappings of the state. Instead, his account of 'government rationality,' or 'governmentality,' amounts to an interrogation of how the practical art of government is envisioned and executed. Here the concepts of 'rationalities' and 'technologies' stand out. A 'rationality' of government refers to 'a way or system of thinking about the nature of the practice of government' (Gordon 1991: 3). Thus, rationalities are the changing ways in which the exercise of political power is conceived. Particularly important to Foucault in this regard is how contemporary governmental rationalities seek to combine processes of individualization with processes of totalization.

'Technologies,' in contrast, consist of those diverse sets of programs and techniques that are the basis for how governance is exercised. Foucault employs a set of historical periodizations to demonstrate some of these different rationalities and technologies of government. He claims that commencing in the sixteenth century there was a 'genesis of a political knowledge that was to place at the center of its concerns the notion of population and the mechanisms capable of ensuring its regulation' (Foucault 1997: 67). This emphasis on populations as the focus of governance continues through his genealogy of liberalism as a rationality.

State Reason and Police Science

Foucault's genealogy of governmentality starts with the concept of *raison d'état*,' or 'state reason,' which arose in the late sixteenth and early seventeenth centuries. It was around this rationality that the art of government first crystallized. State reason is the initiation point for modern governmentality as an autonomous rationality. With it, governance was understood for the first time to be related to rational principles that were intrinsic to the state and were no longer subordinate to the 'divine, cosmo-theological order of the world' (Gordon 1991: 9). State reason is contrasted with the form of government exemplified by Machiavelli's advice to the sovereign in his book *The Prince*. For Machiavelli, governance sought to maintain the principality of the ruler, which was conceived of in terms of the size of the prince's territory and number of citizens under his command. While this form of governance produced periods of relative stability, its embodiment in an individual sovereign meant that there was the constant prospect of a dramatic end to any one system of governance. As the governmental role was increasingly invested in the state, it became more stable and future-oriented, as the aims of governance were now recognized as extending beyond the lifespan of any individual ruler.

State reason was linked to the development of an administrative apparatus and the corresponding emergence of detailed knowledges about the state. One form of knowledge in particular stood out: the 'science of police,' which can be traced to the German states following the Thirty Years War (Pasquino 1991). In this context, 'police' does not refer to our contemporary law-enforcement institution, but is more closely affiliated with our notion of 'policy.' Police science constituted government as an art with its own distinctive and irreducible rationality, which aimed to practically govern the lives of the citizenry for the purpose of fostering secular security and prosperity. As such, police science was a radical departure from the rationality of the prince, which sought to 'hold out' and retain the prince's sovereignty.

The defining attribute of the science of police was its ambition and efforts to produce total knowledge of the functioning of the state for purposes of regulation. The realm of concerns specific to the state extended into every conceivable domain. State knowledge was concerned with an infinite number of unforeseeable and contingent circumstances. This was coterminous with the birth of 'statistics,' which had yet to acquire the distinctive quantitative structure it has today. Instead, statistics referred to the 'science of the state,' which involved descriptive administrative efforts focused on almost anything related to the state (Desrosières 1990: 200). Police science was statistical in the earlier sense of the word, involving 'endless lists and classifications' (Gordon 1991: 10) that articulated myriad decrees about the proper way to conduct one's life. Rather than being a totalitarian form of control, it attempted to foster the utmost happiness in life, involving a productive multiplication of the state's wealth and power – a power that was recognized as lying in its population. Pasquino's (1991: 110) account of some of police science's specific areas of concern provides an appreciation for the breadth of such regulations, some of which pertained to the proper conduct and regulation of religion, customs, health, foodstuffs, highways, tranquillity and public order, science and liberal arts, commerce, manufacture and mechanical arts, servants, domestics and nurses, and the poor. Theoretically, nothing was too mundane to be left beyond the regulatory aims of police science, which went so far as to prescribe the dimensions of saddles and horsecloths as well as to provide instructions on what should be eaten and drunk during a wedding feast.

State reason is intimately related to the availability and use of knowledge about the state. However, these 'statistics' were not yet quantitative, and in this respect governance lagged behind the quantitative revolution that was transforming so many other aspects of European life. In *The Measure of Reality* (1997), Crosby documents the epochal shift from a qualitative to a quantitative form of perception in Western Europe between the late Middle Ages and the Renaissance. This transformation marks the genesis of our contemporary quantitative manifestations of science, business, and bureaucracy. While numbers were used before this period, they were often invoked for their mystical quality and lacked precision. Commencing around 1250 there was an .

acceleration in forms of quantitative perception of time (clocks), space (maps), mathematics (decline of Roman numerals and use of Arabic numbers), music (introduction of musical notation), painting (quantitative relationship to space and perception), and bookkeeping (double entry). Some of the state's earliest attempts to foster quantification involved efforts to standardize weights and measures, an aim shared with the commercial interests of the time. Kula (1986) documents how the state promoted standardized measures for bread, land, and distance that slowly supplanted the previously local, qualitative, and negotiated measurements. These early developments lay the groundwork for a new quantitative problematic of governance.

Liberalism and Statistics

From its inception, state reason was subject to the criticism that it was unrealizable, that its dream of total knowledge was just that, a dream. Out of such critiques emerged a new 'liberal' rationality of governance that advocated a doctrine of governance through wise limits and restraint. It was argued that there were and should be boundaries to the state's power to know and intervene. In lieu of undertaking obsessive efforts to know everything about the population, liberal governance conceives of subjects as having private rights and divides the social realm into a series of self-regulating and relatively autonomous domains. Liberalism conceives of such object-domains as having a kind of quasi-nature with their own specific self-regulating principles and dynamics, exemplified by the 'invisible hand' of the marketplace. Such domains were seen to be beyond the state's legitimate scope of direct intervention. Hence, liberal governance seeks to develop techniques to regulate these 'private' spheres where minute forms of state intervention are seen to be impractical or impossible. Such a form of governance does not prescribe a specific set of policies, but outlines a different approach to the practice of government, an approach with an expanded role for quantitative statistical knowledge.

Liberalism's distinctiveness lies in its attempt to resolve the dilemma of how to govern autonomous domains – without compromising their autonomy – through a unique combination of knowledge, expertise, and the active participation of subjects in their own government (Rose 1993: 290–1). To do this, liberalism focuses on population as the 'ultimate end of government' (Foucault 1991: 100) and relies on a series of knowledges of human conduct derived from the social and human sciences. Governance is no longer the exclusive domain of the state, but involves a host of extra-state professional, entrepreneurial, and reformist agencies that aim to shape the behaviour of citizens in a desired direction (Donzelot 1979).

Foucault's historical analyses alternate between exploring two poles of power: the individualizing and the aggregating. He subsumes both of these approaches under the rubric of governmentality, as both are ultimately concerned with attempts to govern the population. The micro-physics of power he details in *Discipline and Punish* (1977) are the clearest examples of the individualizing, disciplinary form of power, while his work in *The History of Sexuality Vol. 1* (1978) explores how aggregating forms of bio-power target the 'species body.' For Foucault, the individualizing moment is

> centered on the body as a machine: its disciplining, the optimization of its capabilities, the extortion of its forces, the parallel increase of its usefulness and its docility, its integration into systems of efficient and economic controls, all this was ensured by the procedures of power that characterized the disciplines: an anatomo-politics of the human body. The second, formed somewhat later, focused on the species body, the body imbued with the mechanisms of life and serving as the basis of the biological processes: propagation, births and mortality, the level of health, life expectancy and longevity, with all the conditions that can cause these to vary. Their supervision was effected through an entire series of interventions and regulatory controls: a bio-politics of the population. The disciplines of the body and the regulations of the population constituted the two poles around which the organization of power over life was deployed. (Foucault 1978: 139)

If the solitary criminal, isolated in his prison cell and subject to an invisible and potentially constant surveillance, is the archetype for disciplinary power, then aggregate statistics of the population exemplify bio-power. However, commentators on Foucault's work have had much less to say about bio-power than discipline. This is unfortunate given the way in which aggregate statistics promote our contemporary approaches to governance. Statistics are an irreplaceable element in the practice and possibility of liberal governance, and essential to the characteristically liberal idea that there are autonomous realms that obey their own internal laws and inclinations. As Foucault (1991: 99) observes, the historical emergence of statistics 'gradually reveals that population has its own regularities, its own rate of deaths and diseases, its cycles of scarcity, etc.; statistics shows also that the domain of population involves a range of intrinsic, aggregate effects ... such as epidemics, endemic levels of mortality, ascending spirals of labour and wealth.' We can add many things to this list, including the aggregate levels of crime, deviance, and criminal victimization in a population.

Early sociologists such as Durkheim, Quetelet, and Spencer invoked the regularities of statistics on crime, suicide, and marriage to propose that society could be an object of study in its own right (Gigerenzer et al. 1989: 39; Beirne 1993; Hacking 1990). The genesis of the social sciences is related to the rise of liberal practices of governance, as liberalism is intimately tied to the authority of such experts. New statistical knowledges fostered new forms of expertise in the conduct of conduct. For social scientists, liberalism marked the height of what Bauman (1992: 11) refers to as the intellectual's 'legislative' role, a capacity that 'involved the right to command the rules the social world was to obey,' and whose authority 'was legitimized in terms of a better judgment, a superior knowledge guaranteed by the proper method of its production.' Experts in the domain of 'the social' sought to shape behaviour by operating on statistical norms and interventions that worked at the societal level. Hacking (1990: 119) concisely summarizes the role of statistics in relation to the practices of liberal governance: 'We obtain data about a governed class whose deportment is offensive, and then attempt to alter what we guess are relevant conditions of that class in order to change the laws of statistics that the class obeys. This is the essence of the style of government that in the United States is called "liberal." As in the nineteenth century, the intentions of such legislation are benevolent. The *we* who know best change the statistical laws that affect *them*.'

Neo-Liberalism

The final moment in this genealogy of governmental rationalities concerns the development of 'neo-liberalism' or 'advanced liberalism' (Rose 1993, 1996; Rose and Miller 1992). Recent changes to liberal government have been traced to the 1970s and the emergence of a host of extra-state institutions that gained greater prominence in their efforts to govern individual behaviour. Experts affiliated with these institutions employed financial and accounting techniques that overlay statistical knowledge with considerations about cost and efficiency. Situated in dispersed 'centres of calculation,' these experts exercise control at a distance (Latour 1987) through calculative regimes such as accounting, cost-benefit analysis, and auditing (Power 1996). In order to do so, common forms of communication, statistical measures, and units of count had to be fashioned (Rose and Miller 1992). The cumulative effect of such changes was that more entrepreneurial and consumerist forms of social organization were fostered as neo-liberalism forged a vital link between rulers and the private decision-making capacity of individuals.

A defining attribute of neo-liberalism is that citizens are understood as active participants in their own governance. Individuals have a form of circumscribed freedom that involves approaching their life as a project. In the management of this life project they are constituted as free subjects, capable of choosing from a series of expertly mediated options designed to enhance their health, wealth, happiness, and security. As Rose and Miller (1992: 174) assert, when it comes to governing populations, 'personal autonomy is not the antithesis of political power, but a key term in its exercise, the more so because most individuals are not merely the subjects of power but play a part in its operations.' To govern is therefore to structure, contain, and define the possible field of action for individuals while maximizing the rational calculating capabilities of the self. Governance is an ongoing effort to manage the decision-making conditions of individuals, who transform themselves and their life choices in light of these changed conditions. A process of 'prudentialism' (O'Malley 1996) is fostered whereby individuals are expected and encouraged to adopt a calculative attitude towards the management of their own personal risk profile. In the process, governance becomes manifest through the 'regulated choices of individual citizens' (Rose 1993: 285).

Statistics have played a vital role in these different manifestations of the art and practice of governance. Having evolved from their initial manifestation as a massive listing of all matters pertaining to the operation of the state to their contemporary quantitative form, statistics both allow for and foster governance conceived of as a form of actuarial risk management. A caution is in order, however, for although there seems to be an evolutionary quality to this narrative, where one form of governance supplants another, this is not necessarily the case. Governance is a problem-solving activity, and different strategies to manage the population can exist alongside of one another; for example, both liberal and neo-liberal strategies might be brought to bear on a specific problem.

Classification and Governance

Foucault's work continually returns to the relationship between power and knowledge, and his analysis of governance is no exception. The above reflections make it clear that different strategies for governance are related to specific knowledges about the population to be governed. Such knowledges, and the experts who speak on their behalf, promise to 'render docile the unruly domains over which government is to be exercised, to make government possible and to make government better' (Rose 1996: 45). An important and often invisible process that supports the production of statistical knowledge and governmental power is the practice of classification. The production and reproduction of official classifications establishes the contours of the objects to be governed: it renders them knowable and potentially subject to political intervention. Different processes, people, and things are opened up to governance by virtue of the terms established on myriad surveys, censuses, and reports. While they often operate as the unseen background process to the production of knowledge, classifications have their own distinctive power and politics.

Classification is a common practice across different scientific domains and is a cornerstone of human cognition more generally (Lakoff 1987). This does not mean, however, that officially dividing the world into component parts is a straightforward and uncontroversial affair. Classifications often reveal as much, or more, about the assumptions, prejudices, dreams, and aspirations of the classifiers as they do about the objects of which they speak. The historical variability in how our scientific models have divided up nature and her inhabitants reveals that such divisions are conventions, informed by the theory being employed rather than by the way that the world spontaneously divides itself (Gould 1983). However, the fact that we live within the classificatory schemes of our own society makes it difficult for us to acknowledge their conventional status. It is often only when confronted with radically different taxonomies that we recognize the cultural specificity of our own classifications. Consider Foucault's introduction to *The Order of Things*, where he quotes Borges's selection from a Chinese encyclopedia where animals are divided into those '(a) belonging to the Emperor, (b) embalmed, (c) tame, (d) sucking pigs, (e) sirens,

(f) fabulous, (g) stray dogs, (h) included in the present classification, (i) frenzied, (j) innumerable, (k) drawn with a very fine camelhair brush, (l) et cetera, (m) having just broken the water pitcher, (n) that from a long way off look like flies' (Foucault 1970: xv).

To our eyes this is an absurd and laughable way to differentiate those entities that fall under the heading of 'animal.' The point is, however, that this sense of the absurd derives from our adoption of the classificatory schemes that have been institutionalized and legitimated by Western biologists. Some of the categories that we take for granted, that we see as foundational, turn out to be ambiguous or controversial when subjected to closer scrutiny. Take, for example, that apparently most primary of all divisions – man and woman, male and female. Feminists, queer theorists, and activists have troubled this dualism, and raised questions about what, exactly, we mean when we talk about 'sex' or 'gender.' Such questions extend beyond the domain of social theory. Paul Starr (1992: 283) recounts how in San Francisco at least one health-care organization 'requires six categories for its classification of sex, depending on the patient's genetic type, bodily type (which may be surgically altered), and presentation of self.' In the criminal-justice context, a study being conducted by Rosemary Gartner and Bill McCarthy on homicide patterns in four different cities expands the 'sex' of the victim to include four categories, consisting of male, female, male (at birth) transsexual, and female (at birth) transsexual.

An important theoretical line must be drawn between classifications of humans and non-humans. This difference must be accentuated because of the fact that irrespective of the words we use to describe it, the natural world is largely indifferent to how it is labelled (Hacking 1997: 15). From one classificatory system to the next, the thing that we call a goat or an igneous rock remains the same, although a qualification is in order. While the natural world does not transform itself in light of the names we assign to it, this is not to say that how humans classify the natural world is of no consequence. The terms, metaphors, and discourses we employ to delineate 'nature' – which is itself an ambiguous and contested classification (Soulé and Lease 1995) – frequently have dramatic repercussions. For example, the fact that some animals have been assigned to that category of entities that, if consumed in various ways, provides a boost to human longevity, virility, or sexual prowess has had disastrous implications for their continued survival. The same is true for animals deemed 'pests' or 'vermin.' The classifications we employ to delineate the natural world can have devastating and irreversible consequences.

Classificatory indifference is decidedly *not* the case when it comes to delimiting types of people. Whether we discriminate among people by virtue of their nationality, profession, class, ethnicity, or sex, such typologies can be both controversial and monumental in their long-term implications.

Classifications of people can be a lightning rod for political tension owing to the way in which aggregate numbers elide individual differences. Governmental strategies that attempt to ameliorate entrenched inequalities related to group membership often neglect other forms of difference in the process. Such tensions between the individual qua individual and as member of a larger aggregate have introduced a degree of reflexivity into official classificatory practices. As a result, some official classifications of people are encouraged and others tolerated as a necessary evil, while still others are expressly prohibited. Such distinctions have a historical component to them, as different periods have alternately fostered or restricted certain forms of classification.

The terms officially employed to delimit types of people can also play an important role in the production of subjectivities. Our sense of selves and of our potentialities is informed by the terms authorized by statistical agencies. Divisions sanctioned by the state can slowly be adopted by individuals such that they live their lives and conceive of others according to these authorized demarcations. However, statistical agencies do not have free reign to employ any set of classifications they might desire. Although statistical agencies have occasionally overlaid different human populations with classificatory schemes that are entirely alien to those being classified (Anderson 1991, chap. 10), it is more often the case that the ways in which the social world is currently ordered, and how people view themselves and their identities, limit the types of classifications that will be accepted as being accurate. Consequently, the most effective classificatory systems are those that connect with the properties with which a distinct group already identifies (Bourdieu 1991: 135).

Ian Hacking (1995b, 1997) employs the concept of 'dynamic nominalism' to accentuate the interplay between experience and classification. He emphasizes how the categories we use to label and organize people can merge with the 'real' features of individuals to the point that we come to identify with, and live our lives through, such classifications. Such mergings can evolve slowly over time or proceed at an astonishingly rapid pace. His study of what we now call 'multiple personality disorder' (Hacking 1995a) is a telling demonstration of how eagerly people can embrace and remake themselves in light of new diagnostic categories. Such categories are reciprocally informed by the ways that people behave and view themselves: 'The claim of dynamic nominalism is not that there was a kind of person who came increasingly to be recognized by bureaucrats or by students of human nature but rather that a kind of person came into being at the same time as the kind itself was being invented. In some cases, that is, our classifications and our classes conspire to emerge hand in hand, each egging the other on' (Hacking 1986: 228).

Official classifications are informed by existing social divisions and are, simultaneously, partially constitutive of the types of people in the world. However, classification can involve a process of both attractions *and* repulsions. Groups and individuals have occasionally stridently resisted and rejected new classificatory schemes. Political struggles have revolved around attempts to revise existing classifications in the hope of having them better correspond with people's lived reality, or to change the negative connotations associated with one classification to a positive, affirming one. State agencies play an important role in such processes, as they can normalize divisions that are, at root, arbitrary. As Bourdieu (1991: 133) observes, 'It is in the struggles which shape the history of the social world that the categories of perception of the social world, and the groups produced according to these categories, are simultaneously constructed.' Such conflicts bring the politics of classification into the public spotlight. Chapter 4 provides a detailed examination of the Centre's involvement in such classificatory politics.

Governing Criminal Justice

A defining project in criminology and the sociology of deviance has been the attempt to understand the causes of criminal behaviour in hopes of eliminating or reducing crime. An astounding array of factors have been implicated in this search for causes, but the focus of inquiry has regularly returned to the individual criminal. Recent modifications in criminal-justice policy and discourse mark, if not the end, certainly a radical transformation in this individualized approach to crime. Colin Sumner (1994) has gone so far as to write an extended obituary for sociological attempts to discover and eliminate the causes of deviant behaviour.

Supplanting the quest for an etiology of individual criminal behaviour is an official emphasis on crime understood as a routine statistical event with its own regularities and probabilities. Outside of the actions of those pedophiles and pathological killers who are subjected to highly public processes of demonization, most crimes are now approached as a 'normal accident.' As accidents, they are seen to be amenable to interventions aimed at the level of the aggregate rather than the individual. Garland (1997: 186) makes this point in his observation that 'viewed en masse, criminal events are regular, predictable, systematic, in the way that road traffic accidents are. It follows that action upon crime should cease to be primarily action upon deviant individuals and become instead action designed to govern social and economic routines.'

While the statistical risk management of crime has intensified in recent decades, this project was inherent in the earliest beginnings of criminal-justice statistics. From its inception, the collection of such statistics involved an attempt to manage crime risks through an assessment of the probabilities of crimes for classes of people and for specific physical environments. As Deflem (1997: 169) observes, since its development in eighteenth century Europe, 'criminal statistics was essentially description with a purpose: as risk assessment it collected information, and as risk management it predicted the crimes to be expected and prevented. Thus the transformation of crime from danger to risk was a crucial component of criminal statistics.'

In the move towards criminal risk assessment, our comprehension of the individual criminal has also been transformed. Our approach to criminals has moved from a search for the pathological to an appreciation of the normal. Previously understood as fundamentally different from the general population, criminals are now viewed as rational opportunistic actors, involved in a sober calculus of the potential costs and benefits of criminal behaviour. In the process, the criminal 'becomes a statistical individual, understood through his or her relation to a population with a recorded stock of experience and an emergent pattern of behavioral regularities' (Garland 1997: 182). Although a flourishing industry continues to search for the root individual causes of crime, it appears that the bloom is well off the rose for this enterprise, as we move from a concern with individual dangerousness to the management of criminal risks (Castel 1991). The policy aim is now not so much the normalization of the deviant as the transformation of the immediate physical environment, such that conditions that are highly correlated with crime are modified or eliminated (Cohen 1985). This change is most apparent in the increasingly popular criminological enterprises of 'crime prevention through environmental design' (Taylor and Gottfredson 1986; South 1987). Under this rubric a host of amoral techniques are advocated to 'design out' the possibility of crime or reduce its statistical probability. These include the use of environmental design strategies that emphasize technological and informal surveillance as well as target-hardening strategies that seek to make physical locations less susceptible to crime. Such techniques range from the practical to the comical to the deeply disquieting (see Davis 1990, chap. 4).

Neo-liberalism involves strategies of governance that become manifest in the actions of individuals who are free to choose from assorted forms of expertise and techniques provided by state and extra-state agencies. Criminal justice has seen the rapid emergence of a range of private security experts and companies who offer advice and commodities for individuals to consume in their attempts to avoid criminal victimization (Shearing and Stenning 1983; South 1988). A plethora of extra-state experts now advocate on behalf of the criminal risk profile of different groups of victims or potential victims (Rock 1986). Still others concentrate on the risks posed *by* the criminal-justice system itself, accentuating the statistical overrepresentation of different groups in terms of their arrest, conviction, and incarceration rates. Feeley and Simon (1994) have proposed that these broad changes amount to the emergence of a form of 'actuarial' criminal justice, characterized by three factors: (1) the population is taken as the appropriate target for power and intervention; (2) power is aimed at prevention and risk management; and (3) justice *is* increasingly understood as a formal set of rules internal to the system that are akin to a computer program.

One of the most important extra-state agencies involved in such practices is the insurance industry. Both O'Malley (1992) and Reichman (1986) emphasize how the insurance industry subtly coerces policyholders into adopting techniques and technologies to improve the risk profile of their homes and lifestyle. Insurance also prompts a form of 'responsibilization' (O'Malley 1992), whereby individuals are encouraged to adopt a reflexive attitude about the criminal risks they assume in their daily lives, risks that can be reduced by employing various forms of security commodities and expertise.

The knowledge developed by the CCJS and comparable institutions is fundamental to processes of actuarial justice. Aggregate criminal-justice statistics are highly suited to governmental strategies that seek to modify the criminal risks posed by different groups or physical locations. On occasion, the Centre has also actively encouraged the use of its data as a tool to responsibilize the citizenry. For example, in relation to its UCR variable for 'point of entry' on residential break-ins, the Centre proposed that this knowledge 'could possibly initiate a public awareness campaign by local law enforcement authorities to encourage residents to secure doors, windows, etc. when they leave their homes' (CCJS 1990a: 10). Several neo-liberal themes are also articulated in the Centre's claim that the introduction of detailed 'property crime' data elements on its UCRs can be used for 'improving crime prevention programs, developing marketing ideas for security firms, or evaluating the seriousness of specific types of property crime and their economic costs in terms of dollars and property loss' (ibid.: 13). In this one sentence we see an emphasis on crime prevention as an actuarial attempt to responsibilize the public, combined with the prospect of citizens ensuring against their risks of victimization by employing private security firms. Finally, the neo-liberal emphasis on an economic rationality is clear in the concern for the financial costs of crime.

Criminal-justice statistics are also connected with governmental efforts through their role in fostering the notion that criminal justice can itself be understood as a system. This is particularly apparent in the Centre, as many of its statistical indicators concern the performance of criminal-justice components and sub-components. In the 1970s, managers of criminal-justice institutions increasingly recognized the need to employ statistical representations of system performance as a tool of governance, and as a justification for resource allocation. Bottoms (1995) refers to this as a new form of criminal-justice 'managerialism' that involves, among other factors, the creation of key performance indicators and the active monitoring of aggregate information about the system and its functioning. New managerial discourses, increased calls for fiscal accountability, and exponential increases in computational abilities all combined to prioritize statistical knowledge as the basis or justification for decision making. Here a recently retired individual with more than forty years' experience working with Canadian crime statistics reflects on this heightened importance of statistics in criminal justice:

So you can look during the 70's at an increasing awareness of the need for statistics within the criminal justice community. And recognizing that their relationship with the national statistical agency ... was becoming much more significant in terms of the manager's welfare. That the manager was becoming much more dependent on having the right data at the right time ... What we had at the beginning of the 70's was an emerging area of where there were increasing requirements by the central agencies for quantitative data; Operational Performance Management Systems ... These were basically cost-effectiveness tools encouraging the manager to look at results and to quantitatively measure in order to achieve those results.

Aggregate statistics that document processes involved in the operation of various criminal-justice components, such as an organization's caseload, population flows, and cost-per-case, transform the criminal-justice system itself into an object of governance. Possibilities are opened up for intervening in the operation of these institutions at the systems level. In fact, criminal-justice statistics are a fundamental factor in promoting the impression that the relatively independent criminal-justice institutions combine to form a coherent and manageable system.

Statistics as Knowledge Network

The Canadian Centre for Justice Statistics is an intermediary, a statistical clearing house that produces numbers to serve the political and managerial needs of a host of institutions. The knowledge it generates is an important component in the governance of populations and of the criminal-justice system. The importance of the link between practices of governance and the institutional sites where governmental knowledge is produced has been acknowledged in important works by Nikolas Rose and Peter Miller (Rose and Miller 1992; Miller 1994; Rose 1996). These authors frequently mention the role that diverse 'centres of calculation' play in the creation and representation of the objects towards which governmental practices are directed. For governmental knowledge to be developed, people working in such centres must align a diverse assemblage of humans, organizations, and technologies into a functioning whole. Through such networks various forms of action at a distance are made possible, and as Rose (1996: 43) has argued, 'it is only to the extent that such alignments of diverse forces can be established that calculated action upon conduct across space and time can occur at all.'

Despite the recognition that centres of calculation play an important role in relation to practices of governance, little empirical research has explored how such centres operate. A schism exists between prescriptions about how statistical knowledge should be produced and sociological efforts to explore how such numbers are in fact produced. Any randomly selected social-science methods textbook will outline the stock and trade of quantitative methodology: procedural dictates and cautions for how best to produce, justify, and legitimate surveys, experiments, and polls. If we remain within this artificially bounded methodological realm we might be excused for conceiving of the processes of survey design, data collection and organization, system maintenance, and dissemination of findings as relatively straightforward affairs. Furthermore, one might come to believe that knowledge can be produced, and produced correctly, by simply following the rules. Philosopher Paul Feyerabend, in his anarchistic approach to scientific methodology, has challenged this image of science by famously proclaiming that the only valid methodological dictate is 'anything goes' (1993: 19). All other attempts to define the rules and procedures for producing scientific truth unduly restrict what is at heart a chaotic enterprise. A 'method' is simply the means by which something is accomplished. When it comes to the production of official numbers about crime and criminal justice, the method includes an informal set of practices that extend well beyond the techniques enshrined in textbooks.

The CCJS's methodology is a human and organizational affair involving complex inter-institutional negotiations, political acumen, and technical skill. The CCJS is akin to a statistical laboratory, working to produce authorized facts about crime and criminal justice. Although it differs in several respects from the idealized image of an experimental laboratory, we can learn a great deal about the Centre by scrutinizing its practices in light of approximately twenty years of sociological studies of laboratories. This strategy is also in keeping with the admonition from Knorr-Cetina (1995, 1992) that we expand our conception of the types of physical locations that are to count as laboratories. Miller and O'Leary (1994: 470) also entreat analysts to 'address those practices that seek to act upon and transform the world in specific and relatively bounded locales, even if this takes place outside the laboratory populated by physicists, chemists, and the like.'

At first glance it might appear that the analogy between the Centre and laboratory science is strained. Some might object that the staff at the CCJS are not scientists because they are considerably removed from the direct observation of the objects of which they speak. However, this distinction breaks down when we recognize that, like the Centre's staff, laboratory scientists routinely operate on representational forms, assays, and inscriptions that arrive at the door of the laboratory pre-structured and standardized (Latour and Woolgar 1979). Also, like the Centre's activity, much scientific laboratory work is routine, lacking the famous 'Eureka' moment of discovery. In fact, the diversity of endeavours categorized as science cross-culturally and historically is truly astounding. Questions about where to draw the line between science and non-science are frequently contentious and political (see Taylor 1996).

For the purposes of this study, I am not concerned about whether what goes on within the Centre should legitimately be designated as science. Instead, I propose that the similarities between scientific laboratories and the practices of the CCJS are such that it is fruitful to think about the Centre in light of sociological reflections on laboratory science. The parallels between laboratory practices and the Centre's routines will become more apparent in the following pages. However, at this point it is worth accentuating that both enterprises seek to produce acknowledged facts. As part of this fact-producing enterprise, a laboratory serves as a centre of calculation where efforts to mobilize distant places, people, and things are coordinated. Like a laboratory, the Centre is embedded in complex webs of technologies, interinstitutional affiliations, and knowledge flows, which all must be aligned in the hopes of producing facts.

This section continues to set the theoretical stage for the chapters that follow. It first presents the model of truth embraced in this study. This epistemology accentuates the importance of conflict and contingent forms of consensus in the production of truth. As such, it downplays the role typically afforded to how scientific statements are rendered true or false by virtue of their relation to an independent external reality. A series of authors have accented the role that the creation of networks made up of diverse and heterogeneous components plays in the production of scientific truths. The next chapter applies these insights on network construction to the efforts of Centre employees to develop and maintain the UCR survey.

Contested Knowledge

The sociology of science has an ongoing interest in the processes involved in the production of authorized truths. Such processes are approached in ways that are frequently at odds with how scientists account for the truth of their claims, which usually involves some variant of a correspondence theory of truth. Correspondence theories assume that our observations, indicators, and knowledges are true by virtue of the way that they accord with the structure and functioning of the world – a characteristic demonstrated most forcefully in the natural sciences through laboratory experiments. Since Thomas Kuhn's *Structure of Scientific Revolutions* (1962), however, correspondence theories have been increasingly recognized as unsatisfactory descriptions of scientific practice. Following Kuhn's now famous discussion of scientific paradigm shifts, there has been recognition from many quarters that ostensibly the same sensory experience, or evidence, can be perceived in dramatically different ways and be held to support contradictory hypotheses depending on the paradigm in which a scientist is situated. One of the most unrelenting critics of correspondence theories has been Richard Rorty. Taking his lead from Ludwig Wittgenstein, Rorty (1989) argues that our ideas are not true or false by virtue of their relation to the world, but because of how they accord to the rules for producing truth within historically specific vocabularies, or language games. As criterion-governed discourses, language games provide the rules for establishing truth and the types of people authorized to speak the truth (Foucault 1972). As a product of language, truth is ultimately a human creation. One implication of this insight is that sociological accounts of the institutionalization of scientific truths must proceed without easy recourse to claims about how science has managed to get nature 'right.'

Critiques of correspondence theories have expanded on the notion that scientific observations are inherently theory-laden, that the theories we employ shape and constrain our observations. F.A. Hayek's quip that 'without a theory, the facts are silent' is a succinct statement of this position. In a similar vein, others have advanced what has become known as the 'underdetermination thesis,' which holds that different explanatory accounts are possible for the same sensory experience, a fact that allows scientists (and others) to maintain allegiance to a core theory in the face of contradictory observations, providing that auxiliary hypotheses derived from the theory are modified. Evidence does not compel us to adopt a singular and exclusive account of what has been witnessed. Rather, the way that scientists make sense of their observations and the type of research they conduct can be related to their hopes, expectations, interests, and background assumptions (Longino 1990). This point is relatively easy to concede in relation to once-dominant scientific beliefs that have since been superseded or discredited, but is more difficult to recognize when discussing currently authoritative scientific truths. To practising scientists, the sociology of science often appears heretical, in that it seeks to unearth the broader social, cultural, or historical factors that shape, influence, or determine the truth of a claim. If it is not exclusively the nature of the world *as it is* that makes science true, other extra-scientific factors must at least partially account for why claims acquire the mantle of truth.

This study emphasizes the role that social reactions play in the production of truth. Truth is a consequence of the way that humans relate to different claims. Writing in 1907, pragmatist William James (1997: 114) argued that 'truth *happens* to an idea. It *becomes* true, is *made* true by events.' Bruno Latour (1987) has advanced a comparable argument for how scientific claims acquire a degree of facticity, emphasizing how the fate of a claim depends on whether it is embraced or neglected by different audiences. Truth itself is an end-state, achieved when a claim is embraced by other groups and agencies and is no longer subject to attack. Science involves efforts to persuade others to adopt various claims. As claims start to solidify into truth, the social, organizational, institutional, and technological antecedents to the production of a particular fact fall away and the world seems to simply speak for itself.

While this position appears to descend into relativism, Latour sees it as a step away from the relativist abyss. Truth is not relative to anything else, as facts clearly exist in the world. There are things that we generally agree about: 'If there is no controversy among scientists as to the status of fact, then it is useless to go on talking about interpretation, representation, a biased or distorted worldview, weak and fragile pictures of the world, unfaithful spokesmen' (Latour 1987: 100). In the absence of conflicts about a claim's status, the claim is undeniably true. Truth is a *consequence* of the settling of disputes and as such we cannot appeal to the truth of a claim to explain the reason why any particular dispute was settled.

Established truths are by no means permanent. Stable scientific facts can, occasionally with breathtaking speed, dissolve in the face of new claims or magnified critiques. As this happens, what were previously universal, impersonal facts again become associated with the actions and claims of particular people working in specific places.

Although statistics has not been a major empirical focus of science studies, one prominent study used statistical knowledge to explore some of the social factors that can shape the production of true knowledge. Donald MacKenzie's (1981) analysis of the development of statistics in Britain between 1865 and 1930 recounts how the statistical luminaries of this time, Galton, Pearson, and Fisher, were all involved in the eugenics movement. As part of the emerging professional middle class, MacKenzie argues, these individuals found eugenics particularly attractive as it emphasized the need for professional expertise in political decision making and proclaimed the biological superiority of their segment of society. He suggests that this common interest in eugenics became manifest in various ways in their statistical techniques. While it is impossible to fully convey the nuances of MacKenzie's argument here, one of his more intriguing claims is that the very notion of a statistical correlation was intimately bound up with Galton's interest in eugenics. In particular, he details how one of the key questions for eugenics concerned the relationship between the physical and mental attributes of parents and siblings. In effect, this amounted to a concern for the statistical dependence of two variables, and it was this eugenics concern that 'made the understanding and measurement of statistical dependence *as a phenomenon in its own right* a central goal of statistical theory' (MacKenzie 1981: 71). In effect, MacKenzie traces the emergence of a now indispensable statistical tool to the social interests of its creator and his social group.

Actor Networks: Identity Adoption and Ambivalence

A group of authors working under the rubric of 'actor-network theory' (ANT) or the 'sociology of translation' (Latour 1987, Callon 1986, Law 1987) have further radicalized the sociology of science. These authors present a vision of science as involving the complex and contingent interweaving of human and non-human components. They embrace the idea that truth is a status we confer upon ideas, and that these claims are continually subject to critique and opposition. Opponents or sceptics of particular knowledges or technologies will single out any conceivable aspect of a claim in efforts to deconstruct its veracity. Nothing is excluded out of hand in such attacks; if it serves to undermine or raise questions about the authorized status of a claim, it is fair game. Some of the things that can be subject to critique include a researcher's methodology, publication vehicle, rhetorical style, relationship with the media, funding source, scientific credentials, political affiliations, personal reputation, use of technology, and so on. The production of scientific knowledge involves efforts to anticipate such deconstructive strategies in order to circumvent and minimize their efficacy (Fuchs and Ward 1994). Science appears to be as much a battle between interested parties as an impartial quest for truth.

One prominent way in which ANT differs from other approaches in the sociology of science concerns its views on the explanatory force of broader social and/or structural phenomena (Callon and Latour 1992; Collins and Yearley 1992). Its proponents argue that one cannot simply appeal to 'the economy,' 'capitalism,' 'classes,' or 'interests' in order to explain why claims are accepted as true. This is because our understandings of such phenomena are themselves contested and constructed, each emerging out of their respective network (Latour 1993: 95). The stability we afford to such social entities must itself be explained in light of an examination of their respective knowledge networks.

The seminal text in this tradition is Latour and Woolgar's *Laboratory Life* (1979), which explores the role of the microsocial craft work of scientists in the production of laboratory facts. Their book presents an image of science as an ongoing attempt to transform chaos into order, a struggle where scientists employ a range of political, social, and economic resources traditionally evacuated from mainstream accounts of science. Tools are used that extend well beyond the test tubes, statistical analyses, and biological assays that are a scientist's stereotypical stock and trade. As Rouse (1993: 155) observes, 'All of the small local decisions about research materials, equipment, procedures, funding, personnel, skill development, and the like shape the actual development of the knowledges that invest and underwrite the sorts of knowledge claims that philosophers typically investigate.'

The ultimate aim of scientific practice is to produce a form of knowledge that assumes the status of a black box. Here 'black boxing' refers to how the various contingent, local, semiotic, personal, and technological elements originally associated with the production of a fact or technology are made to disappear from the final account. Scientific claims start off as the work of a few individuals doing specific studies in particular locations. As the claims gain credibility they slowly lose reference to these originating conditions and simply become true. The

AUGUSTANA UNIVERSITY COLLEGE
LIBRARY

networks that make the facts or technologies possible are progressively erased and forgotten.

For scientists to extend their truths to new contexts they must negotiate with an ever-increasing numbers of 'actants.' These consist of the myriad component parts of a knowledge network and can include technologies, organizations, assays, inscriptions, funding agencies, and so on. If a claim is to gain strength and move beyond its originating local contexts, these disparate human and non-human components must be patterned into a larger and increasingly complex whole. As Latour (1987: 108) observes, 'The spread in space and time of black boxes is paid for by a fantastic increase in the number of elements to be tied together.' John Law (1987) refers to these efforts to align an indefinite number and variety of elements as 'heterogeneous engineering.' None of these diverse component parts is any more or less important than any other, as all actants must perform their assigned roles faithfully for claims to stabilize. However, some elements will prove to be more recalcitrant than others, requiring intensified or novel strategies to draw them into the network.

Within an organizational centre such as a laboratory, scientific actors draw together natural phenomena, organizations, individuals, and technologies into an operational whole. Callon (1986) has summarized this task as consisting of processes of 'interressement,' 'translation,' and 'enrollment.' How these tasks are accomplished are unique to any particular knowledge network.

In succession, 'interressement' refers to the processes whereby scientists distinguish the types of identities that various actants must adopt for a technology to work or a fact to emerge. It involves imputing a particular role to a person, artefact, or organism that it must fulfil in order for the larger network to function. This is followed by the process of 'translation,' whereby scientists negotiate with the different component parts in an attempt to transform existing identities so that new roles are adopted. In such negotiations, scientists strive to situate their research or technology as an obligatory point of passage for the fulfilment of the interests imputed to these diverse actants. Scientists can attempt to satisfy an almost infinite variety of interests: organizations might have an interest in greater prestige or funding, scientists might be interested in furthering their existing research program, and biological entities can be credited with having an interest in propagating their species. In all of these constructions, the researchers aim to make themselves and their knowledge indispensable to the fulfilment of these interests. So, for example, in his study of an attempt to develop new techniques to cultivate scallops, Callon (1986) documents how scientists attributed a general interest in survival to a species of scallops and then set about trying to advance that interest through the new cultivation practices. Finally, 'enrollment' consists of efforts to stabilize and routinize these relationships. Attempts to control relations and identities exemplify Foucault's observation (1980: 131) that truth is 'produced only by virtue of multiple forms of constraint.' Having translated the interests of entities such that they identify with the knowledge to be produced, scientists must ensure that these entities perform their roles in a routine and predictable fashion. Using various technologies and tactics, social relations are made to assume a mechanical quality – to the extant that originally unstable relationships start to behave like machines.

Scientists who are unable to control and stabilize these roles face the danger that the component parts will revoke their willing participation and withdraw from the network. A series of 'intermediaries' are therefore employed to ensure that the different actants perform their roles faithfully. Intermediaries consist of anything that passes between actors and defines the relationship between them, and can include such things as texts, technologies, disciplined human beings, and money. These elements stabilize the behaviour of different actants and channel their functioning in the direction desired by the orchestrating actor. As such, they give social links shape, consistency, and permanence over time. Murdoch (1995: 747) provides a concise summary of these processes of identity construction and stabilization:

> In order for an actor successfully to enrol entities (human and nonhuman) within a network, their behaviour must be stabilised and channelled in the direction desired by the enrolling actor. This will entail redefining the roles of the actors and entities as they come into alignment, such that they come to gain new identities or attributes within the network. It is the intermediaries ... which act to bind actors together, 'cementing' the links. When there is a perfect translation, or redefinition, of actors' identities and behaviours then these are stabilised within the network. The stronger the network, the more tightly the various entities (human and nonhuman) are tied in.

An intriguing insight that emerges from ANT is that the diverse component parts of a knowledge network are themselves composed of their own networks. For example, laboratory scientists routinely rely on a steady supply of electricity to run experiments. Electricity is itself a black-boxed network of people, schedules, technologies, funding arrangements, and texts. It is, simultaneously, a technological, social, and organizational accomplishment that only arrives in our homes or offices if computerized switching devices function properly, if cables do not freeze or wash away, if emergency crews do not go on strike, and so on. It is only when something goes wrong with any particular 'black-boxed' knowledge or technology that the myriad component parts that make up our scientific networks become apparent.

The upshot of this understanding of actor networks is that it is essentially impossible to map all of the component parts of a network. Any apparently solid entity, institution, person, or phenomenon that one might point to as being part of any particular network is itself the product of its own processes of network building and maintenance. An apparently stable and singular entity is actually always composed of an assemblage of multiple and fluid component parts, which are themselves multiple and fluid (Deleuze and Guattari 1987). Consequently, the analyst's job is not to depict the totality of any particular network but to explore the strategies and techniques employed by scientists to try to interest and control particularly recalcitrant actants. It is through such translations and efforts to control these preferred identities that networks coalesce into a functioning whole.

Actor-network theory conceives of scientists as consciously working to align recalcitrant actants into a functioning network. In fact, the image of human agency emerging out of ANT has at times almost appeared to reproduce earlier hagiographic accounts where monumental scientific discoveries are attributed to the labours and insight of exceptional individuals (see Latour 1988, 1983). However, this image of a sovereign individual producing facts by aligning different component parts through sheer force of will misrepresents the role of agency in ANT. Agency is itself the result of complex processes of network building and maintenance. As Law observes (1992: 384), '[A]n actor is a patterned network of heterogeneous relations, or an effect produced by such a network.' The abilities and possibilities of agents derive from the networks of people, laws, technologies, and artefacts in which they are embedded.

Agency, and therefore power, is precarious and contingent. If technologies, nature, individuals, and organizations do not adopt their ascribed roles, the larger network is unstable and the scientist's ability to produce facts is in doubt.

Conclusion

The Foucauldian analysis of governance and the sociology of science have largely evolved independently of one another. Nikolas Rose, perhaps the most prominent author writing on governance, has acknowledged the importance of actor networks in producing the knowledge that serves as the basis for governmental practice. However, Rose also suggests (1999: 19) that studies of governance are *not* studies of 'the relations that obtain amongst political and other actors and organizations at local levels and their connection into actor networks and the like.' Instead, he urges analysts to concentrate on the rationalities and strategies of rule characteristic of particular styles of governance.

To date, authors writing about actor-networks have not engaged the literature on governance. Given their lineage in the sociology of science, it is not surprising that studies of actor-networks have tended to concentrate on traditional scientific practice. Perhaps the most prominent ANT study is Latour's (1983, 1988) examination of Pasteur's paradigmatically scientific research on anthrax. Nonetheless, in their efforts to produce a general set of methods for studying scientists and engineers, ANT-affiliated authors have provided us with a set of powerful conceptual tools to study knowledge production more generally.

There needs to be a continuing exchange across these two sociological sub-fields. Studies of governance need to concentrate more on the network-building efforts involved in producing governmental knowledge. While Rose might be correct that such studies would not constitute studies of governance per se, they would deepen our knowledge about the epistemological preconditions for governmental practice. Such an exchange would also benefit sociologists of science, in that it would demonstrate how scientific efforts to control and manipulate the natural world are not terribly different in the abstract from the means required to represent and control the social world. The next chapter examines the knowledge network specific to the production of crime data, and is an example of what research that combines the ANT approach and a sensitivity to concerns of governance might look like.

3

Networks and Numbers: The Institutional Production of Crime Data

There is little awareness, except on the part of those directly involved, of the ways in which official statistics are produced.

Government Statisticians' Collective (1979: 130)

To understand liberal governance we must appreciate the practices that make social facts possible. Such facts emerge from networks that generate volumes of inscriptions, that is to say, transportable representational forms such as pictures, drawings, graphs, and so on. Inscriptions flow into a central location, where they are coordinated and emerge as a host of official indices. The importance of the specific operations of these centres of calculation is accentuated by Nikolas Rose (1996: 43), who observes that 'the composition of such networks is the condition of possibility for "action at a distance."' Unfortunately, however, little effort has been expended to unpack the specific means used by these sites to produce their knowledges.

In its efforts to produce knowledge compatible with governmental aims, the Canadian Centre for Justice Statistics imputes identities and roles to different actors, a process of naming accompanied by ongoing attempts to ensure that these actors then conform to these identities. The Centre's success or failure in such endeavours is evident to the extent that it has been able to become indispensable to the different component parts of the criminal-justice system. This chapter examines the power of the Centre – a process that involves 'describing the way in which actors are defined, associated and simultaneously obliged to remain faithful to their alliances' (Callon 1986: 224). As will become apparent, identity adoption and rejection are the extreme poles of a continuum of differential commitment to roles and responsibilities that Centre personnel seek to establish and stabilize. Some actants assume their new roles almost seamlessly, while others are more reluctant and still others fall away completely.

Criminal-justice statistics must have a minimally recognized relationship to the objects they purport to describe for them to be useful for governmental practice. Despite the limitations of critiques of official crime statistics detailed in the previous chapter, the Centre's efforts have remained stable and, if anything, become even more entrenched. Such success can be attributed to processes of network construction and maintenance. For a knowledge network with the scope and complexity necessitated by the Uniform Crime Reports, literally thousands of heterogeneous components must be aligned into a functioning whole. However, this chapter does not attempt to provide a comprehensive map of all the components of this network. The immense scope of the phenomena that make up this network preclude such an effort, as it includes computers, deputy ministers, software specialists, statistical experts, police officers, the public, court clerks, chiefs of police, communication systems, and so on. Instead, the chapter emphasizes the efforts to enrol particularly recalcitrant entities and shows how the Centre's preferred identities for such actants are occasionally resisted. The police in particular are examined, as the identities that the Centre imputes to both police officers and police organizations have at times proved to be difficult to control and stabilize.

Police Organizations

The Centre has a complex set of relations with the police. The latter are assumed to be overseen by rational systems managers who want methodologically sound national crime data in order to compare their force's performance with that of other organizations. Although police forces can produce crime data for their own jurisdictions, different accounting practices across police forces can make it difficult to make national comparisons. The Centre has carved out a niche for itself within the police community by providing nationally comparable crime data.

The presumption that the police are committed to having reliable data on their own internal reporting systems is crucially important to the Centre. Given that the Centre employs a methodology that extracts its numbers from the data on operational police systems, it is important for the CCJS to be able to trust that the police reliably collect data and maintain their systems. Confidence in the accuracy of the data on the police's systems underpins any faith that the Centre can place in its own data. For example, the Centre's 1997 *Juristat* (Kong 1999) on crime statistics noted that an error had been discovered in Toronto's crime data from the previous year (1995–6). This necessitated that the Centre revise Toronto's published violent crime rate for that year from an 11 per cent reduction to a 4 per cent reduction, and revise its property crime rate from a 6 per cent reduction to a 4 per cent reduction. The same publication also noted that in 1997 the Winnipeg police department had discovered that its police officers were not reporting a number of minor offences. Thus, what the Centre had reported as a 2 per cent reduction in Winnipeg's violent crime rate was in actuality a 5 per cent *increase*, while the city's property crime rate had to be revised from a 4 per cent decline to a 3 per cent decline. Combined, these changes meant that what the Centre had publicized as a 2 per cent reduction in the national crime rate had to be revised to a 1 per cent reduction. These examples demonstrate the degree to which the Centre depends on the accuracy of the reporting processes in the jurisdictions.

If the police want national crime data they must provide their local crime data to the Centre. As the police have been providing monthly tabulations of UCR data to the Centre since 1961, it is safe to say that this is now a fairly routine exercise. However, the development of the revised UCRII in the 1980s required considerable effort in the attempt to bring all the police forces in line with the new reporting and systems requirements. During this process the Centre, along with the Canadian Association of Chiefs of Police, became a key advocate for new identities for both itself and the police. The UCRII was to be much more information-intensive, and Centre staff had to overcome resistance from groups and individuals within the Initiative who either opposed the new survey or were sceptical about its utility. A Centre employee who was instrumental in the development of the UCRII recounts the subtle lobbying that had to be undertaken in order to get these parties on board:

One of the challenges ... is we didn't have any microdata surveys at the time. So one of the issues was 'Why do you want microdata? Why do you need data at that level? You are going to have five million records of information every year? To do statistical analysis? Give us a break, we don't need all of this. It is going to be costly, ineffective, how do you plan to do it?' That was a major challenge ... We travelled the country explaining what we were trying to do, talk about the feasibility of doing it. Assessing their systems. Basically getting a buy-in.

One comparatively new identity that the Centre had to foster was that of the computerized police force. While some police organizations already employed computers, many did not or they used them exclusively for administrative purposes. Retrospectively, the drive to computerize may not seem that remarkable, but in the 1980s it was still a serious and risky undertaking for many police organizations who had to deal with questions about data security, costs, and whether to develop a system in-house, or whether they should make the move to computers at all (Ackroyd et al. 1992). The UCRII proposal presented an ideal scenario whereby Canada's major forces would fairly rapidly move towards computerization.

One way that police interests were translated into the UCRII system was through strategic appeals to existing police concerns. The Centre's advocacy for the new UCRII tapped into the police's recurrent complaint that they were being overwhelmed with demands to collect massive amounts of information for a host of different organizations and institutions (Ericson and Haggerty 1997). Centre staff suggested that the move to electronic reporting would make police systems more rational and flexible in reporting information, formatting it, and making eventual upgrades. The importance of computerization to its plans meant that the Centre did not stand idly by waiting for police forces to develop their own systems. Instead, the CCJS worked with the police to secure a particular vision of the future of police reporting. The Centre's Technical Assistance Directorate (TAD) has funds to help jurisdictions establish electronic interfaces and develop information systems. While these funds are spread across the different surveys and cannot be used to purchase equipment, they helped entice some police forces into adopting the UCRII. A senior analyst in the policing-services section recounts how this money has been an important way to interest police forces in moving towards computerized UCRII reporting:

First of all, the police services [of the CCJS] work to encourage going the

new, modern automated route, and money is available. So you get trial
money first of all. It would be open to anybody who wants to buy into it.
With police budget cutbacks [the police] want to use their resources to be
fiscally responsible. So if they can get money to do something, they could.
And if they saw that they are going to have to do it eventually anyway,
and there are more and more demands upon their system, then they
would have a reason for joining us.

A member of TAD recounted how he reads his mandate 'as liberally
as possible' in order to provide extra electronic reporting perks and
systems benefits to the jurisdictions. This is because 'it is those additional benefits that will help provide for buy-in. Without the buy-in
you will not get quality data. That has been the problem all the way
along.'

Within the policing mandate are a variety of different roles beyond
that of the stereotypical 'crime buster.' Officers are alternatively constructed as educators, community activists, problem solvers, philosophers, guides, and friends (Cumming, Cumming, and Edell 1965). In
addition to this array of identities, Centre staff encourage officers to
embrace the identity of faithful recorder and communicator of information. Having established that identity for the police, the Centre
must remain vigilant to ensure that the police maintain that imputed
role. Computer interfaces are useful in this regard because they routinize the relations between the police forces and the Centre. Computerized reporting systems 'background' the relationships between the
police and the CCJS, which means that they function invisibly. As
John Law observes (1991: 174), one of the best ways to stabilize social
relations is to embody them 'in durable materials: relations that tend,
everything else being equal, to generate effects that last.' Computers
can accomplish this task wonderfully. Some police jurisdictions have
established reporting formats that automatically transpose data from
an officer's electronic reports to the UCR categories, so that an officer
may not even be aware that he is providing data to Statistics Canada.
Private software contractors specializing in computerized police systems have furthered this trend by embedding the Centre's reporting
conventions directly into policing software. Not only must the police
have computer systems, they must rationally and conscientiously *maintain* these systems. This includes modifying the UCRII interfaces and
coding conventions as police practices and rules for classifying events
and behaviours are revised.

In their efforts to stabilize a preferred set of police identities Centre employees cannot personally negotiate with the hundreds of Canadian police organizations, let alone thousands of police officers. Instead, they rely on proxy groups who stand in for and articulate the interests of the broader police community. The Police Information and Statistics Committee (POLIS) of the Canadian Association of Chiefs of Police is an important agency in this context. As the national statistical arm of the police community, this body initiates and develops many proposals concerning crime statistics. A former member of the Centre accentuates the importance of acquiring the cooperation of the POLIS committee for any proposal relating to crime statistics:

> So basically, all these guys are representatives from the largest forces. But they do carry a lot of weight. If they say 'absolutely no' then they will get a lot of support for that. So POLIS is critical. It is almost like the lobby group that you have to get on side. But that is only half the battle because you have to get the other 580 forces to agree as well. And you do that by saying 'OK, now we are collecting these data.' Some forces will say 'Fine,' others will say 'No we won't,' others will say 'We don't have it.' So they are just one step. They are a critical part because they give credibility to any data collection function you want to do.

The Centre occasionally applies subtle legal and political pressure in attempts to establish identities. For example, citizens are legally compelled to provide the authorities with knowledge about themselves in certain instances, such as when they are arrested. Such provisions are a condition of possibility for the production of crime statistics, as they allow the police to legally compel individuals to signify aspects of their lives according to the classificatory options embedded on official forms. Canada's Statistics Act also structures the entire Justice Initiative, legally requiring police forces to provide crime data to Statistics Canada. This act broadly frames the relations and obligations between the different institutional players, but in practice it is seldom explicitly invoked. As a senior adviser at the Centre observed, 'You would never go to a jurisdiction and say: "Unless you give us these data we are going to pursue you to the letter of the federal law." It would be ridiculous.' Regular appeals to the Statistics Act would be a sign that relations between the Centre and the jurisdictions had deteriorated to such a degree that the very existence of the Initiative was in jeopardy. However, resistance by some institutional actors to comply with the aims of the Centre can occasionally be overcome through implicit or explicit appeals to political hierarchies. For example, Centre employees can portray such reluctance as contradicting the desires of the deputy ministers who sit on the JIC and have therefore authorized the Centre's data-collection regime.

In practice, the Centre has had varying degrees of success in maintaining these idealized police identities. Individuals, agencies, and technologies have tendencies and inclinations that are often at odds with such new identities. Consequently, there are ongoing struggles to overcome opposition to particular roles. For example, the Centre's attempts to translate the police's purported interest in rational forms of management into an interest in national statistics have occasionally been resisted. Some jurisdictions recognize the importance of such information, while others are less sanguine about the potential benefits. A senior member involved in overseeing the RCMP's operational statistical systems was clearly not sold on the advantages of participating in the UCR: 'If you are asking me how does it benefit the RCMP, I don't see any benefits really coming back that are all that significant when compared to the enormous expenditures that we have to put forward.'

The Centre's attempts to sell the UCRII with promises about how it will reduce the amount of information that police officers have to process is also risky. In legitimating police grievances about the knowledge burden imposed on officers, the Centre actually reinforces police arguments that could be used to undermine subsequent Centre efforts. The Centre is involved in a delicate balancing act wherein it seeks to collect as much information as is practicable while not upsetting the police, who already feel put upon by too many knowledge demands. An officer in the RCMP's data-records division accentuated this point by cautioning that '[i]f [Centre personnel] antagonize those departments sufficiently, and it does become really burdensome, then there is liable to be some political backlash.' A senior methodologist at Statistics Canada reiterated the political risks of asking the police for more and more information: 'There is a real danger that if you keep pushing you may not get anything, or you will get the whole data file. You have to be part politician on this stuff. A project manager has to be careful what they ask for.' We should not underestimate what a catastrophe it would be for the Centre if the police wavered in their commitment to the UCR.

The development of the UCRII has been slowed by the police's halting progress towards computerization. This process has been hindered by a number of factors, including its financial expense. A senior member of the Centre's Technical Assistance Directorate estimated that it was going to cost the RCMP alone over $80 million to adopt the new UCRII. The result of this lag in the adoption of police computers is that many forces have been slow to embrace the UCRII reporting conventions. In 1996 the UCRII registered about 46 per cent of the total volume of recorded crime in Canada. Crime statistics for the RCMP and Ontario Provincial Police continue to be glaring omissions from the survey, but once they come on-line, the UCRII will account for approximately 90 per cent of recorded crime.

As the system developed, however, it became apparent that it was going to be exceedingly difficult to have the remaining small forces adopt the UCRII anytime soon. In light of this, a Centre respondent recounted how the policing services directorate had drawn up a list of police forces 'which would account for 80% of the crime in Canada. The last 20% we weren't going to go after. It just wasn't cost-effective. So to my mind there has always been this idea that we are not going to go after them.' This 20 per cent of crime stems largely from about 200 smaller rural police forces. The Centre ultimately hopes to bring these forces into the survey, but as a survey manager recounted, '[This] won't be in my lifetime and probably not in yours.' Smaller forces continue to provide crime data exclusively on the basis of the old aggregate UCR. The result has been a modification of the original knowledge claims for the UCRII. Instead of being able to document incident-based crime data for all of Canada, the new survey under-represents crime patterns in rural Canada, which tends to have smaller, non-computerized police forces.

The UCRII was also sold to police forces partially on the promise of the greater flexibility provided by a computerized system. Unfortunately, this too has proved to be elusive. An inertia has crept into these computer systems because of their tight coupling with other organizational components of the police and the Centre. Even small modifications can require entire systems to be retooled and reprogrammed. Consequently, these systems are less flexible in practice than their easily manipulated electronic programming might suggest. A member of the policing directorate accentuated this point:

When we want to change something, that means that the police have to change the way that they are doing things. With an electronic interface, we have a load of interfaces that are out there right now. Any time we want to make a change, then, we have to go in with a software developer and rewrite programs. A tremendous amount of overhead is involved. So that becomes a headache. Our edits tend to be very elaborate as well with the micro-data. That means that any changes we make means changes to our edits. So if we are actually making changes to the fundamental requirements of the survey, the trickle-down effect is very big. That means we don't do it very often. That means the survey becomes quite rigid. That is the real down side of it.

Originally constructed as diligent computer-system managers, police administrators have at times neglected this responsibility, or have not taken it as seriously as some members of the Centre would prefer. The computer couplings between the police and Centre work best as black boxes, producing unyielding and automatic exchanges of data. Black boxes can also occasionally break down, and when that happens, they can become considerably more transparent, as previously invisible processes are subjected to intense scrutiny. One issue that the Centre is currently dealing with in this regard concerns what one respondent termed 'interface creep.' The problems derive from the fact that police operational reporting systems evolve over time, requiring ongoing changes to the interfaces with the Centre to avoid reporting errors. Some organizations have not maintained their end of the bargain with due vigilance, resulting in the appearance of obvious errors in their numbers or suspicions among Centre staff that things might be amiss with their data.

The possibility that the police have not committed themselves wholeheartedly to the maintenance of computerized interfaces is perhaps related to how their obligations were originally sold to them. While the Centre works to impress the police with the importance of maintaining interfaces, the amount of time and labour this effort requires is not necessarily accentuated in the early stages of discussion. There is a concern that the police might balk at assuming this ongoing maintenance responsibility if they knew the extent of the undertaking. An individual who establishes jurisdictional interfaces makes this point:

The benefits [of computerization] are easy to come up with, it is the costs that are usually soft-sold. Sometimes you have to do that because if you didn't soft-sell the costs you can't overcome the hurdles. Sometimes once you get over the hurdles, even though the costs are high, they will continue with them because it is in place. An inertia carries it forward. If you didn't soft-sell the beginning you could never get commitment. It is an unfortunate thing that you have to do that, but I think that is human nature. There are political ramifications to everything. If you give every-body all of the negatives they will use that as an excuse, almost every time, to keep the status quo. That is not a bad thing if the status quo is acceptable. I wish there was some other way.

Police Officers

For crime reporting to work, police officers must conscientiously as-sume the role of data collector. In order to institutionalize such an identity the Centre has drawn from, and appropriated, dominant conceptualizations of police work. Such strategic invocations of exist-ing identities are one of the best ways to transform a group into will-ing participants in a knowledge network.

Most police officers conceive of policing as involving efforts to aug-ment public safety through the apprehension and legal processing of criminals. The Centre tries to interest police officers in the practice of data accumulation by equating data collection with crime fighting. For example, the Centre has produced a training video for police officers entitled 'Crime Statistics: Your Silent Partner.' The video commences with a voice-over imploring police officers: 'No matter what part of the country you live in, police officers are all fighting the same war, the war against crime. One of the ways to help fight that war is through the collection and use of crime statistics.' This is a straightforward attempt to translate interests: if police officers want to catch criminals and make the streets safe, they will consistently submit their data according to the Centre's reporting conventions. The video then dem-onstrates how an officer's data are used by police managers to target specific crimes and problem areas, which will ultimately lead to re-ductions in crime. Such efforts to enrol officers into a regime of consci-entious documentation are critical. Officers must alternatively be en-couraged, coerced, and disciplined into taking their paperwork seri-ously if the ensuing data is to be of any value. The entire UCR system rests on this classificatory enterprise, as do any governmental strate-gies that seek to modify crime rates.

While rhetorical moves to construct police officers as data collectors are significant, other factors are more important still. Specifically, po-lice officers assume their data-collection role because it has become institutionalized within police organizations where good police work increasingly translates into producing 'good paper.' A police officer's data-production skills are regularly monitored and evaluated as a component of promotional decisions. Situating officers in a regime of documentary discipline has augmented the classificatory function of police officers. Depending on the force, officers' reports can undergo several levels of detailed scrutiny. Their forms are regularly examined by a 'reader' who scores an officer's reports according to the official UCR reporting criteria. If an officer has omitted information or strayed outside of the reporting guidelines, his or her forms are returned for correction. The training video mentioned earlier gives a glimpse of such lessons in discipline. As the two police protagonists reflect on the fact that their UCR report about a break and entry had been returned to them because it was improperly completed, one officer admonishes his partner, and the audience, 'I think it's time we started taking a little bit more care filling those things out.' By institutionalizing and monitoring data-collection standards, the police organization is doing part of the Centre's work.

Having drawn police officers into the knowledge network, it is now necessary to control their actions. Officers not only have to record occurrences, but they must do so in a predictable fashion. A system in which officers simply provide narrative accounts of what transpired is of little value to a statistical organization or to the aims of governance. Governmental knowledge production becomes predictable through the classificatory options on official forms that structure knowledge into predetermined formats and categories. Such technologies allow central locations to direct the distant observations and actions of complete strangers. Dorothy Smith (1990) highlights how similar procedures are at work in the production of statistics on women with mental illness. These statistics rely on programs that train physicians how to assign individuals into recognized 'types' of mental illness. Individual cases are made actionable according to criteria that are imposed through abstract expert systems that structure patient/physician interactions from a distance. Such official acts of classification ignore or set aside the lived realities of patients, much in the same way that a victim's or offender's subjective understanding of a criminal event is evacuated from the statistical record.

When the police take their classificatory responsibilities seriously, there are often ongoing exchanges between the Centre and police forces concerning how to interpret classificatory rules. One Centre employee is primarily responsible for handling police queries about how to record ambiguous situations. Since the chaos of the world often does not conform to the existing classificatory options, this individual spends a great deal of time trying to clarify the rules for how to score ambiguous situations. This often Byzantine classificatory enterprise occasionally moves into the realm of the admittedly bizarre. For example, one police officer requested clarification on how to score the victim record for a case of 'other sexual assault.' Since he was dealing with an instance of bestiality, the requirement for a victim record proved to be quite comical. As the Centre's documentation on this instance concludes, the prerequisite for a victim record 'works great for the majority of crimes in this catch all, but becomes a problem when a dog is involved. It is rejected when no victim record is submitted.'

Police officers are assumed to resent and resist their role as information recorder. Computers that automatically translate an officer's use of Criminal Code classifications into the Statistics Canada format help overcome such resistance. In forces that lack such technology, police personnel must be trained to classify according to the UCR rules. Individual police forces provide this instruction, with occasional assistance from the Centre. The training, or lack thereof, of jurisdictional personnel in the classificatory peculiarities of many of the Centre's surveys has been an ongoing concern within the Initiative. This is evident in these minutes of a 1994 Liaison Officers Committee meeting: 'Data quality is primarily dependent upon staff training of those involved in information collection and the implementation of system edit checks which identify missing or erroneous data and provide data quality reports. The reality has been that resources for staff training are often insufficient and system edit checks are by-passed to reduce the cost of data input and processing.'

By now it should be readily apparent that the practices of police officers and organizations are a weak link in the extended UCR network. While the police have largely been enrolled, their identities have proved difficult to control. However, such weak points in a knowledge network – places of epistemological ambiguity and contestation – tend to foster new forms of knowledge, practice, and rhetoric. This flurry of activity that emerges at a network's weak point is not unique to the Centre, but is a common scientific phenomena (Rouse 1993: 154).

In attempts to control the production of knowledge by the police, the Centre has instituted a fairly onerous set of formal and informal procedures to scrutinize police data. After the police have checked and verified their files, the files are sent to the Centre, where they are again examined to ensure that they are complete and that the data appear reasonable. The data then go through a complex regime of human and technological scrutiny, including a series of computerized 'logical edits' which ensure that all the crucial data elements are present and that the data are logically consistent. Such edits provide staff with a greater degree of trust in the data and reduce the amount of time they have to spend personally scrutinizing files.

The Centre's efforts to track down potential errors in the statistics have some distinctly Durkheimean resonances. Durkheim (1938) conceived of crime as a normal phenomenon, something that augments social cohesion through public reactions to criminal behaviour. Relatively stable statistical rates of crime and suicide (Durkheim 1951) are therefore actually indicative of a 'healthy' society. It is only when there are radical fluctuations in statistical rates (in either direction) that we should become alarmed, as such swings indicate broader pathological changes in the social structure. As Durkheim (1938: 72) cautions, 'There is no occasion for self-congratulation when the crime rate drops noticeably below the average level, for we may be certain that this apparent progress is associated with some social disorder.' Centre personnel also work on the assumption that crime rates should be relatively stable from year to year. They too believe that they must only account for major fluctuations. As a senior employee involved with the UCR stated, '[W]e assume a certain amount of continuity on the data. So we just test for abnormal data. If something comes up then we take a closer look at it.'

A comparable presumption of normalcy overlays the entire Centre. This working assumption about how criminal-justice statistics should behave informs staff thinking about when to be concerned about potential problems with their data. However, contra Durkheim, Centre personnel do not seek to explain statistical fluctuations by appeal to structural changes to an external normative order. Instead, they look for the influence that police practices, technology, classification, and human error might have had on the data. CCJS personnel assume that such factors will result in statistical fluctuations that make the data stray from the norm. The possibility that errors of classification, system failure, and neglect might actually result in numbers that are in line with anticipated statistical trends is beyond the working practices and conceptual framework of Centre personnel. No effort is made to try and account for why numbers remain stable, as stable numbers are, quite simply, the norm.

This presumption of *normalcy* is embedded in the considerable UCRII technological infrastructure that tracks variations in crime trends over time and across comparably sized police forces. Recently introduced electronic tolerance edits automatically detect and flag statistical trends that fall outside of user-defined statistical standard deviations, a measure of the normal distribution of a set of statistical data. These edits operate by checking how many standard deviations a particular variable strays from the norm. The point at which these fluctuations are deemed to be a problem is a product of institutional routines and decision making. The standard deviation for crimes recognized as having a greater discretionary enforcement component, such as narcotics or prostitution, is set higher than for other crimes. Analysts scrutinize the options that the system flags to see if the data need further investigation. The point where the fluctuations are flagged for greater scrutiny is also established with a recognition of the limited organizational ability to respond to these computer-generated cautions. If they are set too low, analysts risk being overwhelmed by a flood of relatively minor statistical deviations. 'Basically you say "How many records can I review?" And then you cut off at that point' was how one respondent described the process of deciding where to establish these edits.

The use of computerized edits, and the greater reliance on computers more generally, has also produced some unwanted side-effects. In particular, it has introduced a series of complex interactions into an already complex system, and a greater degree of system impenetrability. Charles Perrow (1984: 78) suggests that systems with unfamiliar, unplanned, and unexpected sequences are 'interactively complex.' Such complexity makes systems management and troubleshooting difficult because crucial operations and interconnections are designed to be hidden from the operator. This is exacerbated by the fact that system operators have limited comprehension of some processes and that such systems have unfamiliar or unintended feedback loops. Consequently, operators are likely to experience mysterious interactions among components that designers did not anticipate and operators cannot recognize. Such tendencies were mentioned by some Centre respondents who highlighted the difficulties of monitoring the interactions of computer systems, interfaces, and edits. Here a senior person involved in the production of UCR statistics gives a sense of the difficulties that have emerged as their systems have become more interactively complex:

The systems are what allows us to [produce the UCRII], but it is also the systems that make it that much more difficult to resolve things ... when you have problems, because there is such a heavy systems overlay on the process, they can be much more difficult to find. They can be very invisible. Unless you have a lot of experience with it, you will – if you don't miss it you will have a heck of a time figuring out what caused the problem. If you do miss it then you are lost. If you are not that familiar with the process and all of the intricacies it can be really difficult to fathom why some data are behaving in a particular way with a particular respondent. And a lot of times the respondent won't know themselves. You have to alert them to it that there might be a problem here. For someone who is familiar it could be a two-day resolution process. For someone who is not, it could be a two-week or two-month resolution process.

While individual police officers are embedded in a regime of disciplinary surveillance of their data production, police organizations are disciplined by the computer system. When there are problems with an individual file, the edit checks for the UCRII produce 'error reports.' Police forces are sent copies of these reports so that they can correct the file in question, modify their system, or take greater vigilance in the future. While the percentage of files that prompt an error report is usually relatively low, the high number of total UCRII incidents that some forces submit on a monthly basis means that the total number of error reports they receive can be potentially overwhelming. A senior member of the policing-services program suggested that perhaps 7 per cent of the records generate a message back to the source; but with a force such as the Metropolitan Toronto police, which sends the Centre approximately 25,000 records a month, this can amount to a large number of returned records.

The Centre's power to produce crime statistics is contingent upon police officers in distant locations checking off boxes from official forms in the prescribed manner. If a sufficient number of officers refuse to employ some classifications, the Centre must bring those officers back into the fray or risk losing that particular bit of knowledge. Such a loss would ultimately hamper governmental strategies that are tied to those indicators. Despite efforts to control police UCR reporting functions, officers still occasionally stray from the identity of data collector. A recent example of such classificatory ambivalence concerns the elimination of the UCRII variable that recorded whether a victim or accused had consumed alcohol or drugs before the incident. Although preliminary data indicated that alcohol/drugs were involved in a significant number of criminal events, it had become apparent that key players in the police community were uncomfortable with this data element. Some police representatives claimed that the variable was open to interpretation and hence 'soft.' In situations where an officer had to retrospectively reconstruct the events preceding an incident, including the presence of alcohol/drugs, this subjective element was even more pronounced.

Despite such concerns, some Centre employees were astounded that anyone would think of dropping a data element that appeared to be related to such a high proportion of criminal events. A member of the policing-services directorate summarized his initial reaction to this proposal as follows: 'I was going: "Come on! This is the number one thing [correlated with] the crime [data] that we collect!"' Another Centre employee expressed similar frustrations: 'I'm not happy with some of the changes that are being proposed right now. For example, the presence of alcohol is one data element that is proposed to be cut largely because ... Toronto, has decided not to give us the information. So it is a case where your major respondents are determining what is going to be reported rather than the national standards.'

The above quote indicates that the Centre lost out on the collection of the 'alcohol and drug' variable because of the resistance of a powerful individual jurisdiction. However, there are competing accounts for why the police were keen to drop this element. In addition to questions about its methodological soundness, police reticence also appeared to be a manifestation of clashing police identities. The operating assumption of the Centre was that police officers make a simple decontextualized determination of alcohol/drug involvement. It is an image that ignores the prospective nature of documentation – how police officers anticipate the consequences of their classifications in different institutional settings and modify how they record events in light of such future uses. Consequently, one reason why front-line officers were reticent to indicate alcohol/drug involvement was that they did not want to provide an accused person with a potential legal defence for his or her actions:

[The police] don't want to be committed to saying that there was alcohol consumption taking place because it becomes a reason for *mens rea* as opposed to *actus reus*. The implication being that I was drunk and didn't know what I was doing. Or I was under the influence of a drug and didn't know what I was doing. It becomes a defence for [the accused's] actions. So that is number one why they won't put it down. Number two is that they suspect, nine times out of ten, drug usage was taking place, but they can't prove it. You can't make them blow into a breathalyser to prove that they were under the influence of hash.

The Centre's abandonment of efforts to collect data on alcohol/drugs on the UCRII is instructive; it is an example of a statistical indicator that could potentially be employed in attempts to govern public consumption patterns (Hunt 1996; Valverde 1998) that was *not* produced. Agencies desirous of such knowledge in order to foster new strategies for governance would now have to do without such data or seek out comparable indicators from a more successful centre of calculation. This example is a reminder of the importance of the minutiae of network building as a background requirement for the production of governmental knowledge. The availability or unavailability of such knowledge is not simply a result of new governmental strategies. Governmental possibilities evolve hand-in-hand with specific knowledges, knowledges that are the product of complex processes of network building. The differential successes of such efforts can make governmental knowledge available or, at times, foreclose on the availability of certain potentially useful data. Chapter 4 explores this theme in greater detail in the context of efforts to collect race/crime data.

Centre of Calculation

Governance is frequently coordinated at a distance from the specific objects to be governed. It works upon representations and becomes embedded in texts, institutional routines, and communication structures. Central locales provide a site where knowledge can accumulate and then be dispersed into other networks. At the broadest level, the CCJS constructs itself as a centre of calculation that other interested parties must engage with in order to achieve their desired ends. Centre staff have accomplished this by (1) assuming the status of 'insider,' (2) invoking the image of the Centre as an 'honest broker', and (3) contrasting the Centre's organizational structure with that of statistical agencies in other countries.

Centre staff portray themselves as doing the bidding of other agencies. They work to ensure that they can claim the support of the Justice Initiative or, in the case of the UCR, that they are acting upon the wishes of the Canadian Association of Chiefs of Police. Agencies that lacked this insider status would find it difficult, and probably impossible, to establish a comparable network to replicate, confirm, or dispute the Centre's findings. Being able to claim the cooperation of the Justice Initiative and the CACP also allows the Centre to partially deflect criticism about its being yet another outside agency imposing demands on police officers and organizations. Insider status makes it considerably easier to draw the various criminal-justice practitioners on-line, as one staff member explains: 'One of the things that we are constantly battling with is trying to get the police officers to know that the information that we are collecting is not something that is just for Statistics Canada. It is for the Justice Initiative who wanted national crime data. In fact, it was the Canadian Association of Chiefs of Police who originally came up with the data elements for the UCR. But they often think that they are just collecting statistics for Statistics Canada.'

The second self-characterization recurrently invoked by Centre personnel – that of 'honest broker' – captures the idealized image the Centre holds of itself: an organization that stands above the political fray in order to provide unbiased numbers about crime and criminal justice. While the Centre's numbers are occasionally criticized for methodological and coverage limitations, the CCJS itself is largely seen as non-partisan. Given that by virtue of their subject matter alone, criminal-justice numbers are inherently political, this ability of the Centre to immunize itself against accusations of partisanship has been an important achievement.

Attending a POLIS meeting in 1996 I witnessed a practical expression of the Centre's 'honest broker' status. A police representative there suggested that in light of the fact that new firearms legislation was then proceeding through Parliament, the Centre should conduct a study of the level of firearms usage in criminal incidents. Such a study would produce trend data to allow for pre- and post-legislation comparisons of firearms usage. A Centre representative responded that such a study was currently being done by the federal Department of Justice. The officer replied, 'Yeah, but we want *you* to do this because you are impartial.' For this officer, and his colleagues who nodded in agreement, numbers produce by the Department of Justice on this topic were inherently suspect because that department had introduced the firearms legislation. While they must continually work to maintain this status, Centre personnel have managed to carve out a niche where they stand largely untainted by the odor of political partisanship (see chapter 5).

The third way that the Centre has secured this niche has been by actively accentuating how Centre staff organize the collection of their statistics as compared to how things are done in other nations. Favourable comparisons with the practices of other countries symbolically accentuate the propriety or efficacy of the Centre's practices. For example, the Centre is politically accountable to Statistics Canada, which, outside of its knowledge-production function, is not responsible for criminal-justice matters. In contrast, Centre personnel commonly suggested that crime statistics in the United States and Britain were inherently suspect because the governmental agency that collects the data is also responsible for operating the national criminal-justice system:

> The model in the States and the model in Britain with the Home Office is that justice statistics are within the department which is accountable for the effectiveness of the programs. Therefore the statistics can always be claimed to be suspect because the same minister is responsible. If the minister who is responsible for [collecting] statistics is different from the one [who provides the data, and] whose services or programs are being evaluated on the [basis] of those statistics, then there is a [measure of] political independence.

Sites of knowledge production, operating as centres of calculation, seek to make themselves indispensable. For the Centre, this means that other individuals and groups must draw upon its statistics if they want to advance policy proposals or make public proclamations about crime and criminal justice. Any agency that wants to invoke the national crime rate to further their interests must turn to the Centre, as it has a monopoly on this indicator. A researcher for the Department of Justice who relies heavily on CCJS data pointed out that the Centre is 'the only source of official criminal justice data, nationally. The only crime data ... I mean, there is no other game in town. They are the only real, legitimate source.' This monopoly, combined with a style of governance that draws heavily on statistical indicators, provides the Centre with a considerable degree of organizational security.

The passage of time has made the Centre even more indispensable. It was always assumed that the Centre would draw from the extended jurisdictional networks to produce comparable *national* indicators and that the individual provinces or police forces would continue to produce their own trend data. However, economic retrenchment in many provinces has translated into the release of many analysts, which occasionally has severely reduced a province's ability to produce its own numbers. Consequently, the Centre's profile within the justice system has increased as it has become the de facto producer of some of the jurisdictions' data. This does not appear to have occurred to the same extent in relation to the UCR, as most police forces still maintain reasonable statistical capabilities, but several respondents noted that such increased reliance on the Centre's numbers was a clear trend in the areas of courts and corrections: 'This is another thing, we actually have better access to their data than [the jurisdictions] do. Once they give us data, we have the expertise and access to their own data that they could never ever produce. So if they actually want to know what is going on in their systems, we can do that better than they can now.'

The idealized construction of the CCJS is as an apolitical centre of calculation that has been able to make itself indispensable to a host of individual and institutional actors. But what goes on within the Centre that gives these numbers power and resonance? It is the inscriptions produced by scientific technologies that are vital components of such power. Whether they be photographs, graphs, indices, etchings, or computer printouts, inscriptions are science's life blood. Like scientists, bureaucrats also employ a host of representational technologies to render the world into inscription, thereby making it amenable to analysis and control (Cooper 1992).

A centre of calculation such as a laboratory cannot accommodate the entire population of animals, stars, amoebae, or neurons that it might like to study, so inscriptions are employed to represent these distant phenomena. They mobilize the periphery of a knowledge network in such a way that it can be transmitted great distances without significant reduction in its ability to signify. To be effective, such representations must remain relatively stable as they move through time and space. For example, a microbe might be very delicate, rapidly degenerating as it is moved from its natural habitat. However, reproduced on a photograph, sketch, or standardized form, the microbe can be mobilized and transported great distances without significant dete-

rioration. Once at the centre of the knowledge network (in the laboratory), these representations are most effective when they can be easily
arranged and rearranged in innovative ways that prompt the easy
observation of novelties, distinctions, and similarities. Through cy-
clical processes of accumulation and circulation, centralized locales
gain knowledge about things, events, and persons that are considerably removed from the centre. Such cycles of accumulation ultimately allow a centre of calculation to dominate the periphery, which
lacks such objectified knowledge. Latour (1987: 223) summarizes these
processes:

> By inventing means that (a) render them mobile so that they can be
> brought back; (b) keep them stable so that they can be moved back and
> forth without additional distortion, corruption or decay, and (c) are com-
> bined so that whatever stuff they are made of, they can be cumulated,
> aggregated, or shuffled like a pack of cards. If those conditions are met,
> then a small provincial town, or an obscure laboratory, or a puny little
> company in a garage, that were at first as weak as any other place will
> become centers dominating at a distance many other places.

Scientific laboratories are central nodes in a continuous flow of inscriptions. Just as the heart must be understood in relation to the
circulation of blood, a centre of calculation must be located in the
wider circulation of inscriptions, a process that objectifies the external
world in order to transport it to a distant laboratory. One cannot over-
state the importance of inscriptions as a technology of government.
Inscriptions of births, deaths, health, wealth, and myriad system processes render diverse and distant phenomena into a form that allows
them to be analysed and governed. In the case of UCR statistics, perti-
nent details of a person, place, or situation are extracted from a local
setting, inscribed, and moved along communications networks to a
central locale. There they are combined with many other inscriptions
to produce a new form of knowledge – an aggregate number or ratio.
In the process, the centre comes to know things about the local context
of a faraway place of which even local practitioners are unaware. Such
knowledge then moves outside of the centre, where it is used in reform initiatives or policy discussions.

Outside of the laboratory, scientists are often at a disadvantage relative to their object of study. These objects are frequently stronger than
individual scientists because of their large scale, tight interconnec-

tions, and invisibility. Inside the laboratory, the malleability of inscriptions allows for an inversion of forces. Representative inscriptions allow scientists to isolate these phenomena, inverting the routine play of forces by displacing the normal context in which an entity thrives. In so doing, scientists become stronger relative to their object of study. Rouse (1987) refers to such inversions as the construction of laboratory 'micro-worlds.' Identical processes are at work in relation to producing knowledge about crime, whereby the Centre, for example, removes officially designated crimes from their local context, isolates them, and produces a crime rate, an entirely new phenomenon.

Having secured and stabilized the flow of inscriptions, the Centre now must, paradoxically, work to make them disappear; otherwise, it risks being overwhelmed by their sheer volume. Centre staff, and scientists more generally, now do to the inscriptions what the inscriptions did to their referent – they produce a higher-order inscription. The UCR produces millions of inscriptions relating to criminal incidents, victims, and accused persons. En masse, such numbers are of little value; it is only when aggregated to create second-, third-, and nth-order inscriptions (such as crime rates and incarceration rates) that they provide potentially useful knowledge. Such abstractions reduce the complexity, ambiguity, and chaos often associated with the experience of crime into a set of simple figures and classifications.

A centre of calculation such as the CCJS is a power resource. Our understanding of crime would be weak and anecdotal without the knowledge produced by such locales. We would be swayed by any modern-day Dickens who tells the most evocative tales about the nature of crime and criminal behaviour. The Centre maintains a virtual monopoly over this form of knowledge production in Canada. Indeed, a great deal of the Centre's power derives from its monopoly over phenomena that are its own constructions – the national indicators of crime and criminal justice. Critics can point out myriad reasons why the Centre's numbers might be wrong, limited, or ideological, but if they wanted to assume a radically sceptical stance and test the validity of the numbers coming out of the Centre, they would have to develop a separate but comparable knowledge network. The prospect of creating such an identical network is severely restricted by the legal, organizational, and technological obstacles to establishing relations with the myriad data-providers. More important, if the numbers were to be comparable in any meaningful sense, the new network would have to employ the same classifications and counting rules established by the Centre. In the absence of such alternative networks, crime statistics start to become black boxed.

Black Boxes

Inter-institutional machinations, identity construction, and network maintenance are all conducted to produce knowledge that will be accepted as a black box. Knowledge producers hope to generate facts that can be easily plugged into another network, where 'no matter how controversial their history, how complex their inner workings, how large the commercial or academic networks that hold them in place, only their input and output count' (Latour 1987: 3). Computers, cloud chambers, or statistical indicators become black boxes when scientists and laypeople are obliged to use them to further their own ends while having little or no appreciation for the background processes and networks that make them possible. Only when they malfunction or are critiqued do such knowledges or technologies lose their black-box status, as people again reflect on their originating conditions.

The Centre's numbers acquire a black-boxed facticity when other researchers, politicians, and pundits adopt them uncritically to advance new knowledge claims. At the same time, Centre staff must themselves employ a variety of black boxes. Computers must not crash, communications infrastructures must remain stable, and the capacities imputed to different institutional actors must stay fixed. One example highlights this point. In its publications, the Centre regularly presents its crime numbers as a ratio, the number of incidents per 100,000 people. Ratios allow for comparable measures across locales with different populations. Ratios are also an example of how the Centre relies upon other knowledges to advance its own claims. To produce a crime rate, CCJS staff must employ accepted population counts, but the conditions of possibility for these counts are black boxed in the Centre's publications.

Demographic indices have, in fact, proved to be very controversial in recent years – particularly in the United States (Anderson and Fienberg 1999). In 1996 the U.S. Supreme Court ruled on a challenge to the 1990 census population count. At issue was the refusal by the Bush administration to use sampling methods to compensate for a purported undercount of ethnic minorities in large urban areas. Considerably more was at stake in this dispute than the accuracy of these measures. Population counts are a cornerstone of democratic politics, with political representation and funding for population-based social programs being tied to these indicators. Thus, if sampling methods had been used for this U.S. census, the distribution of seats in the House of Representatives would have been modified to favour California at the expense of Wisconsin. Furthermore, New York would have gained an estimated 230,000 people (Greenhouse 1996). Questions about the limitations and idiosyncrasies of data-collection vehicles are inherent in any attempt to fix limits on something as fluid and ambiguous as 'the population.'

I do not intend to undertake a detailed critique of population counts. Efforts to ascertain valid population indices are a long-standing social scientific concern (Rusnock 1995; Emery 1993; Conk 1987). Instead, I want to highlight how the Centre's use of such measures is a manifestation of the institutionalized forgetting or bracketing of questions about their accuracy. Demographic indices can themselves be unpacked in light of questions about under-coverage, counting rules, and sampling strategies. Centre staff, however, draw on them uncritically as a black box that comes out of Statistics Canada's demography division. When pressed on this point, a respondent asserted that 'we take [those counts] at face value. What they tell us is the population is what we have to go with. But it might be something that we should think about putting a footnote into our reports about.'

If Centre staff were largely comfortable or unreflective about plugging census population counts into their data, this was not the case for everyone in the extended CCJS network. For example, at a POLIS meeting in 1996 a police representative questioned the appropriateness of the population rates used by the CCJS. Working in a port city with a considerable university presence, he wanted more details about when the census count was done. He feared that there could be significant fluctuations in his city's official population level depending on whether the count was done during the school year and whether naval fleets were in port at the time. He claimed that his small city had a seasonal student population of fourteen thousand individuals, and that the NATO fleet could add an extra eighteen to twenty thousand people to the city's population base. While apparently comfortable with the Centre's measure for the total volume of crime in his city, he was concerned that the introduction of a black-boxed population count to produce a ratio would skew its crime rate.

These observations about the Centre's adoption of black-boxed knowledges is not an offhand condemnation of their practices. Plugging in black boxes that mask their background gaps and inconsistencies is inescapable in knowledge production. Even in this study, which attempts to be reflexive about statistical indices, there are instances where measures have been employed uncritically that could themselves have been unpacked and deconstructed. It is imperative that we try to comprehend the social and institutional processes that shape official numbers, but at a certain point this critical impulse must be focused elsewhere if the numbers are to be used at all.

Summary

Contemporary governmental practice relies on statistical knowledge of the objects to be governed. Distant places, people, and things are mobilized through inscriptions. These are returned to a centralized locale where knowledge accumulates and is aggregated into indicators. Reduced to simple indices, the knowledge then circulates to other state and non-state agencies. Thereby, complex and previously invisible processes become objectified and singled out as the target of governance. Although the importance of processes of network building to governmental efforts has been acknowledged (Rose 1996; Rose and Miller 1992), we are only now opening up these centres of calculation to document the minutiae of how governmental knowledge is produced.

From a central locale, the CCJS has produced a knowledge network specific to the UCR that comprises myriad technical and organizational components. To do so, Centre personnel employ a series of strategies and practices that extend beyond what we normally think of as statistical methods, using skills that situate them as political, statistical, and technological actors. Of particular importance for the UCR have been efforts to define and control identities particular to police officers and organizations. The Centre has secured a steady flow of inscriptions from the police and invested the data with an internally defined level of validity. But this image of success should not be embraced too hastily. The component parts of these networks are contingently aligned. Some parts require regular monitoring and attention to ensure that they maintain their preferred identities. The Centre's statistics also continue to be differentially approved, adopted, and scrutinized by different audiences. The criticisms that are raised, and their source, are related to how the trends documented by the Centre intersect with the political and institutional interests of different groups. That said, the Centre's institutional hegemony means that even the harshest sceptic is left with little recourse but to engage with its numbers if she or he wants to talk about the phenomena of 'crime,' even if this only amounts to a summary dismissal of the data.

This chapter has concentrated on some components of the knowledge network specific to the UCR. The other surveys within the Centre, and Statistics Canada more generally, employ broadly similar processes. They too must enrol and control different components and negotiate with groups and artefacts whose representativeness can be challenged. The remaining chapters explore processes of classification, standardization, political negotiation, and knowledge dissemination, which are all components of the Centre's broader knowledge network.

4

Counting Race: The Politics of a Contentious Classification

This has given me the greatest trouble and still does: to realize that what things *are called* is incomparably more important than what they are. The reputation, name, and appearance, the usual measure and weight of a thing, what it counts for – originally almost always wrong and arbitrary, thrown over things like a dress and altogether foreign to their nature and even to their skin – all this grows from generation unto generation, merely because people believe in it, until it gradually grows to be part of the thing and turns into its very body. What at first was appearance becomes in the end, almost invariably, the essence and is effective as such. How foolish it would be to suppose that one only needs to point out this origin and this misty shroud of delusion in order to *destroy* the world that counts for real, so-called 'reality.' We can destroy only as creators. – But let us not forget this either: it is enough to create new names and estimations and probabilities in order to create in the long run new 'things.'

Friedrich Nietzsche (1974: 121–2)

Statistics rest on classifications that can themselves be controversial. Efforts to delineate the specific terms used to divide the population can be challenged or undermined by the politics of classification. This chapter is an extended study of one such classificatory controversy. It examines some of the problems, politics, and practices that can arise when the state classifies, or tries to classify, its population by race. The Canadian Centre for Justice Statistics has expended considerable time and energy exploring whether to collect data on the race of an accused or victim. The staff's preliminary steps in this direction resulted in a public controversy over the authorized terms of governance and self-identity as embodied in ethnic/racial classifications. Questions were also raised about the propriety of the long-standing practice of statistical counting by race/ethnicity. The controversy was resolved when the Centre publicly disavowed its attempt to collect such data. This break, however, was not nearly as complete as it appeared in the press. Instead, the race/crime issue has evolved into efforts to collect data on a single ethnic group – Canada's First Nations.

Scrutinizing the defining events of this controversy and the subsequent attempts by the CCJS to collect aboriginal crime data is important for a number of reasons. The depth of emotion displayed by those who opposed this initiative marks it as a social problem that deserves closer examination. The debate over race/crime data collection also allows us to explore the power of official classifications. While race and ethnicity have become axial political concepts, there is considerable angst over the precise terms to be used in such politics. This is not peculiar to Canada; questions of how to define and count ethnic groupings have received considerable international attention (Booth 1985; Home Office 1996; Petersen 1987; Goldberg 1997; Knepper 1996).

In examining this issue we also learn about how a statistical agency handles controversial classifications and explore (1) how employees conceptualize the relationship between the mundane practice of classification and the world of public politics; (2) how insiders settle on which classifications of people should be adopted; and (3) what social and institutional considerations helped determine whether this was a methodologically or politically feasible endeavour. In the process we learn about some of the competing pressures faced by members of the CCJS. In particular, they had to judiciously manage rival and often contradictory interests in order to develop these statistics. Such efforts again accentuate how the methodology used to produce race/crime statistics includes a host of social, organizational, and political skills.

This account moves beyond the local specifics of this issue to explore some of the broader theoretical concerns related to the power of social classification outlined more fully in chapter 2. The categories that state, and increasingly non-state (Gandy 1993), agencies use to classify individuals and groups operate in complex ways to fashion how we think of ourselves and others. The lines that we use to delineate 'us' from 'them' are informed by bureaucratic ways of dividing up people and the wider social world. Thus, the race/crime controversy provides insights into how classifications contribute to 'making up people' (Hacking 1986).

Racial Numbers

The practice of assigning offenders to racial categories has a long and often inglorious history. The genesis of criminology is bound up in just such an undertaking (Gould 1996). For example, the ordained father of criminology, Cesare Beccaria, employed a racial typology of criminals as part of his search for atavistic evolutionary throwbacks. Since those early beginnings, racial and ethnic variables have remained a mainstay of many statistical agencies, although the justifications for collecting such data have changed. Such classifications have always been political in the sense that they serve as the basis for governmental initiatives (Goldberg 1997, chap. 3). As Edward Said makes clear in his book *Orientalism* (1978), part of the way in which the 'Other' is constituted is through the invention and production of racialized knowledge. It was only in the final decades of the twentieth century that the very practice of counting the population by race became a contentious public issue. Concerns about the accuracy of racial classifications remain, while new arguments challenge the very practice of racialized classification. In Canada this issue acquired peak publicity in 1990 after the Canadian Centre for Justice Statistics proposed the collection of racial/ethnic data on its Uniform Crime Report survey.

During the 1980s, plans were underway to develop the incident-based 'UCRII' crime survey. This survey significantly increased the amount of data available on crimes and created links between the crime and numerous contextual and personal factors associated with an accused, including his or her ethnicity. It was preceded by an extensive process of national consultations. Representatives from various components of the justice system were approached for their opinions on methodology, data requirements, costs, storage capacity, and security. The opinions of the various Canadian police forces and their representative body, the Canadian Association of Chiefs of Police, were particularly important, as their cooperation was essential if the new UCR was going to work. Several respondents identified the Canadian police community as strong advocates for introducing racial variables into the survey. An academic involved in this process recalled how the call for a racial variable 'was a Chief of Police issue. They were pushing for it and they were the ones who really wanted it. I don't think the CCJS has any position one way or another about it. It was just what the Chiefs wanted to put it in, so it was there.' At a later point we discuss in greater detail some of the reasons why race/crime data might have been attractive to the police, politicians, and ethnic groups. At the most basic level, such data offered the promise of knowledgeable forms of governance of ethnic groups and the opportunity to reveal systemic racism within the criminal-justice system. The perceived normalcy of collecting such data was also undoubtedly related to the influence of the United States, as Americans have long collected racialized crime data.

While police support made it possible to collect race/crime data, the Centre agonized over methodological and classificatory concerns until almost the last minute. Centre personnel now had to agree on what would count as a race. The ensuing public debate frequently focused precisely on this question of how an official agency should draw statistical boundaries around the concept of 'race.' Centre staff felt that they had to use categories that already had some public resonance, and that they could not invent entirely new racial classifications. This still left them with a considerable range of potential classificatory options. Pragmatics played a role in this effort. Not wanting to burden police officers with an unwieldly set of classificatory options, they ultimately drew on the common-sense views by which police officers (and perhaps most North Americans) have tended to conceive of race – predominantly by the colour of a person's skin. The result was a category for 'ethnic origin' that was broken down into European origin (white); South Asian; Black; East/South East Asian, Central and South American; and Aboriginal. This last category for 'Aboriginal' was further divided into North American Indian, Inuit (Eskimo), Metis, and Other. The police were responsible for assigning individuals to the most appropriate option, a task they would accomplish by inferring ethnicity from an offender's appearance or from an officer's prior knowledge of an offender.

Some Centre staff members acknowledged the limitations of such a scheme. As a member of the Centre's policing-services program articulated, these classifications ultimately proved to be minimally acceptable because they were 'clear, I will give them that much. They were more color schemes than anything else. Because that is how the cops dealt with things. They don't care about ethnicity, they are talking about identification of a suspect: black, white, oriental, whatever. That is the way they tend to deal with it.'

In institutionalizing such categories, the Centre reproduced existing ways of demarcating types of people – ones that approximated the world-view of the police and other segments of society. As such, this process provides an example of how ingrained categories can acquire an official status, as classifications drawn from the social world are given the bureaucratic stamp of approval. In the process, the Centre was serving 'to give a real existence to that category' (Bourdieu 1996: 25), providing common-sense ways of demarcating people with a formal authority.

Having established the racial categories, Centre staff now implemented these new reporting requirements among the handful of police forces prepared to switch to the new UCR. By November 1991 eleven police forces were providing the Centre with data on racial origin. Just before this new survey became operational, the Centre released an issue of *Juristat* (CCJS 1990), its main publication, to announce the benefits of the new survey. One brief sentence in this document stated that it would now be possible to collect data on the racial background of the accused and victims of violent crimes, that 'for each "cleared" incident, basic demographic information is recorded on all accused persons: sex, age, and racial origin' (13). The nature and intensity of the responses generated by this publication caught everyone in the Centre by surprise. 'We had this little paragraph talking about how we would have crime by race. Well, that is when the Chief Statistician first noticed the word "race," and basically he felt it was inappropriate. And he was going "How could you people do this without notifying me?" Everyone else was going "Huh? What?" Everyone had approved it and stamped it. A hundred page document, who would even notice this?'

As it turned out, many people noticed and voiced their objections. Among this chorus of dissatisfaction were the Prime Minister's Office, city councillors, the Privacy Commissioner of Canada, the media, academics, and myriad community spokespersons.

Objections and Justifications

A.J.P. Taylor has observed that 'history gets thicker as it approaches recent time.' The corollary of this maxim is that as time passes, history tends to become thin, losing nuance until it ultimately coalesces into a dominant narrative. In the telling and retelling, the rough edges are eroded, leaving behind a relatively straightforward and uncomplicated account as the confusion, coincidence, and apparent randomness of experience are washed away. For example, the Centre's succinct account of the race/crime controversy is a story of widespread public opposition to the collection of race/crime data, which was seen to be at best distasteful, and at worst racist. The Centre responded by abandoning the effort entirely. At least that is how the official story goes.

If we pick through the veneer of this institutionalized account, however, we can find multiple interpretations that reveal a more complicated, contradictory, and open-ended series of events. This section roughs up the smooth edges of the institutionalized narrative to reveal competing and often contradictory reasons that were advanced for why such information should or should not be collected. What emerges is an appreciation for the complexity of the issues involved. The plural 'issues' is employed because no single theme encompasses what I retrospectively call 'the race/crime controversy.'

The positions presented below are not intended simply as a review of the arguments for and against collecting race/crime data. Notwithstanding the value of such an endeavour, this is also an opportunity to explore how Centre staff view the merit and potential applications of the numbers they collect. How do they justify the inevitable problems with their data? At what point do these rationales start to break down? As mentioned in chapter 2, their views on the accuracy of their data are contextual. This often involves a pragmatic evaluation of their data-collection vehicles that acknowledges, sometimes in the extreme, the limitations of the data. Such admissions, combined with ongoing efforts to overcome such limitations, are usually sufficient to allow Centre personnel to collect data and publish their findings in good conscience. One reason why the race/crime situation is intriguing is precisely because it represents a pragmatic retreat from pragmatism. The well-rehearsed arguments about the legitimacy and practical necessity of collecting admittedly limited and circumscribed data faltered in the face of other pragmatic threats to the reputation and legitimacy of both the Centre and Statistics Canada itself.

Background

The axiom 'timing is everything' is no less true in a statistical organization than in any other sphere of life. Unfortunately for advocates of the collection of Canadian race/crime data, the timing of public discussions about the issue proved to be particularly inopportune. The release of the draft *Juristat* in the spring of 1990 occurred at a time when racial tensions were exacerbated by words exchanged at Canadian universities and actions initiated in a previously little-known

Québec town. While these events were taking place on the national stage, in Toronto, Canada's largest city, the Centre's efforts were interpreted in the context of a series of highly politicized incidents concerning race and crime. Cumulatively, these created a climate that, if it did not undermine the program from the beginning, certainly made for a more hostile reception.

The first national incident concerned public reactions to the writings of Canadian professor Phillip Rushton, who continues the long-standing tradition of trying to find explanations for criminal behaviour in racial typologies (Rushton 1988, 1990). Employing a tripartite division of racial types consisting of Caucasians (Caucasoids), Asians (Mongoloids), and Blacks (Negroids), he presents statistical evidence of differential involvement in certain types of crime by these three groups that he attributes to their different average brain size. His controversial theories produced a media frenzy about his work in the late 1980s, which, in turn, prompted critical reactions from the public and academics alike (Roberts and Gabor 1990).

Not long after the media tired of Professor Rushton, the greatest civil unrest involving racial issues in recent Canadian history erupted. In Oka, Québec, a group of natives, predominantly Mohawks and some sympathetic whites, blockaded a road to protest commercial encroachment into sacred land. A police officer was shot during a raid on the Mohawk compound, and the Canadian military was eventually called in to resolve the situation. A seventy-eight day stand-off ensued. Canadians received a steady diet of stories and pictures of an armed and increasingly tense confrontation. Commentators incessantly reflected on the prospect of escalating violence in Oka and other First Nations communities. While the incident ended without further violence, racial tensions were strained as at no point in recent Canadian history.

While Oka and the public debates about Phillip Rushton arguably prompted a heightened national consciousness of racial politics and grievances, race relations were particularly strained in Toronto. Tensions lingered between the black community and Metropolitan Toronto Police over the separate police shooting deaths of black youths Michael Wade Lawson and Lester Donaldson. Repeated accusations of systemic racism within the Metro Toronto Police force by the head of the Black Action Defence Committee, Dudley Laws, further heightened these tensions. In the year before the Centre released the *Juristat* issue that mentioned the plan to collect racialized crime data, Toronto had already witnessed an incident that foreshadowed fears about how race/

crime data might be used to the detriment of the black community. In February 1989, Inspector J. Fantino, head of Metro Toronto's 31 Division, publicized statistics that purportedly demonstrated disproportionate criminal involvement by blacks in Toronto's troubled Jane-Finch area. These claims prompted waves of criticism from both the Metro Toronto Police and community activists. Some activists interpreted the release of these statistics as an illustration of police prejudice that would ultimately lead to acts of racist violence against blacks. The depth of distrust between the police and segments of the black community was apparent in the claim by Linda Moroway of the Jane-Finch Action Committee: 'We either get rid of Mr. Fantino or Black people are going to be shot' (Kendall 1989). In a racially charged environment, debate moved quickly from a concern about differential racial involvement in certain types of crime to the spectre of police-initiated homicide against blacks. While Inspector Fantino apologized two days after making his statements, an institutional response was already set in motion. The Metro Toronto Police Department had quickly adopted a policy prohibiting the compilation and release of statistics on race.

In summary, the Centre's proposal to collect race/crime data occurred in a volatile context. At the national level, Oka had heightened concerns about racial politics. This was exacerbated by media attention to Professor Rushton's claims about differential racial/biological predispositions towards crime. In Toronto, public controversies over race and crime had provided community groups with a glimpse of the potential abuses of race/crime data. In response, different constituencies had coalesced into apparently unanimous opposition to the collection of such data. The result of the Centre's entrance into this antagonistic political environment was a series of public recriminations and complaints about the feasibility or propriety of its proposal.

Critiques of Race/Crime Data

Ethnic categories appear to be a cultural universal, frequently situated at the heart of what defines social groupings, setting one group apart from another. As Jenkins (1997: 166) observes, '[I]t is impossible to understand how groups are constituted without a full appreciation of social categorization. There are no groups, ethnic or otherwise, without categorization.' Classificatory systems are used to constitute an individual's sense of self and to distinguish him- or herself from others. Ethnic classifications have long been a mainstay of statistical organizations. In fact, one of the earliest controversies to arise out of the eighteenth century mania over deviance statistics featured debates about different national pathologies as displayed in English and French suicide rates (Hacking 1990, chap. 8).

Official categories are overlaid on people who have already consciously or unconsciously adopted a series of social cleavages. Statistical agencies must arrive at a classificatory scheme that resonates with these existing divisions. That is, official classifications must fit the established common sense if they are to be accepted as accurate. Critics of the race/crime proposal often concentrated on the fact that the proposed demarcations for 'ethnicity' could not precisely capture the diversity of racial and ethnic groupings.

Racial classificatory schemes do more than simply set one group apart from another. They are routinely hierarchical, with different racial groups often being perceived to be differentially suited for socially approved roles or activities. We usually reserve such preferential evaluations for our own group, although this is not always the case, as instances of racial self-loathing would indicate (West 1993). Other ethnic groups are often perceived as being biologically or socially limited, inferior, or prone to myriad types of deviance. Statistics that indicate different levels of achievement in education, salary, and criminal behaviour can reinforce such perceptions of ethnic superiority and inferiority.

Racial hierarchies also inform whether or not we believe a set of racial classifications is sufficiently comprehensive. Given that the ethnic classifications proposed by the Centre were high-level, they inevitably incorporated a host of different self-identifying peoples under a single heading. For example, their classification for 'East/South East Asian' explicitly subsumed nine other ethnic groups, including Chinese, Malaysian, Japanese, and Korean. These, in turn, could be further broken down into other self-identifying groups. The use of such high-level categories prompted calls from some community members for a more fine-grained set of ethnic distinctions. While such calls can be viewed as an attempt to have the classifications correspond more closely with the lived reality of ethnicity, some groups also sought to distinguish themselves from those that they saw as being more unpalatable or criminogenic. For example, here two Centre staff members summarize their interactions with community members on the question of racial typology:

There were some groups that said 'Blacks' is not good enough. There were some Blacks in Toronto who were saying, 'It is the Jamaican Blacks who are causing the problem.'

There were some Chinese politicians in Toronto who were absolutely adamant that we had to have this because it would show that it wasn't the Hong Kong Chinese [who were the problem], it was the Mainland Chinese, the Communist Chinese.

As previously noted, one of the important aspects of official classifications concerns the way in which people come to live their lives in light of these names. The obverse of this, however, has not been sufficiently explored. The ethnic/racial categories introduced by official agencies are not invariably adopted by the identified groups. Individuals may be completely unaware of the way that bureaucracies classify them. Such classifications can fail to put down firm institutional roots, and groups may also resist the specifics of racial-classification schemes or the act of classification itself.

Ethnic divisions and subdivisions became particularly apparent to Centre staff as they sought advice from the local representatives of ethnic communities on how to proceed with this issue. While community members spoke on behalf of their particular ethnic grouping, new factions often came forward to oppose or highlight the limitations of any proposed scheme. Instead of consulting a unified community of support or opposition, the Centre encountered shifting groupings and alliances, which advanced a range of positions held with varying degrees of conviction. This was clear in the Centre's 1991 junket to Toronto, undertaken in the hopes of addressing the concerns of community activists and private citizens. There CCJS staff encountered a plethora of opinions that varied across and within ethnic groupings. As one Centre employee recalled, 'Some of the black community in Toronto really wanted it, some of them were vehemently opposed to it. It really lined up along lines of ideology rather than logic.'

To this point in the account I have used the terms 'race' and 'ethnicity' interchangeably. This deliberate lack of precision parallels the terminological ambiguity in the Centre's race/crime debate. Efforts to classify people according to their skin colour were followed by an attempt to measure ethnicity conceived of as some combination of phenotype and common descent. The UCR documentation proposed that a 'race' was to be understood as a group of persons of common descent and with common features, but did not refer to a person's citizenship, nationality, or cultural identity. However, these different understandings of race are obviously intertwined and can blur at the margins, a fact that produced considerable confusion in public discussion about the Centre's proposal. Such ambiguity is perhaps understandable given that experts cannot agree among themselves on the practical and theoretical relationship between conceptions of 'race' and 'ethnicity' (see Jenkins 1997, chap. 6). One way to understand the race/ethnicity distinction is as a result of a much broader set of classificatory politics and struggles. Historically, conceptions of race were (and are) used by dominant groups to characterize other social groupings, typically with derogatory overtones. Having struggled to acquire their own voice, marginalized and oppressed groups have sought to alter the terms of the debate over group identity, preferring to use the more culturalist conception of ethnicity.

Before either race or ethnicity can be measured, there must be some appreciation for *what* is actually being measured. What attributes were police officers to attend to when they assigned a person to one or another racial/ethnic category? In his critique of the Centre's race/crime proposal, Roberts (1994) points to the practical difficulties bureaucracies have in assigning persons to racial/ethnic categories. Methodological difficulties are posed by the fact that 'race' or 'ethnicity' can be used to refer to a person's self-identity, legal status, place of birth, and physical phenotypes such as skin colour and fuzziness of hair. The problem is most apparent at the classificatory margins, in those places in between and never exclusively 'of' one neatly demarcated category. As one respondent commented, 'You have white people coming forward and saying: "Technically, I am black." How do you answer that sort of question?'

Such ambiguity is only apt to become more pronounced if we accept the prevalent theoretical view that our contemporary situation is characterized by flux, by a series of 'in betweens' and 'not quites.' Thrift (1996: 257) suggests that 'we now live in an almost/not quite world – a world of almost/not quite subjects; almost/not quite selves; almost/not quite spaces; and almost/not quite times.' Identity appears to be much more transient and liminal than in the past, formed across different categories and roles held with varying degrees of commitment. If this assessment of late/post-modern identity is accurate, it promises to offer continuing difficulties for statistical agencies who tend to deal in fixed and bounded identity categories.

Statistical attempts to capture the fractured nature of identity can come face to face with the politics of racialized classification. For example, some Blacks in the United States oppose the prospect of adopting a multiracial variable on the census, as they fear that it might decimate the statistical number of 'blacks' and ultimately undermine their political power (Anderson and Fienberg 1999; Nelkin and Lindee 1995: 117). Given that some people estimate that the number of 'blacks' who could potentially be categorized as 'multi-racial' is as high as 90 per cent, we can understand these fears about the potential effects of a multiracial variable on affirmative-action programs and desegregation efforts.

The term 'classification' actually subsumes two quite distinct processes. The first, which I will continue to call 'classification,' refers to the production of official classificatory schemes. The second involves the day-to-day routine of sorting people into those classifications. This is the task of 'assignment' performed by street-level bureaucrats, pollsters, and enumerators (Starr 1987).

Opponents of the proposal were critical of the fact that police officers were to be the ones responsible for assigning individuals to their respective racial/ethnic category. It was suggested that officers were not trained in such matters, and hence were unsuited to determining a person's race or ethnicity. The degree of difficulty that officers might have had in making such assignments would appear to be related to the number of racial/ethnic options they had to choose from. If police officers were required to assign individuals to one of the more than six hundred ethnic/racial classifications identified by the United Nations, there would be no end of complications. Perceived public hostility to questions about race often prompt police officers to avoid asking individuals for their ethnicity, fearing that such questions might appear insensitive or escalate delicate situations. Consequently, they tend to rely on their own intuition when making racial assignments. Several commentators suggested that for race/crime data to be reliable, this police classificatory discretion would have to be curtailed. Procedures were required to ensure that officers (a) fill out all the assigned boxes on their official forms, and (b) complete the forms in a comparable fashion. Police training was seen as a way to ensure common racial assignments both within and across police forces. Depending on the comprehensiveness of the classificatory system employed, we would then face the prospect of having one component of police training involve lessons in how to correctly identify Poles, Jamaicans, Haitians, and so forth.

The problem of assignment is not nearly as daunting if a more rudimentary classificatory system is adopted. For example, a simple variable for skin colour would be valuable if the aim was to reveal and address systemic racism in the criminal-justice system, as such discrimination would likely be based on an individual's physical appearance. Police officers would certainly be able to make rough distinctions among skin colours. In fact, one of the purported dangers of collecting racial data is that the police already make such discriminations on a regular basis, contributing to the overrepresentation of particular ethnic groups in the criminal-justice system. Consequently, the spectre of a self-fulfilling prophecy has always haunted race/crime data.

It is precisely this prospect of using race/crime data to reveal systemic bias in the criminal-justice system that appeals to advocates of such data. Statistics demonstrating overrepresentation of ethnic groups in criminal justice can be used to marshal arguments about police harassment, over-policing, and target selection. Such statistical demonstrations are a routine component in the racialized politics of U.S. criminal justice, where there appear to be few qualms about collecting race/crime data (Tonry 1995; Miller 1996). Criminologist Thomas Gabor (1994) points out how, in Canada, official crime statistics could be combined with self-report and victimization studies to indicate the overrepresentation of particular ethnic groups in the justice system. For instance, such an effort might prove to be particularly useful in those situations where a minority group has high arrest rates as compared to the majority ethnic group, who, in turn, self-report greater or equal involvement in those crimes. Such a discrepancy would lend itself to arguments about systemic bias by the police.

Some groups have nevertheless wondered about the policy implications of this data; specifically, what would follow if we discovered that certain ethnic groups were disproportionately involved in crime or certain types of crime? Academics and criminal-justice practitioners who attended a workshop on the race/crime issue at the University of Toronto feared that such indices would be naively interpreted as demonstrating some genetic or biological predisposition towards crime (Doob 1991). This is a valid concern in light of long-standing attempts to unearth root causes of crime in people's biological composition. And while participants in the workshop generally favoured the collection of race/crime statistics, they cautioned that biological causes for behaviour could not be derived from such data and that crime trends have to be understood in relation to police enforcement patterns and other social and cultural factors.

While academics raised questions about biology, and the ontological status of 'race,' community groups tended to concentrate on the potential uses of the data. Even if the police accurately assigned individuals to a set of agreeable classifications, what purposes would the data serve? Some argued that there were few policy options to rectify disproportionate levels of crime across ethnic groupings. However, this vision of criminal-justice personnel simply shaking their heads in despair in the face of such data is highly questionable. It is more likely that a host of programs would be developed or proposed to help rectify disproportionate ethnic crime trends. Governance is increasingly concerned with different markers on a person's risk portfolio (such as age, prior conviction, substance abuse, scores on standardized scales, and, potentially, race). These mark people for different institutions, programs, and levels of attention (Ericson and Haggerty 1997; Feeley and Simon 1994). Knowledge about trends in ethnicity and crime would likely be used to inform decisions on how to deploy police resources, and on the types of programs and services that need to be developed and funded.

Opponents to the race/crime proposal, however, were not so sanguine in their views about the potential uses of race data. They did not anticipate that the data would languish uselessly on a shelf or be used as the basis for progressive policies. They feared it would serve illiberal purposes. Conservative and reactionary political groups figured prominently in these fears, as such groups were seen to be predisposed towards making arguments about an ethnic basis of criminality.

Such fears accentuate the degree to which numbers, in themselves, are often inconsequential and malleable. The implications of increasing or decreasing statistical trends does not lie in the numbers themselves but in the way those numbers are skilfully taken up by various parties, who invest them with meaning and situate them in different discourses. Community groups did not so much fear the data as they feared how it would be interpreted, and by whom, and the types of policy implications that would be advanced in light of such interpretations. Ultimately, this is a question of the degree of political power that different constituencies can marshal. A Centre employee summarized the concerns of ethnic minorities as a fear that the data would serve as a means for 'inflicting harm, or that the data would be used for harmful purposes, for racist purposes. Because we couldn't control the way the analysis of the data would be used.'

Segments of the immigrant community feared that statistics indicating disproportionate levels of crime in their community would be used to justify increased police crackdowns or new restrictions on immigration. This concern was reiterated by some members of the Centre, who suspected that precisely such aims motivated police support for these numbers. As a senior member of the Centre involved in the race/crime controversy indicated:

> Now, there was some elements in the police community, and I won't get more specific than that, that have always wanted to do this ... In other words 'Let's nail these guys on the basis of race.' And out of that, whether they had thought it through or not, I don't know, but I'm sure that some of them thought that there would then be [pressure] subsequently brought to bear on immigration officials in Canada to literally disfavour the immigration of people from certain groups who they knew were committing crimes. Whether it was the Caribbean types or the south-east Asian population. I am certain that that was the thinking that went into this. And the police wanted that information to slide it across the table to influence the course of policy development in our society. Where policy would have been most obviously affected was at point of entry. And also perhaps creating pressure on parliamentarians for more permissive legislation regarding deportation and so forth. I'm absolutely certain that that is what a lot of the members of the police community felt. Now that may not have been the majority, but there were some there that were advocating the collection of that kind of information. They didn't see any problem.

Others were also well aware of the potential uses of racialized crime data on immigration policy. Canadian criminologist Thomas Gabor proposed that 'national groups could be ranked as more or less favored based on the danger they have posed to public safety. Groups could be reclassified every few years according to the level of their criminal involvement during a specific period of time' (1994: 162).

While intimately aware of the potential misuses of such data, some community spokespersons pointed out that the majority of the population already assumed there were high levels of crime and violence in their communities. In light of this, these individuals cautiously viewed criminal-justice numbers as a vehicle for enlightenment: 'If the public assumes that blacks commit most of the murders, well, there is no way that we can dispel that if we don't have the statistics. It would be useful in dispelling a lot of myths ... It can be used responsibly to dispel certain myths about certain ethnic groups.' These individuals saw open public discussion about the relationship between race and crime as holding out the possibility of transforming dominant attitudes, rather than reinforcing stereotypes.

A Pragmatic Retreat from Pragmatism

The vociferousness of the opposition to the collection of race/crime data masks the fact that many of the criticisms of this proposal parallel similar issues that Centre and Statistics Canada employees regularly encounter in different contexts. Concerns about methodology, data quality, and interpretation are nothing new to a statistical agency. A routine aspect of producing knowledge involves prospectively anticipating such criticisms and making the appropriate methodological, rhetorical, or organizational moves to dismiss, silence, or undermine critics (Fuchs and Ward 1994). This section outlines some of the ways in which methodological concerns and complaints have typically been countered by the Centre. It allows us to question the presumption that it was the substance of such complaints that resulted in the downfall of the race/crime proposal. In fact, the specifics of the public complaints were largely answerable by Centre employees, and it was a combination of other factors that undermined the race/crime proposal.

Centre staff often respond pragmatically to criticisms of their surveys. Questions and criticisms about the limitations of justice statistics based on methodology, coverage, and classification are met with a 'Yes, but ...' response. Staff forsake any claims about the final authority of their numbers in favour of a much more circumscribed position. In day-to-day life the numbers coming out of the Centre tend to assume the quality of solid facts. And while such numbers are certainly amenable to critique, they solidify over time to become Canada's real crime rate or murder rate. In contrast, Centre staff speak in the language of 'justice indicators' with the important distinction being that facts are apparently immutable, whereas 'indicators' provide a limited but valuable representation of the operation of the justice system. Speaking of 'indicators' provides a rhetorical space for employees to acknowledge various gaps, failings, and qualifications of their data without bringing the entire enterprise into question. Interviewees often invoked this distinction whenever the accuracy, quality, or veracity of the CCJS statistics was addressed. The most common expressions voiced at such junctures included 'But you have to remember, they are only indicators,' or 'There is always shades of grey in every statistic,' and 'Coverage is never one hundred percent.'

Such a pragmatic stance could certainly have sidestepped public concerns about the 'grey areas' of ethnicity – the criticism that racialized numbers should not be collected owing to the classificatory problems exemplified, for instance, by a person born in China to a black father and Spanish mother who nonetheless visibly appears Caucasian. While such problems are obviously a source of concern, the Centre could have argued that those are relatively infrequent situations, and could have invoked the language of 'they are just indicators' to acknowledge such problems, while continuing to suggest that the numbers are useful for certain governmental purposes. The inevitable misclassification of a percentage of the population would not render the statistics useless. Some staff members in fact suggested that racial assignment errors are not a serious problem as long as they are statistically random, that is, as long as there is no systemic bias in how people are misclassified. Many community groups and academics would undoubtedly counter such claims by pointing out that assignment errors would in all likelihood not be random, that the police, for example, would be more likely to assign criminals to ethnic groupings already perceived as being 'criminogenic,' thereby reinforcing dominant stereotypes.

Centre staff also had at their disposal arguments to counter the charge that their racial classificatory systems could not capture all of the world's 'ethnic types.' Statistical agencies are familiar with such claims, which essentially amount to a concern that it is impossible to represent statistically the total universe of diversity in a population. By their nature, statistics obscure some differences in attempts to provide useful numbers at a more aggregate level. The question that must be resolved concerns the level of diversity that one wants to (or can) capture for what purposes. Simply because not every possible ethnic classification would make it onto such agencies' forms does not undermine their more aggregate data. Overall, such questions are one manifestation of the unending interrogation that statistical agencies face about whether the objects they propose to treat as equivalent are in fact equivalent (Desrosières 1990: 200).

Questions about the skill and honesty of police officers are also familiar to CCJS staff. In the context of race/crime, this amounted to a concern about the police's ability to assign individuals to specific classifications. Police officers assign events, places, and people into myriad pre-established classificatory options on the UCR. How well or poorly they accomplish this task is difficult for the Centre to determine (see chapter 2). To date, however, this methodological Achilles heel has not become a fatal flaw in the crime statistics. Instead, it is approached as something that Centre staff should be concerned about and work towards alleviating. In the interim, any concerns about assignment errors are placated by invoking the professionalism of the police, internal auditing systems, and the presumption that police forces have a vested interest in collecting accurate statistics. If the Centre must largely rely on a system of professional trust to ensure that the police properly assign every variable, it is conceivable that such trust could be extended to their ability to assign individuals to ethnic classifications.

Anxieties about the end result of the statistical production cycle – that of interpretation, analysis, and policy development – are also more than familiar to Centre staff. In fact, reservations about how criminal-justice statistics will be used have been a dominant theme of the Justice Initiative. The Centre usually responds by narrowly focusing its efforts on producing as methodologically sound a set of statistical indicators as possible. Centre staff scrupulously avoid making public pronunciations on how such numbers might be interpreted and used. Since its inception, staff at the Centre have steadfastly maintained a policy that assumes it is none of their concern how the numbers are ultimately employed and by whom. Only in situations where the data are clearly misrepresented (which is itself a contextual judgment) does the Centre become involved in attempts to clarify and correct the public record. Centre staff see this position as one way they have been able to maintain an air of objectivity and disinterestedness, setting themselves above partisan politics (see chapter 5).

To this point, this account of the race/crime proposal has attempted to accomplish two things. It has summarized some of the criticisms of the Centre's proposal that have had pride of place in the institutionalized explanation for the proposal's failure. Second, it has suggested that in a different political context the Centre's preferred pragmatic approach to critiques of its methodology and coverage could have answered, side-stepped, or placated the criticism of the race/crime data proposal. The specifics of these criticisms would normally not have been sufficient to derail the collection and production of other types of statistics. We now turn to the final factor that contributed to the failure of the race/crime proposal – the dissolving police network, that is, the failure of Centre employees and police representatives to maintain police support for this proposal in the face of public protest.

The Centre's account of the race/crime issue regularly portrays one individual as having a, if not the, major role in bringing this proposal to a halt. As Chief Statistician of Canada, Ivan Fellegi's position that Statistics Canada should not collect this information ultimately won the day. He summarized his opposition to the collection of such data by highlighting how

> certain kinds of information might be required which society regards as being too intrusive to provide. That is not a once and for all. Those are evolving criteria. Too intrusive or too inappropriate for a statistical agency to inquire about. And that is the tension that we are encountering here. It is a very legitimate requirement and it is found offensive by a large segment of society. So if it is found offensive then we cannot legitimately do it. It has to be an acceptable kind of an inquiry, otherwise it cannot be sustained ... Ultimately if you ask me how I do it I can't explain it because it is a judgment. In every single case of how you arrive at a judgment, you arrive at it.

In defending his disavowal of the collection of this information, Fellegi refers to 'a large segment of society' who opposed its collection. However, no study was ever conducted about the extent of public support or opposition to this proposal. Certainly there was vocal opposition from some sectors, but its pervasiveness remains unknown. Even more peculiar to some members of the Justice Initiative was the fact that while their efforts to collect race/crime data were being stopped, a different section of Statistics Canada was working to include a variable for self-reported ethnic identity on the next census – Statistics Canada's flagship survey.

An edict from the chief statistician immediately ceased the Centre's efforts to collect data based on race for the UCR. Statistics Canada also took the additional and more remarkable step of declaring that there was to be a total rupture in the handling and collection of such information. Any race/crime data that the police had forwarded to the Centre as part of the lead-up to the new UCR were to be destroyed. A total purge of race/crime data took place.

> A: The conclusion was that it was withdrawn. All race data would be, if it was included at the source on the data, on the records that we were

getting from some of the respondents in the UCR survey, we would erase it before it got here. Our instructions were, if possible, erase it at the source. We wouldn't even store it.

Q: That seems rather dramatic.

A: They didn't even want it. The chief statistician wanted to be able to say 'We don't even have it,' as opposed to 'We have it but don't look at it.'

Despite apparent high-level police support for the collection of race/crime data, numerous difficulties arose when it came time to collect and analyse the numbers. For a brief period before the 1991 public outcry, the Centre was receiving UCRII data from a handful of forces. To their surprise, some forces simply refused to forward the race/crime data:

[The Centre] literally tried to collect the data. They had police forces collecting the data ... [T]he main reason they don't collect the data is because they can't. The police turned out to be incapable of sending in these data. Either incapable or unwilling. But I think not unwilling, because they are in favor of it generally.

Police reticence or inability to forward the data bewildered some Centre employees, as the police community had been one of the key proponents of collecting such numbers. The chief statistician, in a letter to the Privacy Commissioner of Canada in August 1990, expressed his confusion about this apparent change of heart:

I must admit that I was surprised, given the explicit endorsation [sic] of the CACP [Canadian Association of Chiefs of Police] Committee following several years of work on this project, by the number of senior police administrators who expressed opposition to the collection of 'race.' I can only conclude that the CACP did not carry out its own internal consultation to the necessary extent, or that views have changed since the decision was taken in 1987 to include racial origin in the UCR survey.

Two scenarios potentially explain this reversal. The above quote alludes to one possibility, which concerns the representativeness of institutional actors. While the police representatives to the CCJS vocally supported the race/crime proposal, the extent to which they were speaking on behalf of the entire police community subsequently came into question. This reversal would thus exemplify how an identity that the Centre imputed to different organizations suddenly and dramatically became problematic. A second, and related, explanation for this change in attitude concerns the timing of this proposal. As previously discussed, between 1987 and 1991 the issue of race/crime had become politically charged. Cognizant of this increased public sensitivity, police forces retreated from their promise to collect and submit the data. This retraction, particularly by major urban police forces, raised difficult methodological problems. The prospect that only a small number of geographically non-representative forces would be submitting racial data made the utility of any resultant data immediately suspect. All of these factors cumulatively prompted the Centre to conclude that the prospects for collecting such data at the current time were not favourable.

Cumulatively, the race/crime proposal was subject to the following criticisms: it did not accurately capture the range of racial/ethnic types; practices of ethnic assignment by police officers were inappropriate and potentially discriminatory; racial typologies are social constructs; nothing politically useful could be done with the resulting numbers; or, alternatively, inappropriate things would be done with the numbers. However, there was no unified voice of opposition. Many of the criticisms were answerable by arguments routinely used by the Centre and Statistics Canada more generally. The failure of these efforts is therefore an example of how as a social and political practice the production of statistical knowledge can be shaped by its cultural environment. In this case, the Centre was working in a context that included pre-existing public anxieties about the relationship between race and crime and a consequent wavering police commitment to the collection of such data.

Transition: A Narrowing of Focus

While the race/crime controversy was apparently an isolated incident that subsequently moved out of the public limelight, there is ample reason to anticipate the return of some variation of this issue. Governmental strategies often focus on the race/ethnicity of the accused and victim. We continue to hear calls for efforts to ascertain the differential involvement in crime by racial/ethnic groupings. Other constituencies want to know how the state deals with offenders from different ethnic/racial backgrounds. The answer to these questions requires knowledge that constructs the objects of governance along racial/ethnic lines.

This analysis therefore amounts to a examination of one moment in an ongoing concern. It is part of the story of an enduring but ambivalent demand for racialized data by governmental actors and political activists. Since 1991 this desire has mutated the race/crime proposal into an effort to gather numbers on one particular ethnic subset.

Aboriginal Data

The phrase 'Native American' was invented by the U.S. government Department of the Interior in 1970. It is an inventory term used to keep track of people. It includes Hawaiians, Eskimos, Samoans, Micronesians, Polynesians, and Aleuts. Anyone who uses the phrase *Native American* is assisting the U.S. government in its efforts to obliterate people's true identities.

Do you want to know what the Indians would like to be called? Their real names: Adirondack, Delaware, Massachuset, Narraganset, Potomac, Illinois, Miami, Alberta, Ottawa, Waco, Wichita, Mohave, Shasta, Yuma, Erie, Huron, Susquehanna, Natchez, Mobile, Yakima, Wallawalla, Muskogee, Spokan, Iowa, Missouri, Omaha, Kansa, Biloxi, Dakota, Hatteras, Klamath, Caddo, Tillamook, Washoe, Cayuga, Oneida, Onondaga, Seneca, Laguna, Santa Ana, Winnebago, Pecos, Cheyenne, Menominee, Yankton, Apalachee, Chinook, Catawba, Santa Clara, Taos, Arapaho, Blackfoot, Blackfeet, Chippewa, Cree, Cheyenne, Mohawk, Tuscarora, Cherokee, Seminole, Choctaw, Chickasaw, Comanche, Shoshone, Two Kettle, Sans Arc, Chiricahua, Kiowa, Mescalero, Navajo, Nez Perce, Potawatomi, Shawnee, Pawnee, Chickahominy, Flathead, Santee, Assiniboin, Oglala, Mininonjou, Osage, Crow, Brulé, Hunkpapa, Pima, Zuni, Hopi, Paiute, Creek, Kickapoo, Ojibiwa, Shinnicock.

George Carlin

The 1991 cancellation of the Centre's plans to collect racialized crime data resolved one problem but exacerbated another. Certain segments of the public were placated, but the information needs of the managers of the criminal-justice system remained unsatisfied. Without racial data it is difficult to answer questions about systemic discrimination or to develop programs to meet the needs of different ethnic groups. These tensions resulted in a compromise solution when the Centre's main governing body, the Justice Information Council, resolved in its June 1992 meeting to have the CCJS develop methodologies to expand the ongoing collection of information on aboriginal persons in the justice system. Centre staff were asked to investigate how such collection might proceed.

This abandonment of efforts to collect numbers on 'race/ethnicity' while instituting the collection of information on 'aboriginals' relies on a peculiar distinction between 'race' and 'aboriginal.' In Canada the consensus would be that the dominant 'ethnic problem' in the criminal-justice system concerns the systemic overrepresentation of First Nations peoples in crime statistics, court appearances, and correctional admissions. Consequently, the logic of abandoning the collection of 'race' data in criminal justice while continuing to collect information on 'aboriginals' is logically comparable to the United States forsaking its efforts to collect data on race but continuing to collect numbers on African-Americans.

Any logical inconsistencies notwithstanding, calls for the collection of aboriginal data came from various locations. At the time of the JIC decision a number of commissions were investigating the place of aboriginals in the criminal-justice system. Two of these commissions advocated increasing the number and variety of statistics on the status of aboriginals in criminal justice (Alberta 1991; Saskatchewan 1992). The Saskatchewan Indian and Métis Justice Review Committee recommended 'the design and implementation of data collection systems to provide detailed information to compare Aboriginal and non-Aboriginal contact with, and treatment by, the criminal justice system' (Saskatchewan 1992: 12). In order for governments to alleviate past wrongs done to aboriginal peoples, they needed aggregate forms of knowledge that singled out these peoples from the broader population.

This section chronicles this latest development in the evolution of Canadian race/crime statistics. While familiar issues about the appropriateness of ethnic classifications are discussed, the emphasis is on questions of group representation. Before Centre staff could proceed with aboriginal data collection, they believed it was necessary to secure the support and approval of different institutional actors. Consequently, they undertook an extensive process of consultation with the police and First Nations groups. The failure of the original race/crime proposal had accentuated the difficulties in determining the representativeness of police spokespersons and community groups. Such problems were all the more apparent in efforts to negotiate with representatives of different First Nations communities.

Attempts to collect aboriginal data mark the return of pragmatics to the Centre's work on ethnicity. The myriad questions about methodology, classification, interpretation, and political utility that had previously loomed so large in the race/crime proposal were now reduced to pragmatic limitations on the data. New problems soon arose, however, as it became apparent that attempts to count people according to aboriginal status were also situated in a larger political context. Thus, a number of new parties were introduced into the knowledge network that the Centre staff sought to align and control. As discussed in chapter 2, in order to produce facts, coordinating actors must create interests among different individuals and organizations. The latter must be convinced of their interest in the knowledge or technology being developed and persuaded that their current ends and agendas would benefit from the new knowledge-production regime.

To establish and extend the knowledge network necessary to produce data on aboriginal involvement in the criminal-justice system, Centre staff had to enrol First Nations groups. One of the first bodies they consulted on this proposal was the Assembly of First Nations, the largest First Nations political organization in Canada. Centre staff argued for the potential political benefits to such numbers, suggesting that First Nations groups could use this data to challenge popular conceptions about high rates of aboriginal criminality, or as a resource to argue for increased programs and services. One participant in these negotiations said that the main benefit for the aboriginal community was that 'it would give them, for once, something based on concrete data. The worst situation was to be confronted by allegations and accusations about the levels of aboriginal crime and have nothing to fall back and say "This is right, this is wrong, this is close" ... so it would give them some solid data.'

The political appeal of such data is not necessarily self-evident. Rightly or wrongly, Centre personnel often assume that their audience can interpret and manipulate quantitative data. It can be difficult to persuade a group of the value of helping produce statistical data if that group believes they lack the training to use the resulting knowledge. During consultations, some aboriginal groups said they were uncertain of their ability to effectively use the data, and feared that others would be able to cynically twist the numbers to advance positions detrimental to the interests of First Nations peoples. To overcome this problem, and hopefully further enmesh First Nations groups into their knowledge network, Centre staff offered to enhance the ability of First Nations groups to interpret and use quantitative data. For example, Statistics Canada conducts a range of specialized courses on how to construct surveys and interpret statistics. Usually reserved for employees of Statistics Canada, this training was offered to members of the Assembly of First Nations in conjunction with the negotiations on providing crime data.

> The other part of what [the Assembly of First Nations] were interested in was to be allowed access into departmental training efforts. So this is one thing that the chief statistician has done for several years was to encourage members of the aboriginal community to apply for and participate in courses like the SSDC – Survey Skills Development Course, or similar things, in order to learn more about how you manipulate, how you analyze and interpret data. How you edit data and do that kind of analysis. So we have gone out of our way to do that as well.

Training groups in the skills of quantitative methods also subtly produces and reinforces a quantitative style of political discourse. Using quantitative measures in political rhetoric, decision making, and protest is now so firmly ingrained that we simply take it for granted. The ubiquity of quantified political claims masks how such a discourse relies on learned forms of quantitative expertise. A numerical world implies quantitatively inclined people who are themselves social and historical products (P. Cohen 1982; Hacking 1990). Implicit in the offer to let First Nations representatives participate in Statistics Canada's courses is the assumption that a major component of politics operates through quantification. To effectively play the political game it is therefore best to have a set of skilled experts on your side who will be able to offer informed interpretations of official statistics and conduct their own surveys about your constituency. In this regard, the Centre sought to 'contribute to the creation of a pool of Aboriginal people with statistical skills and experience, upon which their respective communities can draw' (CCJS n.d.). The offer to allow First Nations groups into these courses helps produce the kind of people, management styles, and political discourse that are the foundation of a statistical agency.

How to Define 'Aboriginal'?

Canada's First Nations peoples are intimately aware that practices of counting and classifying by external agencies are a form of nominal power that has become manifest in their lived identities. Robert Berkhofer (1978) reminds us that the term 'Indian' was itself of European origin, a shorthand term to group together peoples who were differentiated by culture, language, and self-identity. The quote by George Carlin on p. 111 makes the same point for the term 'Native American.' This practice was by no means unique to North America, as Anderson's (1991) discussion of the colonial census in southeast Asia demonstrates. Anderson reveals how a series of extraordinarily rapid changes took place in the official identity categories on these censuses. While these categories were being developed in distant colonial bureaucracies, the people they referred to largely lived their lives as they had always done, unaware of how they were being categorized from outside. Over time, however, these classifications 'put down deep social and institutional roots as the colonial state multiplied its size and functions' (ibid.: 169). As people moved through schools, hospitals, and social-welfare institutions, they were dealt with according to the identity categories on official documents. In the process, what were originally alien classifications slowly acquired a subjective reality.

As in all attempts to measure ethnicity, the Centre faced questions about how to delineate the ethnic variable? How would an 'aboriginal person' be defined? This question is complicated by the intricate web of legal and bureaucratic regimes that bear on aboriginal identity. One can gain an appreciation for the confusing legal and cultural designations pertaining to First Nations people from a quiz in a university textbook (Elliott 1994: 23). Students are asked to connect twelve currently valid categories of First Nations peoples with their legal and/or cultural designation. The categories consist of Non-Status Indians, Inuit (Eskimos), Treaty Indians, Metis, Status-only Indians, British North America Act Indians, Reserve-only residents, Status-Reserve Indians, Band-Reserve Indians, Aboriginal Peoples of Canada, Band-only Indians, and Status-Band-Reserve Indians. The intricacies of this classificatory mania would be laughable were it not such a clear example of the colonial strategy of divide and rule. Where a person falls within this classificatory labyrinth shapes his or her rights and entitlements, and at different times has dictated where people could live and whether they could vote, sign contracts, or purchase alcohol. (Detailed examination of the specific history and legacy of these designations is beyond the scope of this analysis. Readers who would like to learn more about this topic can consult Frideres 1998, chapter 2.)

Contemporary efforts to measure 'aboriginal' crime are only a small component in a much larger state effort to categorize and classify First Nations people. One qualitative difference in this effort that has emerged in recent years is that state bureaucracies that attempt to count the 'Indian' population now consult with First Nations groups on appropriate identity categories. When it came time to contemplate how to define an 'Indian' for the purposes of crime statistics, the Centre sought out the opinion of a number of First Nations groups. Consensus on such matters has not always been forthcoming, but such consultations are an important attempt to have nominal categories correspond more closely to the lived realities of aboriginal identity.

Centre staff advanced a number of scenarios for how the First Nations population could be categorized. The recurrent dynamic of such efforts was that attempts to set stable definitional boundaries around a group were frequently greeted by other individuals who pointed out the inadequacy of the proposed scheme and/or argued that their lived experience of ethnicity was excluded from the classificatory system. For example, the CCJS proposed a tripartite division of First Nations people into 'Aboriginal,' 'Non-Aboriginal,' and 'Metis.' They were surprised to learn that the meaning of the term Metis varied across the country: 'Apparently in the western provinces, Métis is specifically identified as a person with both Aboriginal and non-Aboriginal origin, whereas in certain other areas of the country, Métis is used to identify a person with two different racial origins, Aboriginal or not' (CCJS 1993: 19). While this tripartite classification system had the advantage that it was simple, it was criticized for being inaccurate. However, the level of detail sought by some groups was clearly beyond the practical possibilities of a statistical agency. For example, one national First Nations political organization advised Centre personnel that they should subdivide 'First Nations' into approximately fifty or sixty cultural and linguistic groups.

Contentious Consultations

Centre staff had a fairly concise explanation for why the collection of racial data was impossible or inappropriate, but the collection of aboriginal data was both appropriate and, hopefully, possible. The difference centred on the views and interests they imputed to different communities. Ethnic groups, particularly those in Toronto, were portrayed as singularly opposed to such efforts, while aboriginal groups encouraged the collection of aboriginal data. It was assumed, particularly in light of the recommendations by the aboriginal justice inquiries, that aboriginal communities would support the collection of such data. As one member of the Centre put it, 'The aboriginal communities have been unanimously in favour of continuing [collecting] it.' Despite such claims, it became apparent that there was not unanimous support among aboriginal communities. Instead, some communities proved to be in favour, some strenuously opposed, and still others had given the matter absolutely no thought whatsoever.

Consultations with First Nations groups gave pause to those individuals who believed they would encounter common opinions among different minority communities, as it became apparent that some aboriginal communities were rife with factions. This observation accentuates how the term 'community,' which implicitly assumes a unity and solidarity of opinion, is inappropriate when discussing political issues defined by contestation and by shifting, temporary, and strategic alliances. Here a senior member of the federal Department of Justice recounts how Centre staff became aware of such divisions during their consultations with aboriginal groups in 1995/96:

> The special studies that [the CCJS] has been trying to do on aboriginal justice in Saskatchewan, that has had a very chequered history because they couldn't get enthusiastic participation from the 'on the ground' organizations in Saskatchewan. First they thought they had agreement, then they didn't. And aboriginal groups vary. Some of them think they shouldn't participate in the census, some of them think they have to so that they can define their problems. Some of them want aboriginal designations in the UCR, some of them don't because they think it helps the rednecks see the disproportionate numbers still in prisons.

While consultations might be difficult to arrange and unlikely to produce consensus, they are nonetheless valuable to Centre employees. Consultations allow them to anticipate potential problems and concerns about the data-collection process. They are also a forum where they can advocate to First Nations communities on behalf of national justice statistics generally, and on race/ethnicity variables in particular. Finally, given the often contentious nature of ethnic classifications, any of the Centre's recommendations have a greater rhetorical strength if they can demonstrate that they were arrived at in consultation with aboriginal groups.

In their consultations with some members of Saskatchewan's aboriginal community, Centre staff had to deal with issues of representativeness, politics, and occasionally outright hostility. The Prince Albert

Grand Council (PAGC) in Saskatchewan arranged for meetings between Centre staff and a number of smaller bands within the PAGC's
jurisdiction. The Grand Council appeared eager to develop the study,
as they envisioned deriving political benefits from the eventual production of such numbers. When Centre personnel went to the smaller
communities, however, questions about the representativeness of the
Grand Council quickly arose. The interests of the larger political organization were not necessarily shared by members of the smaller communities, and there appeared to be a history of tensions among the
different representative bodies. 'In some cases there is downright hostility between the communities and the Prince Albert Grand Council.
So we are walking into the midst of something ... The PAGC kind of
paves the way for us, but unbeknownst to us there is a lot of hostility
between them and this particular community. We are kind of inno-
cents. It is a very complicated situation.'

As a consequence, Centre staff were not always particularly welcomed by local bands. The chilly reception is perhaps not surprising
given that the long colonial relationship between aboriginal peoples
and the state has resulted in endemic poverty in some of these communities. People living in such circumstances were not easily impressed
with the urgency of developing national criminal-justice statistics on
Aboriginals. Such indifference is in marked contrast to the world-view
of Centre staff, who often take the value and utility of justice statistics
for granted and who saw these consultations as an opportunity to
demonstrate the importance of such numbers to local communities.
Actually going into some of these small communities prompted at
least one Centre employee to reflect upon such presumptions:

> Somehow, when you spend all of your time in [the Centre], it seems to be
> a natural part of your life to have national statistics. But you have to
> agree when you are sitting in Carrot River – these people are Swampy
> Cree and they were given a rotten piece of land fifty years ago, and it is
> swampy and practically useless for anything. And these people are pretty
> destitute. You drive through the community and it is difficult to imagine
> people living day after day, week, month, year, decade after decade in
> that environment. And then you try and go in there and you try and
> make an argument that it is important to have national statistics. It is a
> hard sell. It is hard for these people to imagine.

Outside of any crisis of confidence suffered by Centre employees,
their advocacy of national justice statistics in these communities proved

difficult for other reasons. First, the problem of discerning the level of aboriginal criminality is largely an urban one. For urban centres that are ethnically heterogeneous, special efforts must be made to determine the differential involvement of ethnic groups in criminal behaviour. Bodies such as the Prince Albert Grand Council, which has a jurisdiction that extends over both rural and more urban environments, recognized how such numbers could help them unpack the degree of ethnic involvement in the criminal-justice system. The usefulness of such data was not so readily apparent to small local bands, who find it comparatively easy to determine the level of aboriginal criminality in their community. Living on reserves with a predominantly homogenous ethnic population and being policed by the RCMP, whose detachment boundaries coincided exactly with those of the reserve, they could safely assume that all crimes in the community were committed by aboriginals, and that all victims would also be aboriginals. This made advocating for aboriginal statistics all the more difficult. Here a Centre employee notes how difficult it was to work up enthusiasm among some small First Nations communities:

> The arguments that [we] used were ones like even though the community itself had available to it data from the RCMP on the number of crimes that were committed on the reserve, in the confines of the community, there was a larger picture that was not available to anybody. And that was at the Prince Albert Grand Council ... So it's basically at that higher level of aggregation where the benefits would be. It was a bit difficult to make that argument. Or, conversely, the people on the other side who were in a position to receive the argument had no time for it, had no appreciation for it and weren't convinced by it.

While Centre staff approached these community meetings with a singular focus on aboriginal justice statistics, they soon realized that discussion would not be confined to that issue. Unbeknownst to Centre employees, some communities situated these consultations in a wider context of political negotiations with the provincial government. Some aboriginal groups saw an opportunity to air assorted grievances about the criminal-justice system – including criticisms about the geographic location of courts and prisons and about insufficient consultation before passing provincial legislation – and called for improved First Nations policing, and increased use of sentencing options that more closely accorded with traditional forms of Aboriginal justice. Here a member of the CCJS summarizes the process of negotiations with First Nations groups: 'It has been rocky. It is really bumpy. It got hung up in a whole series of provincial discussions and negotiations between the aboriginal community, First Nations community and Saskatchewan Justice. There is a lot of negotiations going on on a lot of different issues. The indications I have are that the aboriginal community was using this as a bit of a lever. If they agree to go along with this they would get some consideration for some of their other grievances. So it has delayed things a lot.'

Data is collected on the assumption that it will serve as the basis for governmental action, that policies will flow from the data that will ultimately benefit the various stakeholders. In some First Nations communities, faith in this governmental logic appears to be disintegrating as myriad studies, reports, and data accumulate with little perceived benefit. First Nations people have been the subject of a national royal commission, provincial commissions on aboriginal justice, anthropological studies, and sociological analysis. Statistics Canada has conducted a special census of aboriginal people and now plans to conduct a second. Many ministries and departments have sections dedicated to addressing how well or poorly they meet the needs of aboriginal people and have staff who conduct surveys and studies on various attributes and profiles of First Nations people.

The question now being asked is 'To what effect?' Rather than being seen as a precursor to political action, such studies are now viewed by some as a form of political non-action, a familiar strategy to defer committing to real political change until this study is done or that commission reports its findings. It has reached the point that a regular feature of a national First Nations radio comedy program involves ironically quoting from the scores of unimplemented recommendations of the federal Royal Commission on Aboriginal Peoples. The sentiment that 'We have been studied to death!' has become more recurrent among First Nations representatives, articulating a frustration with the apparent lack of real reform despite the innumerable ways that their peoples have been counted, classified, and scrutinized. Centre staff occasionally encountered manifestations of this frustration, as aboriginal groups had no time whatsoever for their proposals, suggesting that the whole enterprise was a waste of time and money.

The [aboriginal community] Justice Committee members took the consultation as an opportunity to express their deep frustration at the slow pace of First Nation justice reform, and the absence of resources to support their work in particular. In this, the Committee members were critical of a variety of actors, ranging from the federal and provincial governments to the FSIN [Federation of Saskatchewan Indian Nations], the Prince Albert Grand Council and friendship centres. In their view, limited resources were being squandered, and few trickled down to the community level ... Committee members took the view that they had nothing to learn about criminal justice issues from this or any other consultation or data base, and that Aboriginal-specific data were of virtually no value. (CCJS 1996: 15)

At the extreme, the reception of CCJS delegates passed beyond indifference into antagonism. In one community, in an effort to deflect conflict, CCJS staff symbolically and physically aligned themselves with the local RCMP officer who had good relations with the local residents. 'We met with outright hostility in one place. They just couldn't wait to see the end of us. It was just really hostile ... It was kind of strange, we were taking refuge with the RCMP officer: "We are with him. You wouldn't want to hurt us. We are a friend of his, so we are not all bad." It was pretty tense.'

While the Centre has the institutional resources and official sanction to produce authorized statistics, its power to do so is contingent. To produce such numbers a set of common classificatory schemes must be instituted by all survey respondents. This, in turn, requires that Centre staff work to ensure that all of the component parts of their extended networks operate in the prescribed fashion. Contingency enters into this equation because it is not preordained that these elements will operate according to plan, as component parts fail or define their interests differently. Local community ambivalence and hostility show how the identities encouraged and required by the Centre can be resisted and challenged. The identity of 'willing data provider' slips away as local communities dispute the value and utility of such numbers or emphasize more pressing concerns.

At bottom, the race/crime issue amounted to an attempt by an internationally renowned statistical agency to collect a single data element. There is nothing wholly spectacular about such efforts, it is what this agency does – its personnel continually add and delete boxes on forms and surveys to collect certain types of data. As we have seen, however, there can be an intense politics of knowledge surrounding such processes. These politics bring unanticipated phenomena directly to the forefront of analysis. Issues such as police/community relations, provincial/First Nations negotiations, governmental funding, a history of colonialism and cultural genocide, trust of police officers, and political representation are all implicated and must be engaged by Centre staff. Despite such complexities, their efforts to date are a qualified success. In 2000 they published their first report on police-reported aboriginal crime in Saskatchewan (Quann and Trevethan 2000), a publication made possible by the negotiations and consultations analysed above. Developments in this direction have prompted some Centre staff to anticipate the day when they would again try to expand their collection of racial data holdings beyond a simple 'aboriginal' variable.

The Return of Race?

Despite their disavowal of efforts to collect ethnicity/race data, Centre personnel seem to be drawn inexorably towards collecting some form of race/crime data.

Some critics, criminologists, and managers of the justice system continue to see the prohibition against collecting race/crime data as a problem. In a society that privileges quantitative forms of knowledge and makes claims about wanting to improve ethnic equality, it is hard to conceive how such governmental efforts could be evaluated without race-specific data – irrespective of classificatory and ontological ambiguity. A member of the Centre responsible for handling public requests for information made it clear that many segments of the public continue to request racialized crime data and are bewildered to learn that such data are not available: 'The big one of course is race. Why don't we collect race? They collect it in the census, they collect it in the States. Everybody wants it in the States, all of the ethnic groups want it in the States. Why don't you collect it up here? That's always been a real problem one.'

Consequently, some Centre employees continue to believe that it might be possible to reintroduce a racial component to the UCR at a more politically opportune moment. The continuing interest in race was apparent in the Centre's involvement in the Commission on Systemic Racism in the Ontario Criminal Justice System (1995). Members of the Centre assisted this commission by extracting racial data from the Metro Toronto Police database, which was then analysed by academics (Roberts and Doob 1997). Even this relatively 'hands-off' arrangement made some senior members of Statistics Canada uncomfortable, as it appeared to contravene the edict that the Centre get entirely out of the race/crime business.

The stability of this total ban on race/crime data has at times appeared precarious. Members of the Centre and the Justice Initiative frequently suggested that it might be fruitful to revisit the entire issue in the near future now that much of the public furor has subsided. Some staff members think that such information could and should be collected, and that the previous public outcry and police reticence was simply a result of bad timing:

> It may have simply been, this thing in 1990 was not the moment to do things. Even if we hadn't had a problem with Oka maybe it still wouldn't have been the moment to do it. Now the time may be different. Some time in fiscal year 1992–1993 I attended a JIC meeting and the conversation was 'Well, that decision that we took back in 1991 about removing this data was the right one for that moment in time. However, it may be the time to review it.' Now, that has not been done but there seems to be a recognition that maybe there is some value in re-examining that.

Similar sentiments were expressed during consultations with Saskatchewan aboriginal groups, when community members questioned why the Centre would want to collect aboriginal data when it did not collect data on other ethnic groups. The Centre's liaison people responded that in light of the work done by the Ontario Commission on Systemic Racism, they believed this previous ban on collecting racial data would be reversed by the JIC 'as a variety of stakeholders came to recognize the value that such information can have for the development of programs, policy and legislation' (CCJS 1995). However, as the matter currently stands, the Centre is still not collecting racial crime data outside of their work on Aboriginal crime in Saskatchewan.

Discussion

Classifications of people have a curious structure – they are both descriptive and at least partially constitutive of their object. One of the Centre's most important powers is derived from its ability to put classifications into play. When they demarcate types of people, such classifications can provide models for living that are alternatively embraced or challenged. These can be entirely new ways of classifying people or may reproduce existing classifications drawn from the life-world of the population. Irrespective of whether they originate in bu-reaucracies or lived reality, classifications are always bounded – they exist because limitations, ultimately historical and cultural, have been placed on fluid phenomena. Institutionalized on official surveys and embedded on the forms used by state agents, formal identification freezes identities that are always being transformed.

The preceding account accentuates the fluidity of a phenomenon that in day-to-day life is often perceived as being stable and fixed. Ethnic identity is a contingent and historical artefact that can change with social context. In fact, people do not even necessarily identify with a single ethnic label during their entire life-course. A random survey by Petersen (1987: 189) across consecutive U.S. census counts found that one-third of matched persons claimed a different ethnic origin from one survey to the next.

Official classifications of ethnic identity are political in two distinct senses. First, in liberal forms of governance various programs are de-veloped on the basis of such classifications. It is difficult to know if you have reduced racialized employment discrimination or ethnic overrepresentation in prison if ethnic classifications are eliminated from the bureaucratic repertoire. A liberal utopia would not care about how people are classified, but the road to this utopia is paved with a multi-tude of classifications of types of people. In the context of the Cana-dian race/crime issue, it is entirely likely that the same individuals who objected to collecting this data because of methodological diffi-culties and classificatory confusion would also make use of any result-ing data, as it would allow them to make arguments to improve the conditions of minorities in relation to their arrest, conviction, or incar-ceration rates.

The second political attribute of classification concerns struggles to institutionalize desired classifications. Such struggles are undertaken for many reasons, including a desire to formalize a set of terms that correspond more closely with our assumptions about the natural divi-sions in the world. They can also amount to strategic attempts to institutionalize a set of classifications that might improve the social position of your group. For example, recent efforts by Hawaiians to change their classification on the U.S. census from 'Asian or Pacific Islanders' to 'American Indian' are at least partially motivated by the fact that 'some colleges and the Department of Education have minority scholarships that you get through your status as Native American' (Goldberg 1997: 47 n. 12).

This account of race/crime data collection reserves judgment as to the accuracy of the myriad possible ethnic classifications discussed. This posture is assumed quite consciously. In and of themselves racial classifications are not accurate or inaccurate, appropriate or inappropriate. Such evaluations do not result from some form of correspondence to the real state of the world's different ethnic types. Instead, ethnicity is stabilized through plays of power, practices of boundary maintenance, and institutionalization. Even in those instances where groups are given, or take for themselves, the opportunity to advocate for how they want to be classified, this does not guarantee consensus. The representativeness of spokespeople can always be brought into question.

At one level, the public controversy over statistics on ethnicity and crime involved a rather mundane issue: when forwarding their reports to the CCJS would police organizations be required to assign offenders and victims of violent crime to a limited set of ethnic/racial variables? Centre staff must deal with such questions on a regular basis, and usually do so in the context of fairly detached bureaucratic negotiations. In this instance, however, such discussions were complicated by the public politics of classification. In the process, some groups challenged the accuracy of the taxonomy, while others opposed or questioned the propriety of classifying people according to race/ ethnicity. Methodological difficulties did not dictate that this controversy would resolve itself as it did. Instead, the proposal was undermined by a combination of ethnic politics, aboriginal/provincial negotiations, a legacy of colonization and cultural genocide, mistrust, police/public relations, and the questionable representativeness of police forces and ethnic groups. The ensuing controversies accentuate how the availability of governmental knowledge is not dictated solely by the needs and aspirations of governmental actors, but can be shaped by broader political and institutional factors. The efforts by Centre personnel to navigate their way through these controversies also reiterate a larger theme of this study by demonstrating how the Centre's methodology is not confined to what are normally conceived of as statistical methods, but is intimately bound up with more political concerns. This subject is taken up in greater detail in the next chapter.

5

Politics and Numbers

Our mandate is to present the facts in as dispassionate and unbiased [a] manner as possible. We are totally apolitical even though the information and numbers we produce have nation-wide implications. We publish the results of our surveys without fear or favor regardless of the political ramifications for the government of the day.

Statistics Canada (1993: 90)

This chapter examines the different political aspects of, and influences upon, the Canadian Centre for Justice Statistics. It commences with a discussion of the relationship between the Centre and partisan politics. While it is often contended that official statistics are unduly influenced by government, the Centre is determined to remain above such political partisanship. Consequently, it goes to considerable lengths to keep itself at arm's length from direct governmental manipulation. While this means that the Centre has generally avoided partisan politics, it is nonetheless shaped by political factors that are not captured in the idealized image of a strict demarcation between politics and statistics enshrined in the Statistics Canada mandate that heads this chapter. The Centre must negotiate with a complex series of organizational and institutional interests in order to produce its data. This analysis works with a broad understanding of 'the political' in order to accentuate how the mundane day-to-day processes in the production of statistical knowledge can augment or marginalize the interests of different groups. This from of micropolitics includes a range of actions by different parties designed to maximize the opportunities, and minimize the risks, posed by the Centre's activities.

Micropolitics are unavoidable in an agency that is overseen by deputy ministers and their representatives and is reliant on the cooperation of a host of criminal-justice agencies to fulfil its mandate. Inter-institutional negotiations introduce ongoing political tensions over what studies to conduct and release, and questions about who controls the data. Jurisdictional interests are also occasionally apparent in the standardized counting rules employed in some of the Centre's surveys. Efforts to introduce standardized definitions for phenomena such as 'alternative measures' and 'remission' reveal the ongoing and politically interested negotiations that can surround the production of standards.

Politics

The first point to stress is that there was no indication of *any* direct partisan political manipulation of the Centre's numbers. This claim is made up-front and forcefully because it was one of the predominant concerns among the people I interviewed. I was routinely assured that the Centre stood above party politics. There was no evidence that politicians directed the Centre to produce, for example, incarceration rates that would coincide with the political mood or agenda of the day. Such direct interference was strenuously guarded against to the point that it did not appear that politicians even bothered to make such crude requests for statistical duplicity.

The anxieties about politics articulated by Centre personnel parallel those of scientists more generally. Knowledge producers, particularly those who work in democratic societies, must maintain a delicate balance between keeping politics close at hand and not too close (Gieryn 1995), whereby questions about what counts as 'too close' are a contextual matter. Being sensitive to political agendas can help to legitimate scientists and secure financial support. However, politicians value scientific knowledge because of its disinterestedness (Jasanoff 1990), as science purports to stand above personal whim and individual subjectivity. A statistician working in the Department of Justice explains how the Centre's data are only valuable to her work on explicitly political/governmental initiatives to the extent that the CCJS can situate itself outside of politics: 'Their strength comes from being in no one's pocket and promoting no one. On that we can always say that these numbers come from CCJS, they are not our numbers. If they come from us, people will always criticize them, or find them suspect because your influences come into play in how you ask questions and how you collect data. So for me, first and foremost, the Statistics Canada credo of being non-partisan and not being in anyone's corner is its strength.'

Proximity threatens to blur the line between politics and science, however. Born of a governmental need for knowledge, the Centre must work to maintain an arm's length distance from the political imperatives of the day.

While there is no evidence of direct political interference in the immediate production of the Centre's numbers, this is not to say that once criminal statistics are in public culture they are not cynically manipulated. Examples abound of politicians and private agencies selectively or dishonestly invoking statistics for partisan purposes (see Best 1989; Burnham 1997, chap. 4; Baer and Chambliss 1997). Statistics can be invoked to demonstrate just about any point. George Gallup, one of the populizers of sample surveys, bragged that he 'could prove God statistically.' Undoubtedly, he could also give a new quantitative twist on Nietzsche's project by statistically proving the death of God as well. Academics are accustomed to seeing statistics being manipulated, crunched, and massaged to demonstrate quite contradictory points. In fact, it has become common to teach students the basics of statistical methods by teaching them how to 'lie' with statistics (Huff 1955). As inevitably partial representations of the world, statistics are invoked in public culture to demonstrate or refute assorted political arguments. This does not mean, however, that we should abandon statistical knowledge and surrender to Mark Twain's cynicism about there being 'lies, damn lies, and statistics.' Instead, we must acknowledge that statistics are one element in a rhetorical arsenal invoked as part of political argumentation, rather than a form of knock-down proof. Quantification does not make something 'so,' but provides insights, rhetorical possibilities, and opportunities for political strategizing and governmental intervention.

Trustworthy Knowledge

The danger of appearing to be politically partisan is that it can undermine the trust that the public and politicians must invest in knowledge-producing institutions. An invaluable asset for the Centre, trust is only indirectly addressed in its daily routines. Public trust in the Centre and Statistics Canada only comes to the forefront during those relatively infrequent political controversies where trust risks being undermined. This section explores the controversy over the 1993 Violence Against Women (VAW) survey to reflect on the role of trust as an epistemological resource for statistical agencies.

Sociologists recognize that trust fosters social cohesion and is an invaluable component in commercial transactions (Misztal 1996; Govier 1997). Niklas Luhmann (1979, 1988) has proposed that trust reduces social complexity, by 'going beyond available information and generalizing expectations of behavior in that it replaces missing information with an internally guaranteed security' (1979: 150). Given the expanded range of interactions, choices, and opportunities inherent in contemporary societies, trust in our expectations about the behaviour of individuals and complex systems reduces the infinite possibilities inherent in a given situation. Trust reduces complexity, allowing an individual to make his or her way in the world. As Garfinkel (1963) suggests, our day-to-day sense of reality relies on a backdrop of trust, or 'taken for granted' assumptions that other social actors will perform their roles faithfully. Trust is also a vital component in financial arrangements. Even rudimentary commercial transactions require that individuals trust the value of symbolic tokens such as money and credit, as well as the future actions of individuals and institutions.

Not nearly as much has been written on the place of trust in relation to the production of scientific knowledge. This reticence can be traced to the long-standing opposition in modern epistemology between trust and knowledge, whereby to know a matter on the basis of trust was, in all likelihood, to be mistaken. True knowledge presumably derives from first-hand observation, hypothesis testing, and experimentation (Shapin 1996: 69–74). Trust, therefore, stands in sharp contrast to the sceptical attitude towards knowledge claims that Merton (1973a) suggests is characteristic of scientific culture. Merton's image of science's organized scepticism is, however, more scientific self-promotion than an accurate description of science in action. Scepticism about any individual fact ultimately rests on an elaborate edifice of unquestioned trust in other knowledges, technologies, and artefacts that have not been scrutinized by the individual scientist. Georg Simmel (1950: 313) observed long ago that 'existence rests on a thousand premises which the single individual cannot trace and verify to their roots at all, but must take on faith.' The same is true for the routine operation of science, as the individual scientist cannot possibly have first-hand experience of the myriad technologies, artefacts, and knowledges that she or he must rely upon (see Shapin 1994: 17–19; Latour 1987, chap. 1).

Historically, decisions about whether or not to trust a person were related to that person's reputation. You had to know who a person was in order to anticipate how he or she would behave and whether their testimony was valid. In premodern societies, personal reputation was deeply entwined in the day-to-day routines of rural life, where trustworthiness could be ascertained through repeated observations of a person's character and of how faithfully they fulfilled their obligations. In *A History of Truth*, Steven Shapin (1994) demonstrates the historical emergence of the 'gentleman scientist' and the importance of the reputation of individual scientists to the development of early modern science. The validity of a scientist's testimony about experimental results was related to his reputation as a 'gentleman,' and this reputation spoke to the honesty and disinterestedness of his observations, and hence to the validity of his science. Shapin asserts: 'Premodern society looked truth in the face' (1994: 410). Increased urbanization and anonymity, however, severed the tight social networks upon which interpersonal trust and reputation were based. In modern society, trust derived from physical proximity and lengthy relationships has been replaced by a complex system of rituals and markers such as credit cards, academic credentials, polygraph tests, and driver's licenses, which all serve to invest unknown individuals with trust (Nock 1993).

The reputation of individual scientists continues to be important in modern societies, as prominent reputations enhance the probability that a scientist will be heard and taken seriously (Merton 1973b). Increasingly important, however, is the good reputation of knowledge-producing institutions and abstract systems. The public can accept the truth claims of a reputable institution or profession without labouring under the paralyzing assumption that the truths on offer are always suspect. For scientists, trust in established knowledge allows them to build upon an edifice of accepted truths rather than engage in an infinite-regress interrogation of the accuracy of their technologies, the reliability of their assistants' observations, or the purity of their samples.

Within Statistics Canada the role of trust is as important as in any other knowledge-production enterprise. Statistics Canada has fostered a profile as a reputable producer of statistics. This is partially evident in the fact that they have been recognized by *The Economist* as the best national statistical agency in both 1991 and 1994, as is frequently mentioned by CCJS staff. The Centre partially feeds off the excellent reputation of Statistics Canada to enhance its own image. A former liaison officer, commenting on the relationship between the Centre and Statistics Canada, said, 'I think what you see is [the Centre] has the imprimatur of the mother house. If it is published by Statistics Canada it has a sense of reality to it.' Trust allows the consumers of the Centre's products – who, by and large, cannot and would not interrogate the intricacies of their knowledge-production regime – to accept their findings on faith.

Deteriorating trust can have truly astounding consequences. Economies can collapse and solid facts can be reduced to controversial claims if a system's trust is undermined. The Centre recently found itself embroiled in a politically charged public controversy concerning accusations that the Violence Against Women (VAW) survey was motivated by a desire to produce shocking numbers about the abuse of women in Canada. Such accusations seriously challenged the Centre's reputation and threatened to undermine the public's trust in Statistics Canada. They also have the potential to bring the governmental practices that are aligned with such indicators into question. If the knowledge structure of governmental programming becomes suspect, then the programs themselves can be questioned. If distrust spreads, there is the additional possibility that other Statistics Canada indicators and their affiliated governmental strategies will also be questioned.

Health Canada conceived the Violence Against Women Survey in the early 1990s, and in turn commissioned Statistics Canada to undertake the study at a cost of $1.9 million. Centre personnel developed and administered the survey. As a joint venture with another governmental department it was markedly different from most Centre studies. It also employed a survey methodology, in contrast to the Centre's usual use of data culled from administrative systems. A total of 12,300 randomly sampled women across Canada were interviewed via telephone about their adult experiences of sexual and physical assault by marital partners, dates and boyfriends, other men, and strangers. The findings released in November 1993 were startling: over one-half of all women surveyed reported at least one incident of violence since the age of sixteen, while one-quarter reported experiencing violence at the hands of a current or past marital partner (including common-law) (*The Daily*, 19 November 1993). Extrapolated to the entire Canadian population, this study suggested that approximately five million adult women out of a total population of eleven million women could have been victims of some form of sexual or physical violence since the age of sixteen, and that about 2.7 million Canadian women who had ever been married or lived common-law could have been physically or sexually assaulted by their spouses.

For a full year, this survey was praised as a valuable contribution to our knowledge about violence against women. It was the subject of considerable public commentary and a media officer for the Centre claimed that it received more coverage than Statistics Canada's census. As a form of governmental knowledge, it held out the promise of informing assorted strategies to reduce the appallingly high numbers of women who have been assaulted.

Almost twelve months to the day after the publication of the VAW findings, however, John Fekete, a professor of Cultural Studies and English Literature at Trent University, made serious accusations about the validity of these results and the objectivity of the people who had administered the survey. In an eight-page section of his book *Moral Panic* (Fekete 1994: 80–7), he accused the survey of four main failings, and these claims were widely reproduced by the media. First, he said, the study was partisan because it focused only on women and did not look at violence perpetuated on men by women or by women on women. Second, it did not deal with questions about the accuracy of memory recall, which he saw as particularly troubling in light of the fact that women were asked to report incidents of violence that potentially occurred years or decades ago. Third, he harshly criticized the practice of lumping together apparently less serious behaviours with very serious crimes, all under the heading of 'violence.' Finally, he insinuated that by consulting with feminist groups and front-line service providers in developing the questionnaire, Centre staff had rendered the entire enterprise suspect.

Fekete chides Statistics Canada for failing to live up to standards of 'basic scientific integrity and fairness' (1994: 80), but his criticisms are anything but a restrained exchange of scientific opinion aimed at clarification and correction. Rather, they are a frontal assault situated in a larger argument against 'bio-politics' – a concept that resonates with 'political correctness.' His widely quoted accusation that 'Statistics Canada has sold itself to the dark powers of demonization. It has traded in science for voodoo' (86) is itself an attempt to demonize. His tone is unfortunate, because lost in the vitriol are some arguments that deserve further investigation.

As a starting point, I sympathize with Fekete's concerns about how the survey subsumed, under the common heading of 'violence,' what many people would see as trivial acts along with what would widely be recognized as serious acts of criminal violence. This is an example of perhaps the most common criticism levelled against statistical studies: that the things being treated as equivalent are, in fact, not equivalent. However, Fekete's insinuation that the Centre was deceitful in this practice overlooks how the publication did attempt to disaggregate the different levels of violence experienced by women.

The definition of violence employed by the VAW survey was drawn explicitly from the Canadian Criminal Code, and includes 'level one' sexual assaults, which are at the lower end of a continuum of seriousness. Thus, respondents who answered yes to the question 'Has a (male stranger, other man known to you) ever touched you against your will in any sexual way, such as unwanted touching, grabbing, kissing or fondling?' were deemed to be victims of violence. While such acts clearly deserve censure and attention, rolling them into an aggregate number about the percentage of women who have been the victims of 'violence' obviously raises concerns. However, these are not concerns about a statistical agency captured by a political fringe group, but about the relationship between precise legal terminology and the vernacular. Such different understandings of the term 'violence' are an example of the disjuncture between the common understanding of a term and its precise legal definition and implications. While it is fair to question whether the public would spontaneously categorize all manifestations of unwanted sexual touching, kissing, or fondling as violence, Centre staff believed they were legally obliged to employ this classification.

Further reflection on this disjuncture between popular and legal understandings of the term 'violence' leads me to suggest an argument that Fekete did not make. Part of what is occurring with such categorical confusion is an attempt to symbolically invest behaviours that have been traditionally trivialized with greater public concern by aligning them with undeniably serious forms of conduct. One consequence of bringing different levels of serious behaviour together under a common heading is that the less serious behaviours are, by association, seen to be more serious. This is because categories of behaviour, people, and things are understood in relation to the phenomena deemed to be their equivalent. Fox (1993) makes a similar point in her discussion of a study of 'woman abuse in university and college dating relationships' by DeKeseredy and Kelly (1993). She indicates how the authors of this study subsume under a global category of 'abuse' various insults, unwanted kissing, swearing, and put-downs, along with very serious behaviours such as rape. Fox concludes that 'by combining what is debatably abusive with what everyone agrees to be seriously abusive, they stand to trivialize the latter' (322). The opposite is also true, however, in that instances of categorical ambiguity can also invest less serious behaviours with a greater degree of public concern. Although Centre personnel did not explicitly set out to produce such a result, by grouping behaviours together under a common classification they have shaped, by way of association, the way we think about such behaviours.

Returning to Fekete, we must also concede his point that the VAW survey is biased because it does not explore the dynamics of women's violence against men or other women. However, this is true in the same way that it is true that the survey is biased because it does not examine violence perpetuated *by* children, or, that a study of children is biased because it does not study adults. Choice about parameters is inherent in establishing and funding any study, and such choices are unquestionably related to political agendas and lobbying efforts. In itself it is doubtful that this imbalance invalidates the survey's findings, which appears to be Fekete's aim. Managers of the VAW survey suggested that if they were to conduct this survey again, they would include questions about violence perpetuated against men, not because they believed their findings to be invalid as they stand, but as a strategy to circumvent such criticisms. Such an admission accentuates the fact that part of the Centre's knowledge-production regime involves attempts to anticipate and neutralize the deconstructive strategies of their critics.

Fekete's final two criticisms are even less compelling. His insinuation that, by virtue of their consultations with feminist and front-line service providers who work in the area of violence against women, Statistics Canada personnel demonstrated that they had been captured by such groups is spurious. It was not exclusively such 'feminist factions' who were consulted in preparing this survey (Doob 1995). Furthermore, the Canadian public should be legitimately concerned if a survey of this expense and scope had gone forward without consulting people working in the area. In fact, some women's groups were apprehensive about the survey, fearing that if the results indicated a lower level of violence against women than they anticipated it would challenge the credibility of their organizations. These are not the concerns of groups who felt assured that the findings were preordained to support their political agenda.

Finally, Fekete's charge that Statistics Canada did not concern itself with the accuracy of memory recall highlights an important methodological issue. Self-report and victimization studies routinely acknowledge that memory can be faulty, particularly when respondents are asked to think back many years, but the conclusion that Statistics Canada was 'cooking the books' does not necessarily follow. The emerging consensus appears to be that the optimal time frame to ask respondents to recall experiences of victimization is approximately twelve months (Coleman and Moynihan 1996: 79). Fekete's suggestion that faulty memory might bias the resulting data overlooks the fact that respondents actually tend to forget many incidents of victimization that have occurred beyond a twelve-month period – a phenomenon known as 'telescoping' (Hindelang 1976; Durant, Thomas, and Willock 1972). Women have also been known to conceal their experiences of abuse from researchers (Jones, McClean, and Young 1986). Furthermore, many people have claimed (not without controversy) that traumatic memories of abuse are particularly prone to being repressed. It could easily be the case, therefore, that the problems Fekete points to – faulty memory associated with long periods of recall – actually served to reduce the official count of violence against women.

Fekete's accusations amounted to the worst type of attack that can be mounted against a statistical agency, a claim that it is biased and 'captured by a faction' (Fekete 1994: 86). Such allegations are potentially far more damaging than insinuations that the data are wrong or even that personnel are incompetent, as errors can be rectified and incompetence can be weeded out. The spectre of co-optation is insidious, allowing people to dismiss future knowledge claims out of hand. The trust on which any knowledge-producing institution must rely was brought into question when Fekete made it a point to challenge the reputation of Statistics Canada: '[T]he reputation of Canada's number-one number cruncher, the gold standard of the truths about Canadian life, is hostage in all this to the tyranny of pain, grievance, fear and resentment ... The one-sex survey of Canadian women is a completely uncorroborated, worthless waste of money and public trust' (ibid.: 83).

In this one paragraph Fekete implicates both trust and reputation. These themes were echoed in an *Alberta Report* magazine cover story (Verburg 1995) on this issue, which was subtitled 'The Once-Neutral Agency Is Gaining a Bad Reputation for Political Propaganda.' Reputations, both good and bad, allow us to extrapolate from one set of behaviours to future actions. Here, a bad reputation threatened to spread like cancer to other parts of the Centre and of Statistics Canada. A senior member of Statistics Canada's auditing section, who admittedly knew little about the specifics of the VAW survey, expressed his disgust with the survey and feared that the fallout from the controversy would be a generalized distrust: 'All of a sudden people are going to start looking at our economic statistics [suspiciously] if we keep this God damn nonsense up.' A very senior member of Statistics Canada was emphatic about the danger posed by Fekete's accusations, stressing, 'We take any such things very seriously because we have to maintain public support. Our credibility is extremely, extremely, extremely important. So we take any such things very, very seriously.'

The Centre began an exercise in damage control, which included an eight-page response that refuted Fekete's allegations and clarified the purpose and structure of the survey. Between November 1994 and June 1995 the Centre wrote twenty-one letters to the editors of various publications and complained to the producers of CBC *Newsworld* about comments made by Fekete when he appeared on that program. A manager of the VAW also defended the survey in a commentary published in the Toronto *Globe and Mail* (H. Johnson 1994), which she concluded by again returning to the theme of reputation: 'It is ludicrous to think that this agency would jeopardize its worldwide reputation with inflated figures about such a contentious social issue.'

The long-term implications of this incident are not clear. The Centre and Statistics Canada stand by the findings of the VAW survey, which they see as not only valid but groundbreaking. Other countries have used the VAW as a model for their own studies on violence against women. Nonetheless, people who worked on the Canadian survey concede that the public controversy left a bad taste in their mouths, and that reputations, both institutional and personal, have been negatively affected. If one of Fekete's original aims was to tarnish the reputation of Statistics Canada and the Centre, he appears to have had some degree of success.

Agenda Setting

While the Centre purports to be apolitical, its decisions about what studies to undertake are inherently political. In a review of the Centre's publications, Doob emphasizes that its 'choice of what data to present and the manner in which it is presented make the information anything but neutral. The CCJS constantly is making "political" decisions on what it examines and how it examines it' (1993: 13). Decisions about what topics to investigate both reflect and help set the political agenda, as the importance of those issues singled out for attention is reinforced, while topics that are ignored are implicitly seen to be less serious. As governmental strategies are ultimately related to the availability of knowledge about the population and system processes, decisions about what surveys to conduct also influence the types of governmental strategies that can be developed.

If the Centre's choice of topics is inevitably political, whose agenda is being furthered? Whose concerns and priorities are reinforced? Given the organizational structure of the Centre, it is not surprising to learn that the answer is 'the jurisdictions': those institutions of the larger Justice Initiative who provide the Centre with data for its various surveys. The knowledge the Centre produces is primarily in the service of the jurisdictional actors:

> [The deputies] are the people who are the defining factor in this and they want us to coordinate and bring together whatever is necessary from their jurisdictions to achieve defined ends. So our whole process is now designed around that. That is one of the reasons why we try to stay knowledgeable about the so-called policy-management agenda of the partners in the Initiative. We design our products to address that. We design our decision-making items that go to LOC and JIC with that in mind: 'Does this address something they are interested in? Are they pushing for it?' We try to be as responsive as possible to them. I mean, we are in the civil-courts development [area] because they wanted that. We are into the legal aid cost indicators because that is what they wanted. We are working up some possible indicators of justice, social justice, because they want high level indicators of the justice system. We are tying to design our products to address issues that they have.

The Centre's need to be responsive to jurisdictional knowledge requirements is hardly a recipe for radicalism. The studies CCJS personnel conduct are unlikely to seriously challenge vested political interests. As a part of the state apparatus, their ability to expand the parameters of their surveys innovatively is obviously limited. For example, any effort to increase the purview of what counts as 'violence' or 'crime' beyond the definitions established in the Criminal Code in order to make a political point would clearly be unacceptable.

During the consultations leading up to the creation of the Centre it was recognized that a balance of representation was required in order to ensure that people other than official criminal-justice practitioners and politicians could shape the direction of the Initiative. A 'National Users Advisory Council' was proposed as part of the structure of the Initiative. This council was to comprise up to twenty-five members who had an interest in national justice statistics (IWG 1981: 21). An individual who was centrally involved in these discussions and the early establishment of the Centre recounted how this forum was envisioned as a place where groups such as the media, aboriginal groups, women's groups, and prisoner advocates might serve as a corrective to the established interests of system managers and politicians. He also suggests a reason why this proposal never advanced further than the implementation documents:

> It never got off the ground. It was never part of the package which was given to the Implementation Work Group to develop. Presumably that was because when [the chairman] made his recommendations to the deputy ministers, they said 'No on that. If we are putting our resources into this we are going to get out of it what we want, not what they want out of it.' Who wanted aboriginals to interfere in what we are going to do? You know, it's the old story. So it never flew. It was a valiant attempt to try and provide balance in terms of a truly national, rather than a governmental, centre for justice statistics. But it never flew. I guess it never flew because it was killed by the deputies, but that won't be on paper anywhere.

The issue of outsider representation came up again in the 1990s in an LOC discussion about potentially allowing new groups to participate in its meetings. Again, the proposal was turned down, this time on the rationale that in order to be at the table an individual had to represent a jurisdiction; that is, they would have to be data providers and not simply interested parties. This is a pragmatic and understandable decision considering that the current size of these committees already stretches the bounds of manageability. Centre staff members are also conscientious about trying to meet with groups who might have an interest in a proposed study. However, being consulted is considerably different from being a primary definer of the Centre's agenda. An expanded range of individuals and interests represented in the Initiative could transform governmental agendas, as these new groups would likely advocate for the collection of new types of statistical indicators. To make a fairly simple observation, one will search in vain for CCJS national statistics that document the number of complaints against the police or correctional officers. The institutional affiliations of the people in the JIC, LOC, and POLIS would work against any proposal to document and publicize such wrongdoings.

Jurisdictional Politics

The joint federal/provincial nature of the Justice Initiative is the most recurrent source of political tension within the Centre. For the Centre to fulfil its mandate, jurisdictional actors must assume a range of complex identities. Some of the most important of these oversee the Centre's operations on the Justice Information Council and the Liaison Officers Committee. Made up of deputy ministers with justice responsibilities and their liaison officer representatives, these two organizations are the Centre's board of directors. They approve the Centre's operational plan and advise staff on the future of the Initiative and the types of studies to conduct.

The JIC and the LOC are extremely attuned to the political repercussions of just about every facet of the Centre. The political interests of these representatives are not confined to party affiliations but extend to concerns about how work done at the Centre might influence institutional practices, funding, and public profiles. While deputy ministers and liaison officers require statistics as a basis for strategies of governance, they are also concerned about the political implications of the Centre's studies, the classifications personnel employ, and the language they use to report their findings. The pervasiveness of such political concerns can be discerned from the official record of one LOC meeting in 1993. On this occasion, one liaison officer expressed reservations about the plan to produce a *Juristat* on the number of police officers killed in Canada, 'fearing that it may reopen the capital punishment debate.' At the same meeting, the plan to produce a *Juristat* on violence against children 'was canceled due to the potential sensitive nature of the topic and [was] incorporated into the "Compendium of Articles Related to Family Violence"' planned for the following year. Finally, a planned publication on crimes committed by children under the age of twelve prompted one liaison officer to express his concerns 'that the report could reopen the difficult debate over minimum age and his fear that the media could obtain the report.' The fact that governmental knowledges will ultimately become public knowledge raises ongoing concerns about the political repercussions of the Centre's activities.

One extreme example of some of these jurisdictional/political dynamics involves the Centre's above-noted efforts to produce a report about children under the age of twelve who have committed criminal acts. In Canada, the minimum age of criminal responsibility is twelve. Below that age, children who break the law are dealt with informally by their family or referred to social-service agencies. A study that would provide the first official indication of the numbers of children below the age of criminal responsibility who have dealt with the police because they have broken the law promised to provide policy-relevant knowledge. However, the question about the age at which children should be held criminally responsible has been a highly charged political issue since the inception of the Young Offender's Act in 1984. Politicians, victims-rights advocates, and police associations have lobbied hard to lower or eliminate the minimum-age provisions.

A draft of the 'children under twelve' report was introduced at the 1992 LOC meeting, where it was soundly criticized. The liaison officer who chaired the meeting took issue with the study's methodology, and questioned why five years of crime data had been combined to produce a specific table. The Centre's representative suggested that if data from only one year were used there would be a greater possibility that the resulting proportion could be a statistical anomaly, so personnel compiled all of the crime data in question for five years and produced an average rate. While the Chair recognized the importance of such methodological considerations, he was clearly worried about the potential political repercussions of releasing data that would contain a five-year total number of crimes committed by children under the age of twelve, fearing that this figure could create an inflated impression of the level of youthful criminality. Consequently, he advised the Centre to revise the analysis and base it solely on 1991 data, because the data for that year would likely provide a similar proportion of youthful criminality, while the 'absolute numbers would be smaller thus reducing the potential media impact.'

The controversy that surrounded this study continued when it was later introduced at a JIC meeting. One deputy minister objected to the whole idea of the report, citing the fact that by strict legal definition children cannot commit crimes under the age of twelve, so the whole premise of the study was flawed. The official summary of this meeting details how he 'expressed his concern that the report could reopen the difficult debate over minimum age and his fear that the media could obtain the report. He posed the question, is Statistics Canada obliged by law to release [these findings]?' One member replied that while children cannot be charged with a crime, they can certainly commit criminal acts, and this study would provide a valuable indication of the extent of such behaviour. The representative for the police, a constituency that has vociferously opposed the minimum-age provisions, suggested that the police on the street continued to witness an increase in the number of children under the age of twelve who are involved in crime. 'We cannot hide our heads in the sand and pretend it is not happening.'

The diverse concerns pertaining to these data were addressed through a compromise solution. Rather than publicize the information in a *Juristat*, where it could potentially spark an unwanted political controversy, it was to be made available to people who might call the Centre in search of such information. Here a Centre staff member summarizes how the controversy was resolved: 'Instead of releasing the data through normal routes like a *Juristat*, we decided to just have the information available through client services and if somebody wanted the information they could have it. So we did not release that information in the normal way. What that case indicates is the fact that the Centre has seen a long battle over data ownership. Who is allowed to say what goes out and what does not.'

A host of community and political groups are also interested in the Centre's data. At times, they too display the tension between a desire for particular forms of knowledge and a fear that the specifics of that knowledge might operate against their interests. Such discomfort was apparent in the Centre's involvement in the national Violence Against Women survey. In preparation for this survey, the Centre consulted with a number of groups and individuals, including front-line service providers and feminist agencies. As noted earlier, some of these individuals vacillated over this study. While they recognized that a Statistics Canada publication that demonstrated high levels of abuse of women could help focus public attention on the problem, they also feared the potentially disastrous consequences if the survey reported relatively low levels of abuse. As one of the coordinators of this project reported, when the Centre started to develop the survey, 'We were getting it from women's groups. They were so scared that we were going to come out, that women aren't going to disclose. That you are going to come out with low numbers.' In their eyes, lower-than-anticipated levels of reported abuse would detract attention from an important social issue. Such numbers could also potentially be used to chal-

lenge the status of these groups as the legitimate 'owners' of the public problem of women abuse (Gusfield 1989) and their claim to speak
on behalf of a wider constituency of women. One survey manager
summarized the concerns of some of these women's groups about the
prospect that the survey might produce relatively low numbers as
follows: 'If it comes from Stats Canada, you will ruin us.' As it turned
out, the women's groups need not have been overly concerned, as the
findings affirmed their beliefs about alarmingly high levels of abuse of
Canadian women.

In summary, one of the greatest sources of internal political tension
derives from the fact that the Centre, as part of Statistics Canada, must
publicize its findings. The working axiom in the criminal-justice
system is very different from the slogan embraced by politicians
and others on the public stage, that 'any publicity is good publicity.' For jurisdictional actors, publicity also brings with it the prospect of negative political repercussions (see Ericson, Baranek, and
Chan 1989). Consequently, many jurisdictional representatives and data
providers would be more than happy to receive statistical information
about the justice system without having to publicize that knowledge.
As a result, Centre staff members can find themselves in situations
where they have to placate jurisdictional concerns and soothe anxieties about potential public reactions to their different projects. Such
concerns have been central to controversies over who owns the Centre's
data.

Data Ownership

Over the past quarter-century our approach to knowledge has been
fundamentally transformed. No longer exclusively viewed as a social
good, knowledge is now increasingly approached as a commodity,
something that can be owned by some to the exclusion of others (Bell
1973; Stehr 1994; Schiller 1996). For the CCJS, concerns about the ownership of knowledge are not purely the stuff of philosophical reflection, but have been at the heart of pragmatic political struggles,
struggles that again accentuate the dynamic tensions inherent in the
production of governmental knowledge.

In the early 1990s, a number of liaison officers started to suggest
that because the Centre relies on jurisdictional data for its publications, these jurisdictions should have greater say in what material is

publicly released and how these releases are structured. This desire arose out of the perception among some liaison officers that they had repeatedly provided the Centre with the length of rope with which their jurisdiction was subsequently hung. By surrendering their data to the Centre, they allowed the public release of numbers that could, and invariably did, make at least one jurisdiction look worse than all the others. These concerns evolved into a struggle over who actually owned the data, with some liaison officers maintaining that because the data originated in the jurisdictions, it remained, in effect, the property of the jurisdictions, who could do with it as they saw fit. The minutes of a 1994 LOC meeting suggested that the term 'data ownership' came to signify that 'the "owner" of the data retains authority to decide whether and when they are released.'

One Centre respondent involved in these negotiations indicated that the jurisdictional claim to ownership had considerable 'clout' because '[the jurisdictions] can say: "Well, we just won't give you the data." In which case you then have a hole. It is a real barter, give and take whenever the LOC meets.' To augment their claims to ownership, some liaison officers asserted that the provisions outlined in the Statistics Act to protect the privacy of individuals actually extended to the privacy of institutional data providers. This implied that while data could be released, the jurisdictions could not be identified, a situation that could undermine much of the value of national indicators. Such a fundamental weakening of the Centre did not, however, appear to be the aim of the liaison officers, who were more intent on acquiring a greater say in how releases were structured and whether specific reports should be publicly released at all.

For the Centre, the struggle over data ownership was a high-stakes issue, as the prospect of all the jurisdictions acquiring a say on whether or not a report should be publicly released raised the possibility that the Centre's publications would grind to a standstill. Given that some jurisdiction was bound to look worse than all the others on any individual indicator, there was the possibility of protracted political squabbles each time a survey was set for release. Here two senior members of the Centre involved in this issue reflect on what was at issue in the debate over 'data ownership':

It was the ultimate struggle for who owns the data. Now, liaison officer
X, I think reasoned, if we could win the data ownership argument then

we would also have ultimate control over 'Does this go out or doesn't it? Does it go out with my changes or not?' Those kinds of things. 'And I insist on my particular perspective.'

It was a real point of contention because of the anxiety of some of the partners who were less sympathetic to access issues ... It was their data, they gave it to us. The only reason they gave it to us was because they had to, so they own it. If we want you to, as board of director members, if we want you to do a special study on issue X, you only give it to us, nobody else can have it.

After two years of back-and-forth committee work, negotiations, and legal opinions, it was ultimately determined that the Centre owned the data. It was one of the only instances in the Centre's ongoing efforts to secure jurisdictional participation that an explicit appeal had to be made to the Statistics Act. The lawyers who examined the issue concluded that the jurisdictions are legally required to provide the data to Statistics Canada, which maintains effective control over it and is obliged to publicize its findings. Furthermore, they also concluded that, in general, the privacy provisions do not extend to the protection of the identity of organizations, although there was an important caveat on this finding that has been exploited by at least one jurisdiction, as is discussed below.

The general tendency of LOC and JIC members to be concerned about how the Centre's surveys might affect their respective jurisdictions can be even further complicated when discussions are shaped by recurrent federal and provincial tensions. Given that both of these levels of government are represented at the LOC and JIC tables, other political animosities can become part of the unspoken agenda: 'That is the other thing, all of the politics of federal/provincial relations are acted out in these committee meetings. The jurisdiction is mad at Ottawa for whatever reason. They come to these particular meetings and they act out the frustrations of their provincial government on this matter, which has nothing to do with [the issue being discussed].'

Such tensions can shape the availability of statistical indicators. For example, people working in the Centre's courts program frequently commented on one province that combined jurisdictional self-interest with a resentment of initiatives that originate from the nation's capital. A long-standing thorn in the side of attempts to produce national criminal-justice statistics, this province (Province X) was perceived within the Centre as having a 'go it your own way' approach. One place where this combination of reluctant federalism and jurisdictional self-interest manifests itself in the Centre's numbers concerns the courts' 'resources, expenditures, and personnel' (REP) *Juristat*. REP surveys are a mainstay of the Centre, conducted on various segments of the criminal-justice system (courts, corrections, prosecutions, police) in an attempt to acquire an appreciation for the relative costs of these programs and services. Such surveys have also tended to be controversial because of provincial differences in financial accounting practices and acute political sensitivities about expenditures.

Several Centre staff members recounted struggling with Province X to secure detailed information for the courts' REP survey. As it currently stands, the Centre produces a courts REP *Juristat*, but with data elements that are very 'high level' and lacking in detail. In an attempt to acquire greater detail, the Centre sought to develop a 'cost per case' indicator to provide information about the comparative costs of processing a single case through the courts. Several Centre staff members commented on Province X's reluctance to participate in developing this measure, and suggested that, in addition to anti-Ottawa sentiment, there were more practical reasons why this jurisdiction opposed this proposal. Specifically, its aversion was attributed to the fact that this jurisdiction had court costs that were considerably higher than the norm, a fact its officials did not want to publicize any more than was necessary.

This province has been able to sidestep the Centre's desire for detailed courts REP data by invoking a subtle legal distinction concerning privacy. As mentioned, the privacy provisions of the Statistics Act have been interpreted to apply only to individuals and not to organizations. However, Province X has relied on the legal proviso that the identity of organizations *can* be protected if the information being reported is related to their expenses and operations, as opposed to being about their workload. Here a respondent nicely clarifies this distinction:

> You see in the Statistics Act, whether it is individuals or organizations, the confidentiality rule is pretty much the same. An organization can insist upon its confidentiality, and all businesses of course do. Similarly I guess that protection is available to government departments. So this data ownership issue is complicated a little bit ... When the organization is reporting information about itself, that is the financial personnel infor-

mation, it can exercise the confidentiality. If the organization is reporting information about its client's population and caseload, that is entirely secondary, it's not about itself and they are required to report that.

Since the courts' resources, expenditures, and personnel survey is concerned with court expenses, Province X has invoked this distinction to bolster its claim that it need not supply detailed REP information to the Centre. The result has been that the Centre bases its entire publication on the comparatively low level of detail provided by this province. The Centre could, of course, opt to publish the survey with the more detailed data supplied by the other jurisdictions and simply footnote the different reporting conventions for Province X as an anomaly. Some Centre personnel thought that such a strategy might be a means to pressure Province X into complying with the desired reporting conventions:

> The fact is that we only put out the resources, expenditures and personnel in the courts area at the level which province X provides us, because, as I say, to go below that level would be to expose them. So that means quite a limited release ... The only part that comes down to the gentleman's agreement part of it is we could provide more detailed data for all the other jurisdictions with their agreement and leave X to explain itself. The only trouble is that I think X would bring to the table the idea that if you agree to release your data it puts us in an awkward position. They might get some sympathy from two or three other [jurisdictions] on that.

The above quote illustrates how a strategy that would isolate one province could potentially exacerbate tensions and perhaps even give this province some added sympathy from its jurisdictional counterparts. In light of these legal/political complexities, the Centre has decided to continue producing the courts REP survey using the lowest-common-denominator data provided by Province X.

The lengths to which this particular jurisdiction has gone to extricate itself from this reporting requirement are exceptional. It is now generally accepted that the Centre owns the data and that the jurisdictions are obliged to provide the information via the forms and categories worked out among the participants. Nonetheless, the issue does dramatize the fact that senior members of the Centre are constantly in discussion and negotiation about data collection with a powerful committee structure composed of individuals who have vested political interests in the Centre's findings.

Data Dissemination

As it became increasingly apparent that the issue of who owned the data would be resolved in the Centre's favour, discussion in the JIC turned to concerns about 'data dissemination.' The explicit aim of such discussions was to develop more formalized procedures to plan, organize, and rationalize the Centre's publications. Unable to veto or directly control the release of unpalatable findings, the jurisdictions sought more influence over the Centre's communications strategy. More specifically, they sought to develop more routine communication with the Centre, initiate changes to the timing and clustering of releases, and establish an explicit schedule for pre-publication review of *Juristats*. Along with such rationalizations, familiar political concerns were also occasionally manifest in the Centre's communications strategy.

One rationalization that had political overtones was the call for greater reflection on the timing of the Centre's releases. Some liaison officers suggested that inopportune timing of releases could result in awkward moments in the House of Commons or in the provincial legislatures. Consequently, they sought to coordinate the timing of releases more closely with the political imperatives of the day, as the following quote from a 1993 Liaison Officers Committee meeting indicates: 'The Chairman proposed that the timing of Centre products was very important, and the release of these products should be carefully timed to fit the consideration of the issue by the policy-makers. In this context, he suggested that it would be inappropriate to release a *Juristat* on "Prostitution" in the spring of 1993, just after the Deputies will be releasing their report with their policy recommendations.'

Notwithstanding the desires of liaison officers or deputy ministers, the Centre's ability to respond to political concerns about the timing of its releases should not be overstated. Given the amount of preparation and lead time necessary to produce a publication, these releases cannot be rushed to correspond with fast-breaking political developments. Even the prospect of delaying a release is complicated by the fact that the Centre must meet a tight schedule for Statistics Canada releases established months in advance. The politics of release timing can, however, come more explicitly into play in those situations where there is sufficient lead time to make a release coincide with a politically symbolic event. This was the case in 1993 when some liaison officers suggested that specific Centre publications might be timed to coincide with 'Police Week' or the annual meeting of the Canadian Association of Chiefs of Police. There was also a proposal that the release of a

Centre publication on officers killed while on duty coincide with the unveiling of a monument on Parliament Hill commemorating police and correctional officers slain in the line of duty.

Concerns about the topical and temporal clustering of releases also came under the ambit of communication planning. Some members of the Initiative believed that both the timing and topics of the Centre's releases contributed to increased public fears about crime. As one liaison officer cautioned in 1993: 'We must take great care to plan [releases] so that we do not release a whole series of products that raises public concern on matters of safety directly as a result of CCJS information.' Indeed, shocking statistics about crime or other social problems have become a routine part of political claims-making (Orcutt and Turner 1993; Best 1989). While the jurisdictional representatives called for a more 'balanced' coverage of crime and criminal justice, many Centre staff members saw this description as a euphemism for a desire to reduce the number of 'bad news' crime stories in public circulation. The documents from a 1996 LOC meeting suggest that in the selection of topics for study 'a balance be sought between "good and bad news" to foster a more balanced public perception of the justice system.' Given that Centre personnel do not know from one year to the next whether given indices will rise or fall, such advance planning for the type of story they will be communicating is obviously complicated, if not impossible.

If the nature of the story that comes out of the Centre cannot be directly controlled, some politicians believe it best to try to reduce the overall number of releases. For example, the Centre used to produce a separate *Juristat* for the homicide data as well as for the UCR crime data. These were combined into a single release partially out of a concern that having two releases increased public fears about crime. The Centre also used to release a number of publications over the course of a single year drawn from the same survey, in such a way that a preliminary release of crime statistics would be followed a few months later by the final statistics. This approach too was seen to have an undesirable effect on public perceptions of crime, as it could lead to a situation where an increase of crime would initially be reported, and then a few months later the *same* increase would be reported again. Members of the LOC saw this as unacceptable because they believed that the public would be left with the impression that there were ongoing increases in the crime rate when, in fact, only a single increase was being reported. A senior member of the Centre summarized the thrust of these discussions about amalgamating publications to avoid such public misperceptions:

> The points of focus were 'Will this product result in the re-release of data that has already been released in some other product, leading to the impression in the public mind that in July there was a release with a 10% increase in violent crime overall, coming out of the main crime release, and then a "violence" *Juristat* coming out at the end of September in which this 10% increase in violent crime would again be cited in the context of that particular issue being dealt with.' Leaving the public with the situation where they were getting a splash on the newspaper in July, another splash because of the major release in September and then the main crime publication would come out in December once they had all of the data and analysis done to put out the big thing, as opposed to the initial release. And yet another splash in the newspaper with 10%. So the public is getting barraged over and over again with essentially the same number.

While it is understandable that liaison officers might seek to shape the Centre so as to manage public perceptions about crime prospectively, their claims that the Centre was fostering a climate of fear were undoubtedly overstated. Some members of the Centre felt that such accusations amounted to an exercise in messenger shooting. Furthermore, jurisdictional concerns about the possibility that topical and temporal clustering of releases might lead to public misperceptions would undoubtedly not have been an issue if the crime statistics had been steadily declining (which occurred later in the decade) and therefore provided opportunities to reinforce 'good news' stories. Others asserted that the daily media barrage of crime and violence would have a far greater influence on public fears about crime than any influence of a twice- or thrice-released set of statistical indicators. Nonetheless, such attempts to rationalize the Centre's communication plan are another example of how political considerations penetrate some of the Centre's most mundane processes.

Standardization

Measurement systems demarcate the contours of the object(s) being studied. Standardization helps eliminate historically or locally distinct measurement practices and create a community of individuals capable of communicating in the same language about the same phenomena. The standards on CCJS surveys derive from negotiations among Centre personnel and the different jurisdictions. This process can also occasionally introduce political self-interest into the specific details of governmental knowledge.

Ideally, in order for scientific experiments to be comparable, the same measurements must be taken of standardized objects on identical instruments by scientists and technicians disciplined into a regime of observation and documentation. The scientific purifying impulse seeks to remove any variability from the objects operated on by scientists. As Porter (1995: 32) asserts, 'What we call the uniformity of nature is in practice a triumph of human organization – of regulation, education, manufacturing, and method.' Rather than science operating on the raw material of nature, the materials scrutinized and manipulated by scientists usually arrive at the laboratory pre-standardized. For example, the homogenization of nature is the stock and trade of commercial laboratory supply houses who provide purified assays, chemicals, minerals, and animals that have no counterparts in the natural world. Science does not simply find a natural order in the phenomena it studies, but creates uniformity through standardization (Rouse 1987, chap. 4).

A number of generic attributes of standardization play themselves out in the Centre. First, there is often a tension between the desire for uniformity by distant governments or commercial interests and the local investment in particular standards. Second, local standards are more than simply ways to demarcate different phenomena; they are implicated in broader political symbolism, where the use of even antiquated local standards can be a means to distinguish regions symbolically from the desires of distant governments. Finally, standardization involves a process of negotiation, as professionals formalize official rules for how to deal with the particulars of individual cases.

For the Centre, standardization involves establishing common definitions of the world that become formalized in rules for how to count and document events, people, places, and things. When a survey is implemented or revised, considerable time is often required to secure agreement on such rules. Justice officials and practitioners are intimately aware that there are various ways to count an 'alternative measure,' 'correctional admission,' and so on. In their attempts to arrive at a national definition for such phenomena Centre personnel occasionally encounter entrenched political interests, as local jurisdictions consider the consequences of employing one standard over another. New definitions can make jurisdictions appear comparably better or worse depending upon the specifics of their counting rules. Consequently, political reservations about the specifics of standards can occasionally stop a survey from ever getting off the ground or from collecting the level of detail that was initially envisioned.

This section explores some of the politics that influence the Centre's development of standards. The examples are drawn from a number of different surveys, and were chosen because they were relatively current at the time of the research and were still fresh in people's minds. The disadvantage of such an approach is that the final form of these standards remains unclear in some instances. However, the intent is to demonstrate a dynamic *process* more than an end product. A focus on emergent standards provides insights into their negotiated and conventional nature. Once in place, it can be difficult to ascertain why one counting rule was adopted over another, or even to recognize that other standards were ever possible. As a former member of the Centre observed, 'A survey that is in progress has a life of its own. It goes on and people collect it and people send it. It is during those early stages when you are developing a new survey, you are trying to define what the elements are, where things get tricky.'

The Centre is a national impetus to standardization. A former member of the CCJS summarized this aspect of the Centre as follows: 'I think it is to the point where the provinces spend millions of dollars to have their own definitions, their own standardization, but as they then revise their systems down the road, they will then look to implement [the Centre's] standards, if they can. So as a force, the CCJS is very important in pushing forward that common view.'

On my very first day at the Centre I told one of my contacts about my interest in standards. His response was, 'Well, that's what we are all about.' As my research progressed it became apparent that he had not overstated the case. Although efforts to standardize are the norm at the Centre, this is not to say that this process has become routine. The same individual later recounted how, even though the implementation of standards is 'not easy' and is often 'contentious,' CCJS staff must secure a buy-in from the jurisdictions 'or there is no point.'

As with many things related to the Centre, the dynamics of federal/provincial relations can influence the development of standards. The

Centre is often trying to develop a uniform national set of standards for institutions with their own set of local standards that were developed over time in response to localized needs and interests. The specifics of provincial programming or local demands for accountability can make certain definitions of processes and activities particularly appropriate. They can also prompt the development of locally idiosyncratic counting rules. As a result, the national impetus to uniformity can alternatively be embraced, if the national standard corresponds with existing local practices, or resented and resisted if it means that changes have to be made to long-standing local counting rules, administrative procedures, or computer systems. Here a senior member of the CCJS recounts some of the tensions inherent in trying to persuade local agencies to employ the standards developed by the Centre:

> When you come along and say, 'In order for us to achieve our mandate and have comparable information across jurisdictions, that would require these several jurisdictions to begin to think about how they do things differently, define them differently, count them perhaps differently than they are now. Count them where they haven't been counting them before.' And the typical answer you get back is 'This is the way we do business here.' And that has been a major hurdle for a national agency.

Using different standards can also be a way to assume an oppositional stance in federal/provincial relations, a way to assert a distinctive local identity and not bow to the demands of 'the feds.' For some provincial representatives who were more hostile to the federal government, refusing to conform to national initiatives appears to have its own inherent appeal. A senior member of the Centre recounted how one jurisdiction has been 'particularly reluctant to be cooperative, to contribute to this sort of national information initiative ... It is almost as if they still think that there necessarily has to be tension between them and the federal government: "Anything these feds want we have to be suspicious about." You know: "We are only going to cooperate if we can screw them out of this much money."'

The specifics of any particular standard is ultimately related to the needs of the people who produce it. The Centre's development of a Corrections Utilization Study is illustrative in this regard. One aspect of this study was an examination of the phenomenon of recidivism.

The individual given the mandate to develop this component of the study recounted how the overall impetus of the project was largely derived from a concern 'to control prison population and costs.' How the objects under study were to be defined was related to a context in which a continually rising prison population was combined with a political climate of economic retrenchment. This situation prompted fears about the prospect of having to engage in costly prison-building programs. At the time of this research Centre personnel were inclined towards a definition of recidivism as some form of re-contact with the criminal-justice system, although they recognized that a number of other definitions were possible. We gain an appreciation for why they were attracted to this particular, and rather idiosyncratic, understanding of recidivism from the following comment:

> It is really re-contact with the system. Because the main concern about recidivists is that ... it is recidivists that create a real burden on the system through a revolving door. Because there is a lot of evidence around that shows how people are starting off in the Young Offender system and moving from a community based disposition to a custodial disposition, open custody, secure custody, still all within the Young Offender system. Then graduating into the provincial adult systems. Maybe probation right up to doing federal time.

Defining recidivism as 're-contact with the criminal-justice system' was motivated by a political and financial concern with the expenses of the criminal-justice system. So defined, re-offenders are not so much conceived of as a pathological risk, but as a financial burden. This definition is particularly appropriate to the needs of the people mandated to manage criminal-justice budgets. The point is that different standards were available that would have more closely corresponded with the governmental knowledge needs of other institutional actors. For example, some criminologists, victim's-rights advocates, and treatment agencies would have undoubtedly been interested in a standard for recidivism that concentrated on the number of crimes committed by an individual after his or her initial conviction, irrespective of whether they have any subsequent official dealings with the justice system. This would have necessitated not only a new standard, but an entirely different data-collection regime. Ultimately, the specifics of a standard are related to the needs of particular audiences and the anticipated uses of the resultant knowledge. While the same name might be assigned to these different measures, the phenomena under description can be vastly different.

Negotiated Standards

Standardization at the Centre is characterized by a number of attributes. First, there are usually numerous ways to standardize the phenomena in question. Second, different standards actually produce different entities, bringing new phenomena into the world for the purposes of governmental action. For example, a definition of recidivism as individual re-contact with the system as opposed to re-commission of crimes is not simply a different way to measure the same thing, it is concerned with two entirely different phenomena. Third, standards are negotiated in consultation with working groups drawn from the jurisdictions and interested communities. While participants in such consultations often honestly want to create the best possible standard, as representatives of their particular program and/or jurisdiction they also have interests that extend beyond the accuracy of the standards.

People can advocate on behalf of a particular standard because they believe it to be the best, or simply because long use of an existing standard has made it familiar. At the same time, one eye is often on the future political ramifications of adopting a standard, with representatives advocating for measures they believe will make their programs appear more productive and efficient. Jurisdictional concerns about the potential implications of participating in a survey or employing certain definitions or counting rules permeate the Centre. While Centre employees aim to produce the best standard possible, they cannot alienate the jurisdictions for fear that they might receive no data whatsoever.

In situations where standards cannot be agreed upon, the viability of an entire survey can be put into question. One example mentioned frequently by long-time members of the Centre concerned early attempts to arrive at standardized definitions of 'alternative measures' as set out in the Young Offenders Act. Such measures are typically used for less-serious offences, where more informal and expeditious forms of dispute resolution are deemed to be appropriate. One major problem in measuring these programs is their high degree of provincial variability. Across the country alternative-measures programs are operated by different agencies and have different criteria for eligibility. Some programs operate pre-charge and some post-charge, and youths assigned to such programs face a range of different obligations. In effect, the Centre was trying to standardize the counting rules for a group of programs that were not standardized across the country. While there was some desire to standardize the accounting procedures for these programs, various factors worked against these efforts. As one respondent recounted, there was a general unwillingness 'to adopt, in an administrative sense, operational sense, a definition that isn't your own. Or a process that isn't your own. And there is where it breaks down. Because everybody wants to have the predominant methodology or be deemed to have the standard. It is very difficult to do that.'

Efforts to establish standard measures for provincial legal aid plans faced similar entrenched interests. The difficulty in developing such measures was exacerbated by the fact that there are numerous varieties of provincially-run legal aid systems that have developed according to their own logic. Here a member of the Centre involved in one of the earliest legal aid surveys provides a sense of how the different jurisdictions continually contemplated the potential political ramifications of standards:

> So in the early years of setting up legal aid surveys there was all kinds of debate about what it was going to be used for and were the feds going to turn around and use this data to cut back on cost-sharing agreements and all of these sorts of worries. The legal aid plans were wondering whether they should be padding the numbers so that they could get more money. Because 'Is more better? Are we going to get more money if we show more business? Should we count things this way to reflect better on us? Are we going to be evaluated on our effectiveness or efficiency or quality of the services?' So there would be all kinds of arguments about what data were going to be collected for what purposes. And what is this going to show and what are going to be the implications for us. And if we do it this way, what will it mean down the road?

A common dilemma of standardization is that legitimate arguments can be made to count the 'same' phenomena differently, and that different measures inevitably reveal certain attributes of the phenomena under description and neglect others. Several respondents talked about this aspect in relation to the controversy over attempts to develop standardized rules to ascertain the costs of prosecution services across Canada. One jurisdiction whose costs were well above the norm tried to stop the release of the data, arguing that the level of detail the Centre had used was too general and would consequently hide important reasons for differential costs. In particular, they pointed out that prosecutors in their jurisdiction are responsible for laying charges, a task performed by the police in other jurisdictions. Consequently, the provincial representatives argued that the comparative costs for their prosecution services were bound to be higher simply because their prosecutors had to perform this additional time-consuming task. Discussion then moved into the much more explicitly political realm, as a Centre employee recounts:

> It got to a point where we were trying to bend over backwards to explain the reason why costs might be different across jurisdictions. Then it got to the point where they said: 'Can we delay the report? Because our budget is coming out next month, and we really can't afford to have this information out in the public domain because we are going to get slashed when our costs are higher than anybody else in the country.' And it became quite political then. We ended up having to say 'You approved it before, we have to release this. We are accountable to the rest of the liaison officers and we have to get this stuff out.' That kind of thing, when they don't like what they see.

Counting rules can also serve local purposes that individuals and institutions are reticent to abandon. For example, Jurisdiction Y had developed a standard to count correctional admissions that differed from those used in the rest of the country: individuals who left an institution on temporary releases were re-counted as a separate admission each time they returned to the correctional facility. The end result was that this jurisdiction's total number of admissions was significantly inflated compared to jurisdictions that did not employ this rule. I was informed by Centre staff that this jurisdiction was reluctant to abandon this practice owing to concerns about correctional budgets. If they adopted the generally accepted counting rule, their admission count would go down, a result that they feared would detrimentally influence their funding. As one of the members of the Centre observed: 'The way they were counting was good from the point of view of going to their Treasury Board to get more resources, but it didn't make them look good in the statistics ... They didn't want to get away from this because they felt it was important to them in their budget justification.'

In summary, while the Centre may not always successfully develop agreed-upon standards of measurement, they are a harmonizing force, working to foster uniformity in classifications and measurement tools. The counting rules they develop are actually constitutive of their objects of analysis, entities that differ in their specifics depending on which counting rules are adopted. The politics of this process derive from the recognition that standardizing phenomena differently can influence the public profile and future funding of programs. Consequently, negotiations around how to measure different phenomena can embed political concerns in the standards themselves. Thus, negotiations over standards are yet another example of the role that jurisdictional politics can play in the routine operation of the CCJS.

Public Discourse

The knowledge produced by agencies such as the Centre is intended as a resource for strategies of governance. However, the fact that this knowledge is also disseminated to a wider audience through the media has important social consequences. In particular, the form of the knowledge produced by statistical centres of calculation has shaped the broad contours of our public discourses about crime and criminal justice.

It would be difficult to overemphasize the extent to which contemporary criminal-justice politics are intertwined with statistics. Statistics are a bellwether for the success or failure of governmental strategies. Institutional reforms are often undertaken with the explicit aim of modifying a particular statistical indicator, as socially desirable ends are translated into changes to quantitative measures. Since there is no optimal level of crime, violence, or incarceration, the political impetus involves a constant striving to produce statistical indicators that are better than those from previous years or that compare favourably to those of other provinces or institutions. As I write this section, the cover of today's local newspaper has a headline story on the vow made by Vancouver's new chief of police to reduce property crime by 69 per cent and break and enters by 64 per cent (Fong and Bellett 1997). The political goal is to do things that will change the numbers, with the success or failure of the chief and his force hanging in the balance. In the light of such proclamations, is it any wonder that police organizations have often been accused of 'fudging' their data in attempts to appear more efficient? On the table beside today's newspaper lies the *New York Review of Books*, which contains an extended article by James Lardner (1997) on New York's 'miracle.' What could constitute a miracle in this the most cynical of cities? – a reduction in the crime rate of 40%! Undeniably, statistics constitute a major component of the politics of crime.

I shy away from saying that criminal-justice politics are *all about* statistics, and this qualification is necessary because statistics are one pole of an ongoing historical dynamic between aggregate and individualized knowledge about criminal justice. Michel Foucault (see chapter 2) suggests that power over different human populations varies between an individualizing and an aggregating pole. The individualizing moment is characterized by various forms of professional practice that maintain detailed dossiers on individual patients, students, workers, and criminals, who are located in a scrutinizing normative gaze. In contrast, the aggregating pole concerns itself with the 'species body,' and can be traced back to the forms of intervention and control made possible by the statistical forms of knowledge that emerged during the eighteenth and nineteenth centuries.

A similar opposition exists between individualized and aggregate knowledge in political discourse about crime. The individualizing moment is concerned with how the public's knowledge about crime is often read through discrete individuals and events. Historically, what the public knew about crime they knew from first-hand experience, fictionalized accounts, public dramas of capture and evasion of criminals, or media-stoked moral panics about particularly heinous crimes. The development of crime statistics provided an aggregate counterpoint to such individualized knowledges. Statistical crime data provided insights into the mundane reality of crime and the operation of the criminal-justice system, a form of knowledge that acquired political overtones as people began to concern themselves with the social implications of fluctuations in crime rates.

Porter (1995: 77) has proposed that one attraction of the aggregate nature of statistical knowledge about the poor and dangerous classes in early modern Europe was that it abstracted away the individuality of the people being described: 'A method of study that ignored individuality seemed somehow right for the lower classes.' And though criminal-justice politics became increasingly statistical, his claim holds true only to a point, as the meanings and actions of individual criminals and criminal events continue to be of great public import. We continue to have a public lust for rich biographical detail about our most disturbed and disturbing fellow citizens, as our familiarity with the names and actions of Ted Bundy, Peter Sutcliffe, and Clifford Olson attest.

The availability of aggregate data about crime has meant that public accounts about child murderers and serial rapists are now often interspersed with statistical caveats and efforts to locate individual deviants within a larger statistical context. Media-savvy audiences will recognize the conventional and almost choreographed status of these rhetorical moves. The usual scenario is for an individual or group to capitalize on the media parade of heinous individual criminals in order to invest the person with broader meanings about the need for lengthier sentences, changes to the Young Offenders Act, a return of capital punishment, or more police. Such claims are then countered by individuals, often liberal academics, who try to shift the discourse from the level of the individual to the aggregate, suggesting that such horrible individuals or incidents do not represent larger trends. These commentators accentuate how the national or provincial crime trend is actually decreasing, or, in a bad year, emphasize that the indicators for a particular group of people or for particular categories of behaviour are going down, are relatively stable, or are not increasing nearly as much as one might have anticipated. Such ritualized political arguments speak to different ways of conceptualizing the problem of crime, and our familiarity with the broad contours of such exchanges is an indication of the incommensurability of such positions. People engaged in such exchanges have, by and large, different political agendas and are unlikely to be persuaded by the claims of their interlocutors. Indeed, these are not exchanges at all, but performances aimed at converting public opinion.

By virtue of its status as the authorized source for aggregate knowledge about national criminal justice, the Centre becomes a vitally important institution in contemporary political discourses. While Centre personnel do not engage in public claims-making on behalf of specific policy initiatives, the knowledge they produce is a fertile resource, capable of being mined by parties all across the political spectrum in the ongoing public politics of crime and justice.

Conclusion

Politics assumes a variety of forms in the Canadian Centre for Justice Statistics. While Centre personnel are not cynically manipulated by their political masters to produce statistical trends in support of partisan political initiatives, the Centre is permeated with political concerns. Thus, politics is a constant threat. The perception that Centre staff have too close a relationship with government, or any other political groups, can undermine the edifice of trust on which their work relies.

The federal/provincial structure of the Justice Initiative drives much of the Centre's political dynamic. Political interests can be manifest in the topics the Centre studies, the timing and clustering of its releases, the representational structure of the JIC and LOC meetings, and the minutiae of standardized counting rules. While Centre staff seek to avoid being partisan, they are in regular discussion and negotiation with jurisdictional representatives who have interests in the Centre that extend to questions about how the Centre's efforts will influence the funding and public appearance of their organizations.

Public discussions about criminal justice regularly invoke aggregate indicators in a constant back and forth between aggregated and individualized conceptions of crime, law, and justice. Agencies such as the Centre have been instrumental in establishing the broad contours of such a discourse by virtue of their ability to provide the knowledge that informs the aggregate pole of such exchanges.

Many of the examples used in this chapter demonstrate the truth of the old axiom that 'the truth is in the details,' or more precisely, 'the politics of truth is in the details.' The next chapter shows how similar political dynamics can influence how the Centre communicates its knowledge to the public.

6

From Private Facts to Public Knowledge: Authorship and the Media in Communicating Statistical Facts

Don't you know the crime rate's going up, up, up, up, up!

The Rolling Stones

Contrary to the popular expression, the facts never speak for themselves. Numbers cannot tell a story on their own, but must be actively given a voice by others. The discourses in which they are embedded contain different dialects and intonations. Previous chapters documented some of the background processes involved in the production of criminal-justice statistics. They focused on phenomena that are usually beyond the purview of recognized statistical methods, but are nonetheless fundamental to producing the statistical truths upon which practices of governance rest. This chapter continues to explore this theme by accentuating the point at which statistical facts become public knowledge. It examines how the languages used in communicating such facts are shaped by institutional routines, authorship, review procedures, organizational structure, politics, format requirements, and the media.

Two approaches are employed to examine this transition from private facts to public knowledge. First, we scrutinize the Centre's main publication vehicle, the *Juristat*, outlining some of the social and organizational factors that shape how it is written. The second section focuses on the role that the Centre plays as a source of journalistic accounts. This involves an examination of whether the Centre has been able to determine how the media covers stories about criminal-justice statistics.

Juristat

The Canadian Centre for Justice Statistics publicizes its data in a variety of different ways. The most detailed knowledge is available to individuals, typically academics, who secure access to the Centre's database(s) for the purpose of private research. The next level of detail can be found in the full annual publications derived from the Centre's surveys, which can run to hundreds of pages of charts, text, and tables. However, the *Juristat* series is by far the Centre's main publication. Relatively concise, *Juristats* range in length from a few pages to twenty pages of data and analysis. Approximately fifteen are released each year. These are about equally divided between annual or biannual releases that contain information derived from the Centre's regular surveys, and those *Juristats* that focus on occasional or special-topic releases. These latter releases have included, for example, studies of youth recidivism, private security and public policing, breaking and entering, and spousal homicide.

The *Juristat* series provides a summary of trends in criminal justice to a generalist audience. That said, their importance as a knowledge source should not be diminished. Frequently they are the public's main instrument for understanding statistical trends in Canada's criminal-justice system. Professor Tony Doob (1993: 17) accentuates this point in his evaluation of the Centre's publications, which he concludes by observing: '[F]or many people they are the only data that are available on a topic and are used as [sic] archival purposes ... At the moment, a *Juristat* "Service Bulletin" is, more often than not, the publication "of record" for many topics.'

Juristat Writing

Social and institutional routines influence how truths are communicated. Truth is a social accomplishment, and statements become true as a result of how human beings engage them. Scientists therefore use whatever practical means are available to them in order to convince relevant audiences that their claims are valid. In the process they try to anticipate and counter the likely deconstructive strategies of their adversaries (Fuchs and Ward 1994).

Scientific texts are shaped by at least two related sets of processes. The first are the institutional and organizational constraints that influence the form and content of scientists' publications. The second involves the rhetorical conventions employed in efforts to persuade audiences to accept a claim. Both of these processes influence a *Juristat*'s final form.

Many obstacles must be overcome before a set of collected numbers is published. One of the most onerous encumbrances for the authors of *Juristats* is the Centre's distinctive review process. It is a hallmark of science that manuscripts are reviewed by several knowledgeable, but ostensibly disinterested, reviewers before they are accepted for publication in scientific journals. Anonymous reviewers act as gatekeepers, and are one of the most important hurdles to be traversed in the production of legitimate claims. Although there are a multitude of reasons or justifications why reviewers recommend that a paper not be published (see Chubin and Hackett 1990), the idealized image of scientific review conveys that such decisions are based solely on the scientific merits of the manuscript.

The contrast between the idealized scientific review process and that employed by the Centre could not be more marked. First, the number of reviewers is greatly multiplied at the Centre. An author of a *Juristat* formally commences the review process when she gives a copy of the draft to her section chief, although it was probably reviewed and edited by colleagues before this point. After the section chief's comments are incorporated, the draft circulates within the Centre to the heads of the other program areas (courts, corrections, policing), to some senior advisers, and to the executive director of the Centre. After revision, the draft publication now moves outside the Centre, where it is reviewed by liaison officers and jurisdictional partners.

It is widely acknowledged within the Centre, and by policy and administrative personnel I interviewed, that these drafts are routinely photocopied and circulated among appropriate jurisdictional staff for comment and criticism. A select group of sociologists and criminologists have at times also been included in this list of external reviewers. At all stages in this process reviewers have broad discretion to comment on just about any aspect of the draft, including the veracity of the knowledge, the interpretation, writing style, and format. An author of several *Juristats* describes some of the complexities of the review process:

Here we end up with really 40 people who look at it. I write the first draft. It goes through my supervisor and then it goes to my supervisor's supervisor, which is the chief. The chief says 'Well, it is OK' or maybe he doesn't have the time to look at it and says it is OK. Then it goes to all of the chiefs, then the assistant directors then the director, which is another eight people. If they think it is OK it goes to the review process. I can't remember the appropriate names of the review process but you have like a six week review or a two week review. You send it out so that all of the LO's can take a look at it. So you have another 24 people take a look at it. Of those people maybe half a dozen take their job seriously and really do a good job at it. Then it comes back and you send it to translation and updating all these changes. And you really have to appease the LO's, we bend over backwards here to make them happy. If you send them some-thing a little bit controversial that Province X doesn't like, it is gone. If you send them something that just happens to be not phrased nicely ... Then after that review process we go through and we update it again. Then we put it out to the LO's again for a 96 hour review. At that time, just four days before it goes out they have another crack at it. If there is any major thing wrong with the *Juristat* they will let us know ... We also send it to the chiefs of police and policing services as well. So that is another 20 some odd people that take a look at it.

Given the number of jurisdictions that might provide data for any one report there could very easily be local idiosyncrasies with the data that might be overlooked without a jurisdictional check. External re-view is also a way to accommodate the jurisdictional partners who, in the early 1990s, demanded greater input into the Centre's communica-tion strategy. Receiving advance drafts of publications allows them to ensure the veracity of the numbers as well as to develop appropriate political responses to any criticisms they might anticipate flowing from the trends documented in the report. An academic with a lengthy relationship with the Centre concluded that such communications en-sure that the Centre is 'not going to have some province screaming at them. Or, if they are going to have a province screaming at them, they are going to know it beforehand and have already decided that they are going to do that.'

The Centre's review process also differs markedly from scientific peer review in terms of the disinterestedness of the reviewers. Re-viewers for academic journals are theoretically only interested in a manuscript's scientific merits. While they may stray from this ideal in practice, the Centre cannot even maintain this pretension of disinter-estedness. Many of the jurisdictional reviewers have clear political interests in the knowledge being communicated. One Centre employee characterized the approach adopted by liaison officers to draft *Juristats* as follows: 'They are quite vigilant in terms of "Would this hurt us or help us?"' Chapter 5 noted how the vested interests of individuals on the Centre's governing bodies have occasionally shaped the Centre's production of knowledge through the choice of topics to be studied. In particular, these individuals have attempted to strike a balance between 'good news' and 'bad news' stories about criminal justice. In a 1996 LOC meeting this approach was articulated as a desire 'that the evaluation criteria used for selecting and assigning priorities to topics include the consideration ... that a balance be sought between "good and bad news" to foster a more balanced public perception of the justice system.'

This desire to produce 'good news' stories can also appear in a reviewer's comments on the minutiae of how the Centre's data are presented. For example, one liaison officer recounted expressing his discomfort at how a draft *Juristat* had contextualized a decline in the national crime rate. The manuscript had documented Canada's fourth consecutive annual decline in the crime rate. However, this decline had been preceded by many years of steady increases in the crime rate. While the reviewer recognized that this claim was accurate, he suggested that the author concentrate more on the 'good news' component of the story, which was the fact that crime had decreased. Here the liaison officer summarizes his concerns: 'The way that was initially worded, that was a big "but." Instead of focusing on the fourth annual decline in crime, I think we took away from that positive message by flagging the increases ... The language could be tempered a little.'

Another member of the Centre also recounted how political concerns about terminology became apparent in relation to a study he was conducting on the use of temporary absences from prison. The initial title for one aspect of this study was something akin to 'The Use of Temporary Absences to Manage and Contain Prison Overcrowding.' The political apprehensions of others ultimately resulted in him changing this heading. He observed that although financial concerns about overcrowding were undeniably the impetus for the study, the jurisdictions 'were a little bit excited once they saw that in print. Seeing this in big words, because even though it happens, they don't like to see it phrased as using temporary absences to manage overcrowding, because they want the spin to be much more that they use temporary absences for rehabilitation and programming gradual release and the benefits of that ... So that had to be cast in a better light.'

Despite the complexity of the Centre's review process, questions remain about its merits. Some senior members maintain that internal review is occasionally lax precisely because there are so many reviewers, prompting any individual reviewer to assume that errors will be caught by someone else. Others complained that the substance of the comments that come back from the jurisdictions often have little to do with the numbers per se, but instead concentrate almost exclusively on which trends should be accentuated and how the findings should be worded. One Centre staff member concluded: 'There is very little in terms of people taking the time to get into the nuts and bolts of the actual numbers and verifying the numbers. Which I think is kind of scary.' Several authors believed that some external reviewers were engaged in an unnecessarily painstaking and occasionally self-interested attempt to rewrite publications so that the poor statistical performance of their jurisdiction or organization would be cast in a better light. All of this places the author in a difficult situation, as he or she has to accommodate as best as possible a range of demands that are often in tension:

> I just finished writing a *Juristat* which came out about a month ago with Jane Doe on correctional trends. And that was hilarious because she had been given ... well she had been given new instructions about what the *Juristat* should now look like: 'They should be accessible, they should have interpretation, they should have clarity. They shouldn't be boring.' She had these very precise instructions ... So we did what I thought was a very nice job on taking that *Juristat* and constructing it in a much clearer way with nice bullets, little boxes and all that sort of stuff. And then it went around and you would not believe the editing and the re-editing and the interpretation and the adding and the deletion that went on. I was out of the loop. I just got a new edition every other day and she was pulling her hair out ... [S]he was receiving different advice from ten different directions.

Any act of writing is inevitably an act of editing information, one that accentuates some things and neglects others. With justice statistics decisions about what trends to present and how to present them are pragmatic, made in light of an appreciation for the types of things that are important to communicate as well as those that are potentially controversial. Authors of *Juristats* often face complex pressures related to their desire to present their findings honestly while not offending powerful institutional interests. For example, they want to accurately represent jurisdictional variations on statistical indices, but in so doing cannot afford to alienate individual provinces. Writing such publications is not an abstract scientific endeavour removed from social considerations, but is enmeshed in attempts to anticipate the sensibilities of different powerful audiences. As one author proclaimed: 'You are given four months to write a *Juristat*, and you spend a good part of that time appeasing people and playing a political game, rather than concentrating on your analysis.' The following two respondents accentuate how, in the writing of *Juristats*, political choices are made so as to not antagonize different jurisdictions:

> Depending on what you choose to highlight may drastically determine which of the jurisdictions look [to be at] the top or the bottom of the heap in whatever display you are talking about. So you have to be sensitive to those selections in making sure they are the ones that are fair and the ones that are important from a national perspective. Not that you want to protect PEI and the Yukon and the NWT in every case, but you don't in a series of fifteen *Juristats* give each specific rate, they are going to look – certainly the Territories – they are going to look abysmal on all of them. You don't have to hammer them over the head twelve times with the same message, that's abusive. But it is difficult to make those judgments and those selections.

> When there is sensitive information, let's say, Newfoundland is highlighted this year on the violent crime because there was a big increase of 20%. They don't want to see that. It might be true, it might not be true but they don't want to see it published. We might have to re-word it so that it doesn't stick out like a sore thumb. We don't want to hide the information but we certainly don't want to embarrass anyone. So if something like that would happen we would state it in such a way that perhaps it was explained.

Writing Science

Analysts of various theoretical leanings increasingly recognize that science has a rhetorical component (e.g., Gross 1996; Bazerman 1983; Simons 1989; Selzer 1993; Gusfield 1976). To different degrees, these authors all emphasize science's literary quality, and how the truths of science cannot be separated from how they are articulated. While authors of scientific papers seek to inform and educate their audience rationally, they also employ distinctive linguistic and rhetorical techniques to increase the likelihood that their claims will be accepted. This is clear from the linguistic styles and conventions employed in writing a *Juristat*.

Given that the aims of the Centre's publications generally parallel those of scientific writing, it is not surprising to find that their prose also parallels scientific literary protocols. The scientific ideal for writing up findings is a 'style of non-style' (Gusfield 1976: 17), characterized by an absence of literary imagery or tropes. Richard Rorty (1997: 309) has described this as a style in which 'the words in which the investigator "writes up" his results should be as few and as transparent as possible.' This approach is adopted by the Centre. The epistemological importance of this technique is that readers are steered away from the image of human subjects lying behind the claims being advanced. In fact, it is a defining attribute of modern conceptions of scientific objectivity that the taint of an individual's subjectivity should be removed from scientific practice (Daston 1992). Clear, unambiguous, and non-literary writing purports to allow the world to speak for itself (Gilbert and Mulkay 1984: 56).

Another commonality between scientific writing and the Centre's style of presentation concerns the conferral of relatively unambiguous facts. In a famous article, Medewar (1963) accuses scientific papers of being 'fraudulent' because of how they represent scientific practice, in particular how the social, institutional, and chance factors inherent in any act of scientific discovery are removed in favour of a retrospective account emphasizing the rational unfolding of the scientific method. Latour and Woolgar (1979) describe the same process in terms of the progressive 'forgetting' of the originating research and researchers. Similar processes of forgetting are at play in relation to how the Centre's knowledge makes its way into public culture. Most of the ambiguities and limitations that inhere in the Centre's data are dropped out in the interest of clarity. In the *Juristats*, blunt facts come first; for example, on the cover page, where highlighted 'bullets' tell us that 'The police-reported crime rate decreased by 5% in 1994,' or 'The violent crime rate decreased by 4.1%, the largest annual decline since the survey began in 1962, and the third consecutive annual decline.' These are unequivocal facts completely removed from organizational routines, political interests, methodology, coverage limitations, and human intervention; facts that simply *are*. In effect, the conditions of possibility for statistical knowledge that have been one focus of this inquiry are completely absent at this point.

Moving into the text of the publication, one is apt to encounter a methodology section. As recently as 1990, the preliminary *Juristat* for crime statistics did not mention the limitations of official crime statistics, and only had a single brief footnote to indicate that the offences listed in the publication were only those reported or known to the police. Now there is, routinely, an attempt to accentuate the data-collection methodology and make some mention of the familiar criticisms of official crime statistics: for example, authors will draw attention to the fact that the numbers do not address the 'dark figure' of unreported crime, and can be influenced by legal changes and police practices. While one might assume that such qualifications detract from the authoritative status of a scientist's claims, the exact opposite can be the case. Methodological caveats are a routine component of scientific prose, particularly in the social sciences, and are a standard technique in the production of truth. As it is widely recognized that no study could be perfect, pointing to some limitations portrays an image of scientific honesty while still maintaining that these problems do not seriously interfere with the knowledge being produced – that they are limitations but not fatal flaws. In the Centre's case, methodological caveats about how the facts are related to organizational routines allow *Juristat* authors in good conscience to return to treating these constructs as facts. Methodological criticisms become normalized in the very act of acknowledging them.

The text of the *Juristat*s contain a more detailed, although still seriously restrained, discussion about the data. The findings are presented in assorted tables and graphs that are connected in a narrative summary of the data. This summary often amounts to a listing of which regions, crimes, and events are most or least prevalent as well as of some of the more dramatic year-to-year fluctuations. The narrative structure of these accounts was aptly characterized by one respondent as an 'up and down story,' because of their tendency to provide a straightforward account of the direction of statistical trends across different jurisdictions and over time. This approach has changed somewhat in recent years owing to efforts to provide more discussion of the social, legal, and organizational factors that might account for statistical fluctuations. In practice, however, their claims remain very restrained; the texts tell a story about different factors that *might* account for the changes, rather than attempt to advance an argument for the influence of one or another cause. Nonetheless, this practice is still a significant departure from what was permitted in the past.

Writing a *Juristat* inevitably brings an author face-to-face with questions about what things to accentuate and how to present the findings. What comparisons to employ and which statistical timelines to use are common concerns in the presentation of any statistical data, and different presentation styles allow authors to tell very different stories. One contentious presentational issue for the Centre concerns cross-national comparisons. Difficulties are inherent in attempts to make such comparisons owing to the different reporting regimes, cultural sensibilities, and legal frameworks that influence the statistical data. That said, we continue to be a fascinated by comparisons of our crime and incarceration rates with those of different countries. This fascination has introduced a recurrent source of unresolved tension concerning which countries should be included in cross-national comparisons. Here two authors of *Juristats* comment on their experiences of dealing with this issue. The first highlights his discomfort with comparisons of incarceration rates with different countries, and with how Canada can be made to look better or worse depending on which group is used as the basis of comparison. The second respondent comments on how his efforts to include a comparison between the crime data for Canada and several different countries were vetoed by a more senior member of the Centre, who was uncomfortable with attempts to compare Canada's data to that of any country other than the United States:

> There was an incarceration rate comparison and they were quibbling over which countries should be included. That always provokes a bit of a debate. It shifts Canada up or down depending on if you include Angola and Slovakia, then Canada is pretty low. If you stick to western industrialized nations then Canada is number two.

> In terms of the box on international comparisons there is always a question about how many other countries we can compare ourselves to. There is never agreement and it comes down to who is most influential. [The Director] said 'out' so out it goes ... We had settled on, I had put in three countries. Canada, the U.S., England and Wales. We had spent some time compiling the data and I selected those countries based on the fact that the information was current and more comparable and pretty standard.

We wanted something more than the United States, because we are criticized because we are comparing ourselves to the worst case scenario. So
we wanted to look at the European situation.

One walks away from reading a large number of *Juristat*s with the
impression that what makes them truly remarkable are the things that
are, or have been, absent from the text. For example, authors have
traditionally been required to remain tightly tied to the data being
reported from a particular survey or study. This requirement to draw
exclusively from the study being reported seems to be related to the
scientific ideal that scientific papers should only report new findings.
Only recently have authors in the Centre been encouraged to abandon
this presentational style, which one respondent characterized as
'dustbowl empiricism,' in an effort to liven up their publications. While
this change was justified as a way to make the texts more accessible
and enjoyable to readers, it was also a way to increase the epistemological weight of the publications by allowing them to circumvent
potential criticisms that the numbers are inaccurate or incomprehen-
sible. One respondent observed that the desire to invest their publications with more context and meaning was a way to address the situation where 'people either won't use [the publications], will use them
badly, or will badmouth the Centre, saying the numbers are just wrong
or don't make any sense.' Clarity and simplicity of presentational style
increase the truth value of claims directed at a generalist audience.
Therefore, authors are now encouraged to draw from different surveys and data sources in order to provide a more comprehensive picture of trends in a particular topic area. For example, a recent *Juristat*
on violent crime employs data from the homicide survey, the UCR,
and Statistics Canada's General Social Survey. Other authors have
gone beyond Statistics Canada materials to reference trends documented in academic studies.

While authors have welcomed this call to integrate other knowledges
into their publications, the practice brings with it certain difficulties.
Anyone who hopes to situate new criminal-justice statistics in relation
to 'the facts' as they appear in the academic literature will soon recognize that such 'facts' are not clear and unambiguous. Trends outlined
by academic researchers are often confusing or contradictory, and how
one interprets incompatible evidence often has more to do with political and ideological commitment than to an ability to sort through the
data objectively. In addition, any facts that Centre authors might wish

to document from academic sources must first percolate through the review process, where they are apt to be criticized by reviewers for personal or political reasons. As one author protested: 'It is almost like we have to have a stack of literature backing up a certain point of view. The person who is commenting will say, "Well, I don't like it." All the person has to do is say, "I don't like it," and we have to get rid of it. To argue a counterpoint we have to have a stack of information to back up our point of view. Ultimately it is just a clash of points of view.'

Authors of *Juristat*s must be cautious about which studies and surveys they reference and incorporate into their publications. They do not want to align their publications with controversial or questionable studies. This caution presents a problem, however, for while authors are intimately aware of the strengths and limitations of their own data-collection regime, they cannot be so certain about other data they might rely upon. Here an author provides an example of the considerations that go into deciding which materials to reference:

> The message here now is that it is no longer acceptable to simply report on that one survey. Get out there and find secondary information that helps conceptualize a bit more for the reader ... You have to be comfortable with the information. In a lot of cases we are using Statistics Canada information, so minimally you have to understand the methodology that compiled it, and make a decision based on 'Is this acceptable?' I remember one, I think there was one on child abuse that was being done here. One of the sources that was provided was through an organization that came up with some figures on child abuse rates. And their numbers were incredible, but they had a wealth of statistical information. Then when we got into the methodology we thought this was absolutely insane, it will never stand up on its own. So it was dismissed.

Authors' presentational style also continues to be restricted by an express prohibition against making statements on matters of policy. They must shy away from any hint that they believe a specific law, organizational structure, or funding regime is better or worse than another. There can, however, be considerable ambiguity as to where the line between policy and non-policy matters will be drawn in any particular instance. One author summarized these tensions by observing how, while authors were being pressured to make their publications more 'punchy,' they were 'not allowed to put anything in there that would be the least bit controversial, and it has to be only related to the data. It is a balancing act.'

Finally, perhaps the greatest source of ongoing anxiety for authors concerns the degree of interpretative latitude they are permitted. Statistics Canada has traditionally circumscribed the amount of interpretation authors could place on data, preferring a simple recounting of the findings of a study or survey. In the CCJS, the result of this policy has been a series of publications that contain a great deal of information as to the 'who, what, when, and where' of criminal-justice trends, but are notoriously short on addressing the question of 'why.' The roots of this reticence are related to the desire to avoid controversy. Recent attempts to make publications more topical and engaging mean that there is some increased, although still limited, room for interpretation. The specifics of what all reviewers will accept continues to be an issue:

> [Interpretation] is the double-edged sword. It has to be worded in a very diplomatic manner. It is like hiding behind the words. You have to word it in such a way that you don't come out and say that some particular jurisdiction is higher or lower because of this particular reason. Somehow you have to put in words between the lines. It is a tricky business because you have to appease these people. It is a very political organization, the way the Centre is organized. But it is all based on co-operation so it has to be that way. If your respondents aren't happy you don't get very much data.

The prohibition against commenting on policy, combined with the limited scope for interpretation, has meant that an informal division of labour has emerged between the Centre and academics. A select group of Canadian criminologists and sociologists work closely with the Centre. Some of these individuals occasionally contract with the Centre to write *Juristats* or, more commonly, attempt to explain to the public, via the media, why statistical trends are behaving in a particular manner. Centre personnel often refer media inquiries about the meanings and implications of their statistics to these academics, some of whom occasionally receive draft copies of publications so that they will be better prepared to answer such questions. One Centre employee concluded, 'If we are forthcoming with the academics it makes their job easier and it makes the media's job easier. And it gets the message out like we want it out.' In practice, this means that in order for Centre personnel to articulate the truths about trends in criminal justice as they see them, they must draw upon a different organization, one that has more interpretative latitude and that is not explicitly aligned with the Centre. Although formally distinct from the Justice Initiative, these academics are an important part of the Centre's extended knowledge network – offering the interpretation that is structurally impractical or impossible for CCJS employees to provide.

Official limitations on interpretation are not due to an inability of CCJS employees to provide informed opinion, as many of them have a detailed appreciation of the data, derived from a lengthy involvement with a particular survey and subject area. One academic who frequently had media calls directed to him by the Centre observed: 'I may not know the answer either, but [Centre staff] will certainly be closer to the data and be able to give as much of an explanation as I could.' Here another academic comments on how the Centre has relied on her as a means to sidestep potential controversies over interpretation:

> I think they refer press calls to me at times where they feel uncomfortable giving an interpretation of things or even talking, let's say, about provincial variation, because they know provincial variation is the kind of thing that one or both of the provinces is going to be upset [about]. One province is going to be upset because it is high and another is going to be upset because it is low or average. So there is real trouble for them saying very much. So they refer it to me first of all because they know ... I will give an interpretation that they are comfortable with.

The fact that authors of *Juristats* are closely involved with the production of the survey can also mean that they might have insights on the data that would be unavailable to academics. Such insider knowledge actually posed a minor dilemma for one author who was preparing to report a comparatively small annual fluctuation in the crime rate. It was apparently a fairly routine story as, while crime rates may change over time, they do not tend to demonstrate dramatic year-to-year variations (Martin and Ogrodnik 1996; Wright and Fedorowycz 1996). This respondent was concerned that the *Juristat* he was writing would report a 1 or 2 per cent decrease in the national crime rate. His methodological/ethical dilemma derived from his belief that such small statistical fluctuations could very well be within the normal range of error and variability inherent in the data, but that such errors and limitations were generally not publicly acknowledged:

> I have a hard time reporting statistics that have a change of 1 or 2 per cent. I mean, that is stable. But we have a tendency, in policing services anyway, to say that this is a definite decrease or increase ... I am going to have a very hard time saying that there is a decrease of crime of 1% in my own *Juristat*. Ethically, from my own personal viewpoint ... when you look at how we collect our statistics and the number of imputations that we do and the number of last minute fixes that we do, we are definitely playing with more than 1% when we come down to the crunch.

The fact that crime trends have been going *down* can also present authors with unique difficulties about how to present their data. Authors are well aware that they are not simply communicating knowledge, but are involved in rhetorical attempts to persuade occasionally unreceptive audiences. When the knowledge being espoused corresponds with prevailing perceptions, it is comparatively easy to have claims accepted. However, in those instances where the facts being documented clash with such perceptions, readers and commentators are more prone to question their validity and search for reasons why they might be wrong – a situation that the Centre generally aims to avoid. One author who was in the process of writing a *Juristat* that would document a small national decrease in the violent-crime rate commented on how this indicator contravened the prevailing public sentiment that crime and violence were on the increase. Consequently, he believed that in order to have the Centre's claims about statistical decreases in violent crime rates more readily accepted, 'we are going to have to give people some credit for their feelings of insecurity.' In order to acknowledge these insecurities, while still pressing the truth value of the Centre's claim about a decrease in violent crime, he chose to employ a presentation style that would outline some of the complexities of the data that might account for this discrepancy. This approach included highlighting the fact that crime rates are averages, that the actual level of violence may be higher in particular local communities, and that public perceptions of violence can be shaped by particularly heinous crimes that are not representative of statistical trends. Overall, he suggested that his aim in employing such rhetorical strategies was to urge the readers: 'Don't stop believing us, just look at it in the big picture.'

In addition to being an institutional and personal practice, authorship in the Centre is now also a documentary reality. It was only in the mid-1990s that the *Juristats* began to have authors' names attached to them. Before this they were simply authored by the 'Canadian Cen-

tre for Justice Statistics.' Respondents recounted how this change was
the result of a lawsuit from a member of another section of Statistics
Canada. Apparently, this individual had sued to have his name attached to the products he was writing in an attempt to acquire academic or professional authorship credits. This documentary change is
grudging institutional acknowledgment of the fact that the production
of statistical knowledge is mediated by human intervention. However,
the Centre's publications are so structured by format requirements,
political concerns, and reviewer comments that some authors have
said they had little personal attachment to the product that went out
the door. This places authors in a precarious situation, one where they
are responsible for a publication that, at the end of the day, they may
feel they have played little creative role in producing.

Authors are encouraged to stand by the strength of their convictions
in writing a *Juristat*, but there can be professional repercussions for
such determination. One author recounted how in an upcoming *Juristat*
he hoped to compare the data on crime with data derived from an
immigration database. While he believed that this was both possible
and valuable, he remained reticent to present such knowledge. The
potentially controversial nature of such a table made him fear for the
implications it might have for his career: 'It really comes down to how
much do I believe in it and how much do I really want to push it. And
is it a risk to my career? Am I going to come across as a pushy SOB
who will only do things his own way and is not cooperative or will I
be viewed as someone who really believes in what he does and sticks
by his guns? There are just many ways you can twist it.' Authors walk
a fine line between communicating important information to the public but not surrendering entirely to how other people want the information structured. This is evident in the following exchange between
two respondents over the precarious situation of *Juristat* authors:

A1: You are held accountable for ideas and interpretations that are not
yours.
A2: Your neck is on the line. And it may be on the line because of a
particular [Liaison Officer] that you didn't agree should be in the *Juristat*
to begin with ... I remember we had this big controversy when I very first
came to Statistics Canada. The director was addressing the division, talking about *Juristats* in particular and he said ... : 'You are the author of this
Juristat. If you feel like you want to include a certain text then you do so. It
is your name on the product.' That is theoretical, that is not how it is done.

A1: You try to get your first draft in the way you want it, because you know that you will be fighting to get things left in. If it doesn't suit somebody it will be out. And it is very difficult to add things once it goes around for comments. If what you want to add is not directly related to what people have already seen. Because if you give them new stuff they will just have more stuff to comment on.

The Media

The act of writing is shaped by an author's presumptions about his or her audience. One of the main audiences for Centre publications are the news media, a set of institutions that informs the format of Centre publications, its communication strategy, and also the nature of the comments coming from reviewers. The Centre's relationship with the media marks the transition point from private to public knowledge. If the Centre's claims are to be accepted by the public, they must first be reproduced by the media in a way that does not excessively challenge their truth value.

The media frame public discourse and focus political attention. Through them we acquire much of our knowledge from and about different institutions. Increasingly, the media are recognized as a significant component in the organization of criminal justice (Ericson, Baranek, and Chan 1987, 1989, 1991; Schlesinger and Tumber 1994). This section documents the Centre's distinctive relationship with the media and how concerns about the media prospectively shape the specifics of the Centre's knowledge production.

The Centre exists primarily to produce knowledge for the institutional players in the criminal-justice system. Its relationship with the media derives from the larger Statistics Canada mandate to publicize its findings. From the vantage point of the Centre, the media are yet another set of heterogeneous institutions and actors that must be patterned into its extended knowledge network. Following the template developed by Latour (1987) and Callon (1986) outlined in chapter 2, the media must first be made to be 'interested' in the knowledge developed by the Centre. This process appears to be relatively simple, given the media's long-standing fascination with matters of crime and justice. The Centre must then establish means to control the media's role as an uncritical disseminator of the Centre's findings. This role has been partially stabilized by the Centre's use of specific formats, presentation styles, and dissemination vehicles.

A theoretical question derived from accentuating these inter-institutional linkages concerns the degree to which the media uncritically reproduce the CCJS's knowledge. Within media studies, 'dominant ideology' theorists have argued that the media are subservient to official sources in terms of the type of coverage they provide. In relation to criminal justice, official sources feed the bureaucratic and economic logic of news production, where deadline pressures and the requirement to fill newspaper space prompt a dependency on information from official criminal-justice sources (Fishman 1980). The media tend to treat official accounts unproblematically as 'the facts,' and in so doing reproduce the dominant ideology of sources (Hall et al. 1978). Countering this approach is one derived from research on the practices of journalists, which emphasizes the contingent and negotiated character of media-source relations (Ericson, Baranek, and Chan 1987, 1989, 1991). These authors have demonstrated that while sources are a vital component in how media accounts are structured, reporters do not necessarily uncritically reproduce a source's preferred version of events. Alternative sources allow journalists to produce stories that run counter to the narrative preferred by official sources. The degree of latitude for alternative accounts varies among different sources, with, for example, political legislatures having relatively little control over the types of stories produced, the police effecting more control, and prisons effecting still more control (Ericson, Baranek, and Chan 1989; Doyle and Ericson 1996).

Despite the fact that statistical agencies are one of the most authorized sources of knowledge about crime and criminal justice, and despite the frequent appearance of official crime statistics in media reports, media analysts have largely ignored such institutions. This section partially addresses this lacuna by drawing from interviews with Centre personnel and two prominent journalists to outline the contours of the relationship between the Centre and the media. Seeing as the following analysis neglects the day-to-day routines of journalists, it tends to accentuate the degree to which the Centre has been able to control the media. However, these interviews also document quite distinctive fears among Centre personnel about the possibility of critical coverage, and these fears reveal how the media maintain a degree of discretion over the final form of a story.

Respondents recounted how in the early and mid-1980s the Centre had few formal dealings with the media. Over time, however, Centre staff increasingly recognized that the media were interested in their data. Consequently, as one senior member of the Centre recalled, 'There was a push to make some of these things appear in the press more, and this was reflected in how things were presented.' Some of their national indicators, such as the crime rate, were particularly attractive to the media. One respondent even went so far as to proclaim: 'What actually *is* the national crime rate? What do you *do* with it? You put it in the newspaper and put a headline on it.' In fact, Maltz (1977) suggests that one of the original motivations behind the development of UCR statistics in the United States in the 1920s was to provide journalists with information about crime.

As they forged a closer relationship with the media, Centre staff soon recognized that some of their knowledge was perhaps *too* attractive to the press. For example, one individual recounted how when he became chief of the Centre's policing section, he halted the practice of releasing a table that detailed the ten Canadian cities with the highest homicide rates. Although this knowledge was accurate, he saw it as being too amenable to sensationalism and, therefore, not something he wanted to accentuate. As he recalls, 'There were instances where the press just took that table and put a graphic of a smoking gun over it and ran it. This was something that was clearly sensationalistic and we were not going to give them that table any more. The numbers are available, but now they have to do the digging themselves if they want them.'

Today, the media influence on the Centre is pervasive, informing the timing of releases, their wording, the degree of statistical sophistication, and the types of knowledge presented. The desire to make the Centre's publications more 'punchy' and approachable by public audiences largely translates into a concern to make things more accessible to the media. One author declared that the entire intent of writing for the Centre is 'to make it as reader-friendly and user-friendly in that journalistic style as possible. Make sure that they are able to take what we say and publish it.' This includes the use of bite-sized facts and simple graphics amenable to easy media reproduction. Here two members of the Centre comment on how the relationship with the media has informed the writing of Centre publications:

When there is a release it goes out on the wire and journalists write their stories from that. That is the way we have been asked to write our information now, to know what is news-worthy. That is kind of the perspective we have to look at now rather than just the basic mundane number crunching. We have to make kind of a story out of it. Which some people see as a problem ... It forces us to look at things in a journalistic view rather than an academic kind of view. Before it used to be facts and only facts, now we have a lot more contextual information ... We've got sexy bullets now at the beginning of each section to catch people's eye, the media's eye, in terms of newsworthy items. So that has changed ... It is to the point where newsworthy kinds of things, only those kinds of things are in there. And they are short. There can be nice little graphics in there to catch your eye rather than five pages of tables.

Our major audience is journalists. So you have to give them all of the facts that they would find of interest right up front. The idea is to make it as readable as possible so they don't misinterpret the information right off the bat. One thing we have to do is avoid any footnotes in the highlights because we know that they won't be read and they won't be reported. If it is not crystal clear it is not going in the highlights.

The Centre's appreciation of what constitutes a good public release of its data is related to the type and extent of media coverage that data receives. The Centre's understanding of good publicity focuses entirely on its institutional authority. Within broad limits, Centre personnel simply do not care about how people interpret the data or manipulate it for partisan purposes. They fully expect that their numbers will be employed for diverse and contradictory ends and will be finessed by people located at every point along the political spectrum. Such uses do not pose a problem, just so long as the numbers are taken at face value. For example, two Centre officials independently used exactly the same words to define a successful release: 'We didn't have a lot of people challenging the data and saying that we were making it up.'

Echoes of the classic liberal approach to free speech resound in this view of the uses and potential abuses of such data. While they recognize that statistics can always be consciously or unconsciously abused, Centre staff rely on the prospect of free and public debate to ensure the ultimate triumph of truth over malicious and fraudulent claims. In this institution dedicated to the production of numerical data, one can even find individuals who believe there are benefits to conscious public misrepresentations of their numbers. A manager of one of the Centre's surveys displayed just such a logic when he observed: 'I think it is positive when someone misuses data. The beauty is they come out and make the argument and they get attacked by a dozen people with good data saying why this is what we are doing. That is education. I think you actually have a net positive outcome. You have actually corrected the record on something.'

Centre personnel work to ensure that the type of coverage they receive does not tarnish their reputation. Any reports that go beyond simply reproducing their numbers to implicate the Centre are seen as a potential hazard. To again emphasize this point, yet another member of the Centre commented on a recent release by observing how, 'in previous years when the media did not like the numbers they tended to say they were wrong, that the Centre had somehow manufactured the numbers ... There is now more of an emphasis on trying to explain and understand them, so that is progress.' Quite simply, and understandably, the Centre aims to avoid the charge that, for any number of reasons, it has gotten the numbers wrong.

The media provide both opportunities and dangers. They are a means to communicate the Centre's facts and are a source of institutional legitimization, but they can also single the Centre out for criticism. Consequently, the Centre strives to control the type of coverage that its releases will receive. As is increasingly the case in relationships between the media and news sources, control of the media is not secured through secrecy, but through prospectively engaging the media to provide accounts in preferred formats (Ericson, Baranek, and Chan 1989). A member of the Centre described how the writing style for the *Juristat* is related to the relationship of Centre staff with the media: 'We don't want the journalist screwing up the data so we spoon-feed them as much as possible.' The use of highlighted bullets on the first pages of their publications is a prime example of such 'spoon-feeding,' as these present facts, easily reproduced by journalists, that are removed from the intricacies of the surveys and background processes that make them possible:

Q: Do you often get situations where [the media] are essentially pulling the bullets right from the publication?
A: We want them to do that. We often say that when we don't get a lot of calls it is because the data is well-written. They have just ripped off of it what they need. That is good, that's a good sign.

The Centre works to constitute journalists as passive recipients and verbatim reproducers of its data. It has had considerable success in this regard, as media reports often simply recount the story told in the Centre's releases. Here one of the few Canadian reporters who specializes in legal and criminal matters emphasizes the journalistic dependence on the knowledge that emanates from the Centre, and the way that knowledge is phrased: 'The form the media reports take is completely dependent on the Centre. No reporter is going to go through and crunch the numbers. If the Centre says, "Crime is down 2% from last year," that is what the story is going to be. If the Centre says "Crime is still at a ten year high, even if it went down one or two percent," that is the story. Given constraints and time the spin is generally what the Centre puts on it ... We are completely dependent on them.'

However, this individual overstates the case. While journalists are undoubtedly structurally subordinated to the Centre's truths, there are several instances where reporters have presented the Centre's numbers only to then suggest that they were suspect, wrong, or out of touch with reality. Such a critical stance can partially be attributed to the objectivity requirements for journalists. Loathe to appear as the simple mouthpiece for the state by simply reproducing official statistics, journalists also generally lack the statistical training to independently evaluate these numbers. In the tradition of the 'point-counterpoint' approach to journalistic objectivity, they resolve this dilemma by seeking out other groups to comment on or critique the Centre's numbers (Sacco 1998). Such stories seem to be particularly common in those jurisdictions that report comparably high levels on unfavourable indicators. They also seem to be more prevalent in those situations where the numbers are at odds with prevailing public perceptions about trends in criminal justice. In such circumstances it is not uncommon for journalists to question the validity of the Centre's numbers and methodology. The extent to which these stories are seen to seriously challenge the Centre's reputation is a contextual matter, related to the specific media outlet and commentator making the accusations and to the tone of the allegations.

Media criticism is most damaging when it can draw from authorized sources who challenge the numbers. One example was Professor Fekete's (1994) accusations, detailed in the previous chapter, that the Violence Against Women survey was politically biased. Another incident occurred following the 1993 release of the crime and homicide *Juristat*. At that time Toronto's chief of police sparked a controversy by publicly accusing the Centre's numbers of being 'out of touch with reality,' a claim supported by the fact that the statistical trends documented by the Centre for Toronto did not mesh with those collected by the Metropolitan Toronto police force (Christopoulos 1994). This discrepancy appears to have resulted from a methodological oversight by the Centre and a lack of communication between the CCJS and the Metro Toronto police. It also prompted efforts to control the future possibility of such authoritative challenges to the Centre's data. In particular, the Centre instituted a policy whereby it now requires police forces to 'sign off' on its data to indicate that it is accepted as accurate. Centre officials believe that the police will be less apt to publicly criticize the Centre's findings if they have already formally approved the data.

The Centre has established relatively stable links with the media. On the day of a release, some staff members spend a considerable amount of time simply faxing publications to the media. Other media outlets acquire summaries of these publications through Statistics Canada's daily electronic-mail release system, The Daily. The Centre also employs an 'information officer' who communicates with reporters, a development that parallels the larger trend in criminal justice to designate individuals who will provide the media with stories accompanied by the preferred institutional interpretation (Ericson 1994; Schlesinger, Tumber, and Murdock 1991). Although the information officer must avoid the hint of controversy, and has an interpretative latitude that is largely confined to what was written in the report, he gives a human face to impersonal processes. As Giddens (1991) emphasizes, in a society pervaded by complex abstract systems, there is still a need for face-to-face interaction between the public and the human representatives of these systems. In these encounters the human 'face work' that is necessary to reinforce the trust we must place in abstract systems is accomplished. For the Centre, the information officer provides the mediated human face for a complex statistical knowledge network, one whose truth claims most of us must simply take as a matter of faith.

The Centre is highly sensitive to the volume and nature of media coverage received by its reports. As a result, staff produce internal summaries of the coverage their major releases receive, its prominent themes, and any controversies that might have developed. Again, their concern is not with the myriad ways that their data are politically manipulated. Rather, their summaries are an attempt to monitor the type of coverage and search out those instances where the numbers were deemed to be fraudulent or where the Centre or Statistics Canada was singled out for criticism. In extreme instances they write letters to editors that detail what they see as unfair coverage, and have held meetings with journalists in attempts to clarify how their various surveys operate. These efforts are more than a way for the Centre to lend the media an educational helping hand; they are also meant to avoid future controversies by informing journalists about the operations and limitations of the surveys and in so doing keep the critical focus off of the Centre.

From the perspective of the Centre, the media coverage of criminal-justice statistics appears to be a relatively straightforward exercise. Journalists receive the publications on the morning of the release and use these data as the basis for a story about trends in particular statistical indicators. More enterprising journalists contact the Centre's information officer for a human retelling of these trends or seek out academics or other institutional sources, who provide commentary and interpretation. Outside of the infrequent controversy that prompts focused attention on the Centre, the routine reporting of summaries drawn from its publications is the full extent of the Centre's public profile. There is no journalistic 'statistics beat' comparable to the police beat or the courts beat.

The media do not explore the day-to-day routines involved in the production of statistical knowledge. The work of statisticians and analysts simply does not accord with a media template that ideally requires action, controversy, and, particularly in the case of television, dramatic visuals. The Centre does not offer anything like the gripping possibilities of riding in a police car or attending court. It is a professional, bureaucratic, knowledge-producing organization whose most dramatic activities are meetings. Exacerbating this lack of media attention is a general statistical antipathy among journalists. The professional background of journalists is much more likely to have been creative writing than statistics or criminology. Furthermore, they are writing for an audience that is generally understood to have a minimal degree of statistical sophistication (Paulos 1988). One Centre respondent recalled how years previously he had invited journalists into the Centre's offices in order to receive feedback about how they might better meet the media's needs. He left this meeting impressed by the media's requirement for statistical simplicity. One journalist put a fine head on this point by telling him: 'We don't know anything about numbers, so don't swamp us with numbers.' Although it would be almost impossible for a statistical agency to avoid swamping people with numbers, the Centre has done its best to meet journalists' needs by providing concise statistical facts and relatively uncomplicated analyses and representations.

In summary, the Centre finds its relationship with the media useful, but also potentially dangerous. Centre personnel require the media to disseminate their findings, but in so doing face the prospect of having their authority challenged. A number of strategies to formalize and routinize the relationships between these two institutions have developed. Cumulatively, such efforts are further evidence of Ericson's (1994: 109) argument: 'The news media and source institutions are best conceived as *part* of each other, mutually influencing their respective ways of classifying, organizing, thinking and acting.' Some of the ways in which the Centre has formalized these relations are by releasing its data directly to media outlets, presenting the data in a media-friendly format, making individuals available who can provide a human face to impersonal numbers, and referring requests for interpretation of the numbers to a preferred group of academics. Such efforts are an attempt to ensure that the media reports the Centre's numbers in a fashion that is both honest but also does not question its authority. Although the Centre has been comparatively successful in this regard, the ongoing fears among Centre personnel about the risks inherent in public release speak to their inability to completely control the types of coverage they receive. Alternative sources such as academics, nonprofit organizations, and the occasional jurisdictional representative allow journalists to produce stories that run counter to the Centre's interests. An image emerges of ongoing tensions and strategic interactions between the Centre and the media, rather than the more deterministic image, as portrayed by the 'dominant ideology' theorists, of journalists being captured by authorized sources.

Conclusion

We have now reached the point where the fate of the Centre's knowledge claims are, by and large, outside of its immediate control. Centre employees have worked to produce knowledge that will be accepted as authoritative by building a complex knowledge network composed of heterogeneous elements. They have followed accepted methodology, built networks, navigated through institutional politics, and enticed others to become interested in the data. The final act in this drama is to write and communicate their findings.

In this context, however, writing can be a complex social accomplishment, informed by institutional interests, authorial concerns, politics, and a complex and distinctive review process. Authors work their way through these elements to produce reports that will be accepted as authoritative by different audiences. In order to do so, they employ a literary style that makes their claims relatively easy to digest and removes the role of human and organizational factors in the production of knowledge. Among these authors' main audiences are the journalists who serve as their primary conduit to a wider public. Their relationship with the media informs the types of knowledge conveyed, as well as the format, language, and statistical sophistication of their communications. The media are also a source of constant tension, for while they publicize the Centre's claims, they can also potentially question its data and in so doing challenge its institutional legitimacy. Consequently, the Centre has tried to align itself prospectively with the media in order to structure the types of accounts that reporters produce. While Centre personnel have been comparatively successful in setting the agenda for the coverage of criminal-justice statistics, they recognize that the final contours of a story are ultimately beyond their control.

Conclusion:
Statistics, Governance, and Rationality

This concluding chapter provides an opportunity to briefly reflect on two issues. First, it considers the modifications that this study suggests to the dominant approaches to the study of governance; or, more precisely, how the study of governance can benefit from engaging with an expanded range of issues and approaches. These concluding reflections on governance are largely directed at some of the positions advanced by Nikolas Rose, who has been the most prolific and insightful commentator on governance. This chapter accentuates three themes that relate to the analysis in this book pertaining to how governance operates and how it might be studied in the future. These include the need to reinvigorate the study of the state, which should concentrate on how explicitly political concerns might influence the form and availability of governmental knowledge. Such a stance would itself require engaging with (or in) more realist sociological approaches than are usually embraced by governmental analysis. The book concludes by abstracting from this study to raise broader questions about the potential future role of agencies such as the Canadian Centre for Justice Statistics. It does so by situating the Centre in the context of a continuing increase in the volume and specialization of knowledge, and of a political turn towards more sensational and emotive criminal-justice policies.

On Governmentality and Sociological Analysis

Liberal governance seeks to shape the behaviour of autonomous subjects in the directions desired by authorities. Statistics about both the population and system processes are vital epistemological resources for such efforts as they delimit the contours and tendencies of the objects to be governed. Abstract liberal ambitions about increasing the security or wealth of the population, or the efficiency of particular systems, are transformed into specific strategies that are evaluated according to whether they modify a multitude of statistical indicators in a desired direction. These statistical objects of governance are themselves the product of the network-building practices of various centres of calculation that produce a host of quantitative indicators. In the case of the CCJS, these include, among other things, rates of criminal behaviour, prison admissions, and legal aid costs-per-case measures. Without such measures, contemporary liberal techniques for governing crime and the criminal-justice system would essentially be unthinkable.

This text has not, however, provided a traditional study of governance per se. Instead, it has concentrated on the institutional production of knowledge about criminal justice. As a result, it differs from traditional governmentality approaches in three ways. First, it demonstrates the continuing importance of approaching the state as a key site of governmental analysis. Neo-liberal governance relies on a plurality of governmental agencies, of which the state is only one (Rose and Miller 1992). Agencies such as the CCJS are a vital component in the ongoing production and reproduction of the state, and in fostering governmental practices by both state and extra-state agencies. However, perhaps in reaction to the traditional hegemony of the state depicted in Marxist thought, studies of governance have tended to downplay the continuing importance of the state. Instead, they have emphasized the ways in which myriad extra-state 'social' (Donzelot 1979) agencies work to shape an individual's self-governing capacities. While the state should not be reified, we need to continue to explore the network-building processes and capacities characteristic of state agencies. This is particularly the case in those instances where the state demonstrates unique abilities to produce governmental knowledge.

Contemporary talk about globalization and the related crisis of the nation-state tend to focus on how the state's sovereignty has been eroded in the face of powerful transnational influences. This emphasis on the global, however, tends to downplay the continuing importance of the state's ability to coordinate a plethora of knowledge-production networks. Admittedly, this is a task that the state increasingly shares with various corporate and transnational organizations that control massive amounts of data about citizens and institutions (Gandy 1993; Ritzer 1995; Turow 1997). However, the knowledge produced by an agency like Statistics Canada cannot be easily duplicated by non-state agencies. Complex issues of political jurisdiction, combined with the taint of self-interest that plagues private forms of knowledge production, mean that it is unlikely that anything but a state-affiliated organization would be able to produce legitimized national numbers on criminal justice, health, education, the economy, and various other topics. Consequently, extra-state forms of governance are still bound to the state to the extent that they rely on knowledge that only state agencies can produce.

In producing official statistics, the state creates and reproduces various classifications. It finances the agencies who produce official classificatory systems and legitimates official forms of classification. Untold numbers of state bureaucrats, demographers, and statisticians enact official ways to view and delineate the world. In the process, 'the state establishes and inculcates common forms and categories of perception and appreciation, social frameworks of perception, of understanding or of memory, in short state forms of classification' (Bourdieu 1994: 13). Through the options established on different surveys, censuses, and reports, a protean reality is objectified for the purposes of governmental scrutiny and intervention. The state must therefore remain as an analytical focus, as it is in its centres of calculation where many of the specific epistemological objects of governance are produced.

The second contribution that this study makes to traditional governmental approaches concerns the role that explicitly political factors can play in shaping the form and content of governmental knowledge. In his book *Powers of Freedom*, Nikolas Rose (1999) dedicates an entire chapter exclusively to 'Numbers.' There he distinguishes between American and European approaches to the study of statistics, and aligns governmentality analysis with the latter tradition. The American approach amounts to a form of political sociology, and is concerned with why some things are counted rather than others. Decisions about what should be counted, and how, are located in the context of struggles between different interest groups. In contrast, the European tradition situates the analysis of numbers and politics in a Foucauldian conception of power. Authors working in this tradition focus on how the quantification of politics transforms democracy as a 'mentality of government and a technology of rule' (Rose 1999: 215).

The emphasis is therefore on the link between government and knowl-edge/information and on the development of particular rationalities and strategies of rule.

This study of the CCJS demonstrates that this demarcation between European and American approaches to quantification is unnecessary, and ultimately limits a broader understanding of how governance operates. To appreciate the dynamics of governance one must also engage with the micro-politics of knowledge production. The governmentality literature has paid little attention to how political struggles, special interests, or pure chance might play a role in shaping the specifics of governmental knowledges. The minutiae of how certain classifications come into being or, alternatively, of how the potential development of certain knowledges is forsaken in the aid of more explicitly political considerations has not been adequately explored. Consequently, one can be left with the impression that the specific forms of knowledge that emanate from diverse centres of calculation were preordained. This study demonstrates that the epistemological resources of governance have their own history and micro-politics.

Recognizing that governmental knowledge can have a political dimension should be a spur to further explorations into the production of the epistemological resources of governance. However, any such studies must break with another divide that has been erected in the governmentality literature. Studies of governance tend to be 'histories of the present,' which chart the changed rationalities that culminate in our contemporary understandings of the self and of the aims and practices of governance (Stenson 1998). Such studies are set in opposition to more 'realist' forms of sociology. In fact, Nikolas Rose has expressed an antipathy towards sociological efforts to explain how different systems of governance operate in practice. Rose (1993: 288) suggests that studies of government should eschew sociological realism in lieu of a concern to examine how authorities have conceived of what it means to govern and how governance is made possible. In a programmatic statement on this issue, Rose (1999: 19) proposes that 'analyses of governmentalities are empirical but not realist. They are not studies of the actual organization and operation of systems of rule, of the relations that obtain amongst political and other actors and organizations at local levels and their connection into actor networks and the like.' He continues this vein of thought by proposing that studies of governmentality are concerned with 'the conditions of possibility and intelligibility for certain ways of seeking to act upon the conduct of others, or oneself, to achieve certain ends.' It is this antipathy towards realism that appears to be at the heart of Rose's earlier-mentioned disavowal of American approaches to studying quantification, as that form of political sociology has tended to provide accounts that are more realist than Rose appears to be comfortable with.

This study has tried to break down this division between studies of rationalities of rule and more realist approaches to the study of the social and political preconditions of governance. In this regard, it shares David Garland's (1997) belief that there can be a useful dialogue and cross-fertilization between sociology and studies of governance. Ultimately, the strict demarcation between realism and studies of governmental rationalities is both artificial and unhelpful. If, as Rose suggests, governmental studies seek to understand the 'conditions of possibility' for certain ways to act on others and oneself, the exclusive emphasis on rationalities ignores how governance is made possible precisely through the various network-building processes that produce governmental knowledge. The ways in which these networks are manufactured, the various interests that coalesce around new ways of demarking the world, can be studied sociologically. This effort would require acknowledging that more-realist studies can inform our understanding of the preconditions for particular governmental rationalities and strategies.

Knowledge, Expertise, and Rationality

This analysis has focused on the internal operations of the Canadian Centre for Justice Statistics. To the extent that it strays beyond the confines of the Centre's walls, it does so in order to examine the diverse elements that Centre personnel have sought to pattern into a larger knowledge network. These final, more speculative, comments situate the Centre in a broader social context. Here we are concerned with how the knowledge produced by the Centre might be deployed in the future. Knowledge is a tool used to fulfil specific purposes. This means that social, political, and cultural changes can transform how knowledge is deployed. Social processes are now at work that appear to work against the type of rationalist use of statistics on crime and criminal justice that originally motivated their production.

Statistical institutions are icons of rationality. Their philosophical roots can be traced back to the Enlightenment ideal of deploying objective knowledge to confront bias and ignorance (Deflem 1997). They were to produce the knowledge through which a host of rationally thought-out policies for the betterment of society were to be developed. Today, however, we face questions about the continuing salience of this vision. Citizens face increasing restrictions on their ability to engage meaningfully with this knowledge, while there has been a political turning away from the use of statistics as the basis for rational criminal-justice policy developments. Instead, statistics increasingly appear to be a rhetorical resource in emotional and often reactionary public claims-making. At the same time, official efforts to confront crime and criminal victimization tend to rely more and more on forms of hyper-technicist expertise.

Originally this book was going to conclude with an admonition that the general public needs to learn more about the specifics of how criminal-justice statistics are produced and communicated. The motivation for such a plea is the recognition that subtle methodological and political factors must be appreciated to fully understand official statistics, or any knowledge-production regime. The more knowledgeable citizens are about the vagaries and nuances of how knowledge is produced and disseminated, the less apt they are to be swayed by dubious studies or cynical manipulations of findings.

By now, such cautions are routine. As political discourse has become increasingly quantified, citizens are expected or encouraged to become better versed in this statistical language of power. Subject-matter specialists who are intimately aware of the complexities of particular data-collection vehicles frequently suggest that the public needs to enhance its understanding of how knowledge is produced. Only then can people fully appreciate the intricacies of any specific issue. Such admonitions are occasionally combined with the suggestion that citizens require greater mathematical and methodological skills to understand the statistics that shape their lives (Paulos 1995, 1988).

It is precisely the routine and predictable nature of such cautions, however, that prompts me to abandon what would have been a relatively straightforward conclusion. We now live in a numerical world where we are routinely confronted with a host of statistics derived from an apparently unending stream of studies and surveys. Every workday, for example, Statistics Canada releases *The Daily* via an electronic mailing list. Subscribers to this list receive a summary of the studies and publications that Statistics Canada is releasing that day. In one typical week in 2000, this included studies or publications pertaining to the consumer price index; particleboard, oriented strandboard, and fibreboard; air travel between Canada and the United States; the changing face of conjugal relationships; inter-corporate ownership; refined-petroleum products; new motor-vehicle sales; exports by country; steel primary forms; shipments of rolled steel; dairy statistics; changes to municipal boundaries, status, and names; consumption of containers and other packaging supplies by the manufacturing industries; Canada's balance of international payments; railway carloadings; civil-aviation financial statistics; building permits; employment, earnings, and hours; monthly survey of manufacturing; informatics professional-services price index; industry price indexes; travel between Canada and other countries; shipments of office furniture products; historical labour-force statistics; science statistics; federal government personnel engaged in scientific and technological activities; and stocks of frozen poultry meat.

It is worth reiterating that Statistics Canada, which produces this weekly outpouring of numbers, is only one organization responsible for the official statistics for one country and its inhabitants. Even in this relatively underpopulated nation a host of other studies and surveys flow from governmental departments, commissions, private think-tanks, advocacy groups, academics, non-governmental organizations, and businesses. If we multiply these by the number of countries in the world it becomes clear that the claim that we now live in a 'knowledge society' (Stehr 1994) is more than empty sloganeering. We are surrounded by, enmeshed in, and constituted through knowledge, and a significant percentage of that knowledge is quantitative.

What implications does this massive outpouring of knowledge have for the public? How might citizens relate to a world permeated by ever-increasing amounts of specialized knowledge? The sheer volume of knowledge means that conventional calls for the public to inform themselves about the specifics of the knowledge used to develop social policy is little more than empty rhetoric or wishful thinking. Consider this study alone; in more than 200 pages it has explored the background processes involved in producing national statistics about crime and criminal justice in one small sub-component of a statistical organization for one country. Although it raises issues about the methodology and politics involved in producing such numbers, it would be a rare layperson who would read such a text. Furthermore, even this extended inquiry does not purport to address anything approaching all of the important methodological caveats, subtleties, and micro-politics related to the CCJS and the surveys it produces.

Despite this proliferation of knowledge, some citizens have managed to learn the nuances of the knowledge structures that pertain to issues that interest them or that affect them directly. One can think of the detailed knowledge of some citizen activists about the risks posed by genetically modified foods or nuclear energy. Such individuals have dedicated the time and energy to becoming non-credentialized experts. There are obvious limitations, however, to such efforts which make it unlikely that any but a fraction of the population will acquire lay expertise on any particular issue. Citizens face structural impediments to developing a detailed appreciation of the plethora of knowledge regimes that influence their lives, and such limitations are quite independent of their intelligence. Time is often not available to learn a specialization unrelated to a person's employment. Citizens also often lack the methodological or statistical training to appreciate the subtleties of these numbers. Furthermore, as this study has demonstrated, many of the decisions that shape how knowledge is structured, including decisions about what knowledge is produced and how it is communicated, take place in bureaucratic offices well beyond the scrutiny of even the most strident activist.

Another paradox is inherent in the development of expertise. As individuals focus on one particular policy issue or scientific specialization, they necessarily have less time to learn about the specifics of other issues. Sociologists have long recognized that one consequence of specialization is that individual experts face an attendant trade-off in more general forms of knowledge (Rueschemeyer 1986). Although some of the technical skills acquired in learning about one issue can be generalized, learning the specifics about how the data pertaining to one particular issue are collected, analysed, and communicated comes at a loss in a comparable appreciation for other issues. Such a narrowing of focus poses a dilemma for citizens of increasingly complex societies. Individuals now witnesses an apparently unending procession of social problems move across their television screens and across the pages of their newspapers (Hilgartner and Bosk 1988). Each issue seems to beg for some form of immediate response based on informed opinion.

In the face of such difficulties, citizens routinely turn to the advice of experts who perform the role of complexity reduction (Abbott 1988;

Freidson 1986; Nock 1993). As citizens are not able to evaluate criti-
cally all the various knowledges that impinge on their daily lives,
experts provide guidance on how to develop opinions and outline
personal courses of action. Liberal governance is itself intimately bound
up with the skills of experts (T. Johnson 1993). Neo-liberalism constitutes individuals as free to exercise a circumscribed form of freedom.
Individuals are to make decisions about how to govern their own lives
with the assistance of a host of state and extra-state experts. The freedom to choose among expert opinions masks the fact that we have
become profoundly dependent on experts and expert systems (Bauman
1992). A host of mundane decisions pertaining to the governance of
our own lives, including decisions about where to live, who (and how)
to date, and how to construct our homes, transport our children, secure our vehicles, and configure our computers, are now done in light
of considerations about crime and victimization. Such decisions bring
the public into contact with expert systems concerned with private
security, computers, architecture, realty, policing, alarm manufacture,
and insurance.

Studies of neo-liberal governance have tended to focus on the *form*
of governance, emphasizing how a distinctively rational epistemological space is carved out so that citizens can make decisions pertaining
to the governance of their lives. It is assumed that citizens will act
rationally in their own best interests to govern a range of different life
decisions pertaining to crime, health, finances, and so on. However,
not enough has been said about citizens' actual decision-making practices. In this space of rational governance, do citizens actually behave
rationally? How do they choose among the various competing forms
of expertise that might be available, and do they follow that advice?
Individuals often encounter ambiguous situations when it comes time
to choose among expertly mediated options. Expert opinion can be
incredibly fractured. In fact, a defining element of some of our most
pressing social problems is that there is an array of experts presenting
various often-contradictory opinions, critiques, and findings (Jasanoff
1995). In criminal justice this can be seen in those situations where a
host of experts offer a range of advice on the success of policy initiatives, the nature and extent of the crime problem, the best way to
secure your home or child, or the proper course of criminal-justice
reform.

What the governmental focus on rationalities elides is the role of
irrationality in decision making. It loses sight of various symbolic,

reactionary, or 'common sense' elements in how people make decisions, and ignores how accepting expert advice is akin to a leap of faith, a surrendering to trust in that individual and the expert system she or he is aligned with (Giddens 1991; Shapin 1994). Decision making is not strictly rational, directed inevitably towards the most logical options on offer from various experts. Instead, decisions can be shaped by a host of irrational and emotive factors. Such a focus on the emotional and symbolic is clearly the case in criminal justice, where various fears and passions inform how people evaluate decisions about security, policing, and punishment. In recent years we have seen a degree of irrationality in the vocalization of fairly reactionary sentiments about issues of criminal justice among segments of the public. In the face of a largely impenetrable mass of knowledge, and the difficulties in evaluating competing expert opinions and interpretations, individuals rely on personal and cultural factors to make decisions. Culture, the shared meanings of a group, works much like expertise in that it helps reduce complexity in decision making. People turn to 'common sense' and long-standing practice for guidance about how to proceed. Interestingly, it was precisely the biases of such belief systems that the production of official governmental knowledge historically aimed to thwart. The irony is that the epistemological tools for rational decision making have proliferated at such a pace that most citizens have little recourse except to rely on emotional, ideological, and cultural discriminations to decide among proper courses of action on matters pertaining to criminal justice.

Such public tendencies would be less disconcerting if those charged with policy development were themselves committed to a rationalist approach. The past two decades, however, have seen a political retreat from rational forms of criminal-justice policy development. The causes of this trend at the party-political level are more related to political expedience than to the increased quantity of knowledge. Politicians have the advantage of having an array of experts at their disposal to make sense of developments in crime and criminal justice. Furthermore, they have the resources, staff, and time to allow for reasoned reflection on various expert opinions. Nevertheless, it has become a matter of political expediency in recent years to push for more retributive and symbolic forms of criminal-justice policy. Thus, it has reached the point that there is a disconnection between the policy advice advanced by criminologists, those individuals who are often the most intimately aware of statistical trends in criminal justice, and these more sensational and retributive criminal-justice policies (Garland and Sparks

2000; Brodeur 1998). In the 1970s, as the issue of crime became increasingly politicized, a 'race to the bottom' commenced, where politicians clamoured over one another to offer the most harsh and reactionary criminal-justice policies. This process has been particularly marked in the United States, but continues to have spillover effects in the United Kingdom and Canada.

What is interesting about such developments for our purposes is how they go against the accepted wisdom of most criminologists. Indeed, it would be difficult to find a critical mass of criminologists who advocate the wisdom or rationality of some of the most important and high-profile criminal-justice policies of the past two decades. The 'three-strikes' laws, extensive prison-building programs, prisoner chain-gangs, reintroduction of capital punishment in several American states, expanded police powers of stop and search, warehousing of prisoners, militarization of policing, boot camps, and an intensified war on drugs all seem to have developed in opposition to the main currents of criminological thought. Such policies appeal to what Bottoms (1995) has referred to as 'popular punitiveness.' This amounts to a political attempt to tap into, and exploit, public insecurities that are more attributable to the late-modern breakdown of a host of other social security systems than to the explicit risk of criminal victimization. In the process, criminal-justice priorities have moved from an attempt to develop policies rationally to more visceral and ideological 'get tough' posturing. As Bauman (2000: 215) observes, today 'the spectacularity – the versatility, harshness and promptness of punishing operations matter more than their effectiveness, which – given the endemic listlessness of public attention and short life-span of public memory – is seldom tested anyway. It even matters more than the actual volume of detected and reported crimes.'

However, it is not entirely accurate to say that there has been a complete evacuation of rationalist criminological approaches. Instead, it is more appropriate to think in terms of Max Weber's (1978) ideal-type division between formal rationality and substantive rationality. For Weber, formal rationality is singularly concerned with the most efficient means to accomplish a particular task, in contrast to substantive rationality, which has a broader focus on the value of the goals themselves. Increasingly, where the state and corporate interests now tend to engage with criminological expertise, it is in its most formally rational manifestations. This strand of criminology emphasizes how to do familiar things better, where 'better' involves questions of efficiency and doing more with less. What we witness in the process is the further entrenchment of programs singularly concerned with the monitoring of people and places, managing the flows of accused, inmates, and parolees, and further opening everyone's life up to surveillance (Haggerty and Ericson 2000). In the name of political expediency, policy-relevant criminological expertise becomes profoundly narrowed to focus on solving a host of officially defined problems, but loses its broad agenda-setting role. The criminologist's role as 'legislator' (Bauman 1992), concerned with shaping the direction of policy, cedes to a technical-rational emphasis on efficient 'crime busting.'

These developments have implications for the role that institutions such as the CCJS will serve in governance and public culture. Since their inception, institutions that produce criminal-justice statistics have been situated at the intersection of rationality and political expediency. On the one hand, they are an icon of rationality, designed to thwart forms of ignorance and bias, and to assist in the level-headed development of policy. At the same time, the statistical knowledge they produce can be approached not as science, but as a language that offers opportunities for persuasive rhetoric. The numbers that come out of these locations can be cynically manipulated in ways that most citizens neither understand nor have the time to investigate. These rationalist and rhetorical elements of statistical knowledge are simultaneously interwoven in a site such as the CCJS. Historically, it has been presumed that rhetoric would ultimately be thwarted by truth, as represented by the rational use of criminal-justice statistics. However, the trends over the past decades should give us pause to consider whether the scales might not be shifting.

The sheer volume of knowledge about criminal-justice issues, combined with a turning away from the rationality of criminological thought on policy development towards forms of 'popular punitiveness,' would indicate that the role of rational evidence as exemplified by official statistics is increasingly taking a back seat to emotion, rhetoric, and political symbolism. Although there will undoubtedly continue to be a role for agencies such as the Canadian Centre for Justice Statistics, it is possible that they will increasingly be approached not as resources for data that can assist rational policy development, but as sources for data to be invoked in support of narrowly technicist crime-fighting endeavours or as a justification for broadly symbolic or even reactionary policies.

References

Abbott, A. 1988. *The System of Professions: An Essay on the Division of Expert Labor*. Chicago: University of Chicago Press

Ackroyd, S., et al. 1992. *New Technology and Practical Police Work: The Social Context of Technical Innovation*. Buckingham, Eng.: Open University Press

Alberta. 1991. *Justice on Trial: Report of the Task Force on the Criminal Justice System and Its Impact on the Indian and Métis People of Alberta*. Edmonton, Alta.: The Task Force

Anderson, B. 1991. *Imagined Communities*. 2nd ed. London: Routledge

Anderson, M., and S. Fienberg. 1999. *Who Counts? The Politics of Census-Taking in Contemporary America*. New York: Russell Sage Foundation

Baer, J., and W. Chambliss. 1997. 'Generating Fear: The Politics of Crime Reporting.' *Crime, Law and Social Change* 27: 87–108

Barry, A., T. Osborne, and N. Rose, eds. 1996. *Foucault and Political Reason*. Chicago: University of Chicago Press

Bauman, Z. 1992. *Intimations of Postmodernity*. London: Routledge

– 2000. 'Social Issues of Law and Order.' *British Journal of Criminology* 40: 205–21

Bazerman, C. 1983. 'Scientific Writing as a Social Act.' In P. Anderson, J. Brockmann, and C. Miller, eds, *New Essays in Technical and Scientific Communication*, 156–84. Farmingdale, NY: Baywood

Beirne, P. 1993. *Inventing Criminology: Essays in the Rise of 'Homo Criminalis.'* New York: SUNY

Bell, D. 1973. *The Coming of Post-Industrial Society*. New York: Basic

Berkhofer, R. 1978. *The White Man's Indian: Images of the American Indian from Columbus to the Present*. New York: Knopf

Best, J. 1989. 'Dark Figures and Child Victims: Statistical Claims about Missing Children.' In J. Best, ed., *Images of Issues: Typifying Contemporary Social Problems*, 21–37. New York: Aldine de Gruyter

Booth, H. 1985. 'Which "Ethnic Question"? The Development of Questions Identifying Ethnic Origin in Official Statistics.' *Sociological Review* 33: 254–74

Bottoms, A. 1995. 'The Philosophy and Politics of Punishment and Sentencing.' In C. Clarkson and R. Morgan, eds, *The Politics of Sentencing Reform*, 17–49. Oxford: Clarendon

Bourdieu, P. 1991. *Language and Symbolic Power*. Cambridge, Mass.: Harvard University Press

– 1993. *The Field of Cultural Production*. Cambridge, Eng.: Polity

– 1994. 'Rethinking the State: Genesis and Structure of the Bureaucratic Field.' *Sociological Theory* 12: 1–18

– 1996. 'On the Family as a Realized Category.' *Theory, Culture & Society* 13: 19–26

Brodeur, J.P. 1998. 'Expertise Not Wanted.' Paper to the Max Plank Institute, Schloessman Seminar on The Expert in Modern Societies: Historical and Contemporary Perspectives. Stuttgart, Germany

Burchell, G., C. Gordon, and P. Miller, eds, 1991. *The Foucault Effect: Studies in Governmentality*. Chicago: University of Chicago Press

Burnham, D. 1997. *Above the Law: Secret Deals, Political Fixes and Other Misadventures of the U.S. Department of Justice*. New York: Scribner

Callon, M. 1986. 'Some Elements of a Sociology of Translation: Domestication of the Scallops and Fishermen of St. Brieuc Bay.' In M. Callon, J. Law, and A. Rip, eds, *Power, Action and Belief*, 196–233. London: Routledge and Kegan Paul

Callon, M., and B. Latour. 1992. 'Don't Throw the Baby Out with the Bath School!' In A Pickering, ed., *Science as Practice and Culture*, 343–68. Chicago: University of Chicago Press

Castel, R. 1991. 'From Dangerousness to Risk.' In G. Burchell, C. Gordon, and P. Miller, eds, *The Foucault Effect: Studies in Governmentality*, 281–98. Chicago: University of Chicago Press

CCJS (Canadian Centre for Justice Statistics). 1990a. *The Future of Crime Statistics from the UCR Survey*. Ottawa: Statistics Canada

– 1990b. *The Development of Data Quality Assessment Procedures for the Uniform Crime Reporting Survey: A Case Study of Calgary-Edmonton*. Canadian Centre for Justice Statistics, Law Enforcement Program. Ottawa: Statistics Canada

– 1993. *'Aboriginal Origin' Variable in Justice Services: Summary of Recommendations*

– 1995. 'Memorandum: Aboriginal Data Consultations.' Ottawa: Canadian Centre for Justice Statistics

– 1996. *The Collection of Data on Aboriginal Persons: Phase 1 Report*. September

– n.d. *Determining the Criminal Justice Information Needs of Aboriginal Groups: Background Documentation*

Christopoulos, G. 1994. 'Hogwash! Top Cop Brands Crime Stat's "Out of Touch with Reality,"' *Toronto Sun*, 24 August: 4

Chubin, D., and E. Hackett. 1990. *Peerless Science: Peer Review and U.S. Science Policy*. New York: SUNY

Cicourel, A. 1965. *Method and Measurement in Sociology*. New York: The Free Press

– 1968. *The Social Organization of Juvenile Justice*. New York: Wiley

Cohen, P. 1982. *A Calculating People: The Spread of Numeracy in Early America*. Chicago: University of Chicago Press

Cohen, S. 1985. *Visions of Social Control: Crime, Punishment and Classification*. Cambridgeshire: Polity

Coleman, C., and J. Moynihan. 1996. *Understanding Crime Data: Haunted by the Dark Figure*. Buckingham, Philadelphia: Open University Press

Collins, H., and S. Yearley. 1992. 'Epistemological Chicken.' In A. Pickering, ed., *Science as Practice and Culture*, 301–26. Chicago: University of Chicago Press

Commission on Systemic Racism in the Ontario Criminal Justice System. 1995. *Report of the Commission on Systemic Racism in the Ontario Criminal Justice System*. Toronto: Queen's Printer for Ontario

Conk, M. 1987. 'The 1980 Census in Historical Perspective.' In W. Alonso and P. Starr, eds, *The Politics of Numbers*, 155–86. New York: Russell Sage

Cooper, R. 1992. 'Formal Organisations as Representation: Remote Control, Displacement and Abbreviation.' In M. Reed and M. Hughes, eds, *Rethinking Organisation: New Directions in Organisation Theory and Analysis*, 254–72. London: Sage

Coull, J. 1995. *Data Quality Review of the Incident Based Uniform Crime Reporting Survey*. Ottawa: Statistics Canada

Crosby, A. 1997. *The Measure of Reality: Quantification and Western Society, 1250–1600*. Cambridge: Cambridge University Press

Cumming, E., I. Cumming, and L. Edell. 1965. 'Policeman as Philosopher, Guide and Friend.' *Social Problems* 12: 276–86

The Daily (Statistics Canada). 1993. 'The Violence Against Women Survey.' 18 November

Daston, L. 1992. 'Objectivity and the Escape from Perspective.' *Social Studies of Science* 22: 597–618

Davis, M. 1990. *City of Quartz: Excavating the Future in Los Angeles*. London: Verso

Dean, M. 1999. *Governmentality: Power and Rule in Modern Society*. Thousand Oaks, Calif.: Sage.

Deflem, M. 1997. 'Surveillance and Criminal Statistics: Historical Foundations of Governmentality.' *Studies in Law, Politics and Society* 17: 149–84

DeKeseredy, W., and K. Kelly. 1993. 'The Incidence and Prevalence of Women Abuse in Canadian University and College Dating Relationships.' *Canadian Journal of Sociology* 18: 137–59

Deleuze, G., and P. Guattari. 1987. *A Thousand Plateaus: Capitalism and Schizophrenia*. Minneapolis: University of Minnesota Press

Desrosières, A. 1990. 'How to Make Things Which Hold Together: Social Science, Statistics and the State.' In P. Wagner, B. Wittcock, and R. Whitley, eds, *Discourses on Society: The Shaping of the Social Science Disciplines*. Dordrecht: Kluwer Academic Publishers

Donzelot, J. 1979. *The Policing of Families*. London: Hutchinson

Doob, A. 1991. *Workshop on Collecting Race and Ethnicity Statistics in the Criminal Justice System*. Toronto: University of Toronto Centre of Criminology

– 1993. *Understanding Crime and Criminal Justice Statistics: Examining the Reports of the Canadian Centre for Justice Statistics*. Ottawa: CCJS

– 1995. 'Understanding the Attacks on Statistics Canada's Violence Against Women Survey.' In M. Valverde, L. MacLeod, and K. Johnson, eds, *Wife Assault and the Canadian Criminal Justice System*, 157–65. Toronto: University of Toronto Centre of Criminology

Douglas, J. 1967. *The Social Meanings of Suicide*. Princeton: Princeton University Press

Douglas, J., ed. 1970. *Understanding Everyday Life: Toward the Reconstruction of Sociological Knowledge*. Chicago: Aldine

Doyle, A., and R. Ericson. 1996. 'Breaking into Prison: News Sources and Correctional Institutions.' *Canadian Journal of Criminology* 38: 155–90

Durant, M., M. Thomas, and H. Willock. 1972. *Crime, Criminals and the Law*. London: Office of Population Censuses and Surveys

Durkheim, E. 1938. 'The Normal and the Pathological.' In *The Rules of Sociological Method*, 47–75. London: The Free Press of Glencoe

– 1951. *Suicide*. New York: The Free Press

Elliott, D. 1994. *Law and Aboriginal Peoples of Canada*. 2nd ed. North York, Ont.: Captus

Emery, G. 1993. *Facts of Life: The Social Construction of Vital Statistics, Ontario 1896–1952*. Montreal, Kingston: McGill-Queen's University Press

Ericson, R. 1981. *Making Crime: A Study of Detective Work*. Toronto: Butterworths

– 1982. *Reproducing Order: A Study of Police Patrol Work*. Toronto: University of Toronto Press

– 1994. 'An Institutional Perspective on News Media Access and Control.' In M. Aldridge and N. Hewitt, eds, *Controlling Broadcasting*, 109–33. Manchester: University of Manchester Press

Ericson, R., P. Baranek, and J. Chan. 1987. *Visualizing Deviance: A Study of News Sources*. Toronto: University of Toronto Press
– 1989. *Negotiating Control: A Study of News Sources*. Toronto: University of Toronto Press
– 1991. *Representing Order*. Toronto: University of Toronto Press
Ericson, R., and K. Haggerty. 1997. *Policing the Risk Society*. Toronto: University of Toronto Press and Oxford: Oxford University Press
Feeley, M., and J. Simon. 1994. 'Actuarial Justice: The Emerging New Criminal Law.' In D. Nelken, ed., *The Futures of Criminology*, 173–201. London: Sage
Fekete, J. 1994. *Moral Panic: Biopolitics Rising*. Montreal: Robert Davies Publishing
Feyerabend, P. 1993. *Against Method*. 3rd ed. London: Verso
Fishman, M. 1980. *Manufacturing the News*. Austin: University of Texas Press
Fong, P., and G. Bellett. 1997. 'Vancouver Police Chief Vows to Cut Crime 69 Per Cent.' *Vancouver Sun*, 25 September: A1
Foucault, M. 1970. *The Order of Things: An Archaeology of the Human Sciences*. New York: Vintage
– 1972. 'The Discourse on Language.' In *The Archaeology of Knowledge*, 215–37. New York: Pantheon
– 1977. *Discipline and Punish: The Birth of the Prison*. New York: Vintage
– 1978. *The History of Sexuality Vol. I: An Introduction*. New York: Vintage
– 1980. 'Truth and Power.' In *Power/Knowledge: Selected Interviews and Other Writings, 1972–1977*, 109–33. New York: Pantheon
– 1991. 'Governmentality.' In G. Burchell, C. Gordon, and P. Miller, eds, *The Foucault Effect: Studies in Governmentality*, 87–104. Chicago: University of Chicago Press
– 1997. 'Security, Territory, and Population.' In *Foucault: Ethics, Subjectivity and Truth*, 67–71. New York: The New Press
Fox, B. 1993. 'On Violent Men and Female Victims: A Comment on DeKeseredy and Kelly.' *Canadian Journal of Sociology* 18: 321–24
Freidson, E. 1986. *Professional Powers: A Study in the Institutionalization of Formal Knowledge*. Chicago: University of Chicago Press
Frideres, J. 1998. *Aboriginal People in Canada*. 5th ed. Scarborough, Ont.: Prentice Hall Allym and Bacon
Fuchs, S., and S. Ward. 1994. 'What Is Deconstruction and Where and When Does It Take Place?: Making Facts in Science, Building Cases in Law.' *American Sociological Review* 59: 481–500
Gabor, T. 1994. 'The Suppression of Crime Statistics on Race and Ethnicity: The Price of Political Correctness.' *Canadian Journal of Criminology* 36: 153–63

Gandy, O. 1993. *The Panoptic Sort: A Political Economy of Personal Information.* Boulder: Westview

Garfinkel, H. 1963. 'A Conception of and Experiment with "Trust" as a Condition of Stable Concerted Action.' In O. Harvey, ed., *Motivation and Social Interaction: Cognitive Determinants*, 187–238. New York: The Ronald Press

Garland, D. 1997. '"Governmentality" and the Problem of Crime: Foucault, Criminology, Sociology.' *Theoretical Criminology* 1: 171–214

Garland, D., and R. Sparks. 2000. 'Criminology, Social Theory and the Challenge of Our Times.' *British Journal of Criminology* 40: 189–204

Giddens, A. 1991. *The Consequences of Modernity.* Stanford: Stanford University Press

Gieryn, T. 1995. 'Boundaries of Science.' In S. Jasanoff, et al., eds, *Handbook of Science and Technology Studies*, 393–443. London: Sage

Gigerenzer, G., Z. Swijtink, T. Porter, L. Daston, J. Beatty, and L. Kruger. 1989. *The Empire of Chance: How Probability Changed Science and Everyday Life.* Cambridge: Cambridge University Press

Gilbert, N., and M. Mulkay. 1984. *Opening Pandora's Box: A Sociological Analysis of Scientists' Discourse.* Cambridge: Cambridge University Press

Goldberg, D. 1997. *Racial Subjects: Writing on Race in America.* London: Routledge

Gordon, C. 1991. 'Government Rationality: An Introduction.' In G. Burchell, C. Gordon, and P. Miller, eds, *The Foucault Effect: Studies in Governmentality*, 1–51. Chicago: University of Chicago Press

Gould, S.J. 1983. 'What, If Anything, Is a Zebra?' In *Hen's Teeth and Horse's Toes*, 355–65. New York: Norton

– 1996. *The Mismeasure of Man.* 2nd ed. New York: W.W. Norton & Co.

Government Statisticians' Collective. 1979. 'How Official Statistics Are Produced: Views from the Inside.' In J. Irvine, I. Miles, and J. Evans, eds, *Demystifying Social Statistics*, 130–51. London: Pluto

Govier, T. 1997. *Social Trust and Human Communities.* Montreal, Kingston: McGill-Queen's University Press

Grainger, B. 1996. 'Data and Methodology in the Area of Criminal Justice.' In L. Kennedy and V. Sacco, eds, *Crime Counts: A Criminal Event Analysis*, 21–39. Toronto: Nelson

Greenhouse, L. 1996. 'High Court Rules Results Are Valid in Census of 1990.' *New York Times*, 21 March: A1

Griffiths, C., and S. Verdun-Jones. 1994. *Canadian Criminal Justice.* 2nd ed. Toronto: Harcourt Brace

Gross, A. 1996. *The Rhetoric of Science.* Cambridge, Mass.: Harvard University Press

Gusfield, J. 1976. 'The Literary Rhetoric of Science.' *American Sociological Review* 41: 16–34
– 1989. 'Constructing the Ownership of Social Problems: Fun and Profit in the Welfare State.' *Social Problems* 36: 431–41
Hacking, I. 1986. 'Making Up People.' In T.C. Heller, M. Sosna, and D.E. Wellbery, eds, *Reconstructing Individualism*, 222–36. Stanford: Stanford University Press
– 1990. *The Taming of Chance*. Cambridge: Cambridge University Press
– 1991. 'How Should We Do the History of Statistics?' In G. Burchell, C. Gordon, and P. Miller, eds, *The Foucault Effect: Studies in Governmentality*, 181–95. Chicago: University of Chicago Press
– 1995a. *Rewriting the Soul: Multiple Personality and the Sciences of Memory*. Princeton: Princeton University Press
– 1995b. 'The Looping Effects of Human Kinds.' In D. Sperber, D. Premack, and A. Premack, eds, *Causal Cognition: A Multidisciplinary Debate*, 351–83. Oxford: Clarendon
– 1997. 'Taking Bad Arguments Seriously.' *London Review of Books*. 21 August
– 1999. *The Social Construction of What?* Cambridge, Mass.: Harvard University Press
Haggerty, K., and R. Ericson. 2000. 'The Surveillant Assemblage.' *British Journal of Sociology* 51: 605–22
Hall, S., C. Critcher, T. Jefferson, J. Clarke, and B. Roberts. 1978. *Policing the Crisis*. London: Macmillan
Hilgartner, S., and C. Bosk. 1988. 'The Rise and Fall of Social Problems: A Public Arenas Model.' *American Journal of Sociology* 94: 53–78
Hindelang, M. 1976. *Criminal Victimisation in Eight American Cities*. Cambridge, Mass.: Ballinger
Hindess, B. 1973. *The Use of Official Statistics in Sociology*. London: Macmillan
Home Office. 1996. 'Race and the Criminal Justice System.' London: HMSO
Huff, D. 1955. *How to Lie with Statistics*. London: Gallancz
Hunt, A. 1996. 'The Governance of Consumption: Sumptuary Laws and Shifting Forms of Regulation.' *Economy and Society* 25: 410–27
Hunt, A., and G. Wickham. 1994. *Foucault and Law: Towards a Sociology of Law as Governance*. London: Pluto
IWG. 1981. *Report of the Implementation Work Group on Justice Statistics: Towards the Establishment of the Canadian Centre for Justice Statistics*. Ottawa: Statistics Canada
James, W. 1997. 'Pragmatism's Conception of Truth.' In L. Menand, ed., *Pragmatism: A Reader*, 112–31. New York: Vintage
Jasanoff, S. 1990. *The Fifth Branch: Science Advisors as Policymakers*. Cambridge, Mass.: Harvard University Press

– 1995. *Science at the Bar*. Cambridge, Mass.: Harvard University Press

Jenkins, R. 1997. *Rethinking Ethnicity*. London: Sage

Johnson, H. 1994. 'The Reality of Violence against Women.' *Globe and Mail*, 19 December: A23

– 1996. 'Violent Crime in Canada.' *Juristat* 16(6)

Johnson, T. 1993. 'Expertise and the State.' In M. Gane and T. Johnson, eds, *Foucault's New Domains*, 139–52. London: Routledge

Jones, T., B. McLean, and J. Young. 1986. *The Islington Crime Survey*. Aldershot: Gower

Kendall, D. 1989. 'Lastman Blasts Race Committee.' *Toronto Sun*, 23 February

Kingsley, B. 1996. 'Assault.' In L. Kennedy and V. Sacco, eds, *Crime Counts: A Criminal Event Analysis*, 99–113. Toronto: Nelson

Kinsey, R., J. Lea, and J. Young. 1986. *Losing the Fight against Crime*. Oxford: Basil Blackwell

Kitsuse, J., and A. Cicourel. 1963. 'A Note on the Uses of Official Statistics.' *Social Problems* 11: 131–9

Knepper, P. 1996. 'Race, Racism and Crime Statistics.' *Southern University Law Review* 24: 74–112

Knorr-Cetina, K. 1992. 'The Couch, the Cathedral, and the Laboratory: On the Relationship between Experiment and Laboratory in Science.' In A. Pickering, ed., *Science as Practice and Culture*, 113–38. Chicago: University of Chicago Press

– 1995. 'Laboratory Studies: The Cultural Approach to the Study of Science.' In S. Jasanoff, et al., eds, *Handbook of Science and Technology Studies*, 140–66. London: Sage

Kong, R. 1999. 'Canadian Crime Statistics, 1997.' In *The Juristat Reader*. Toronto: Thompson Educational

Kuhn, T. 1962. *The Structure of Scientific Revolutions*. Chicago: University of Chicago Press

Kula, W. 1986. *Measures and Men*. Princeton: Princeton University Press

Lakoff, G. 1987. *Women, Fire and Dangerous Things: What Categories Reveal about the Mind*. Chicago: University of Chicago Press

Lardner, J. 1997. 'Can You Believe the New York Miracle?' *New York Review of Books*, 14 August: 54–8

Latour, B. 1983. 'Give Me a Laboratory and I Will Raise the World!' In K. Knorr-Cetina and M. Mulkay, eds, *Science Observed*, 140–70. London: Sage

– 1987. *Science in Action: How to Follow Scientists and Engineers through Society*. Cambridge, Mass.: Harvard University Press

– 1988. *The Pasteurization of France*. Cambridge, Mass.: Harvard University Press

- 1993. *We Have Never Been Modern*. Cambridge, Mass.: Harvard University Press
- 1999. *Pandora's Hope: Essays on the Reality of Science Studies*. Cambridge, Mass.: Harvard University Press

Latour, B., and S. Woolgar. 1979. *Laboratory Life: The Social Construction of Scientific Facts*. Beverly Hills: Sage

Law, J. 1987. 'Technology as Heterogeneous Engineering: The Case of the Portuguese Expansion.' In W. Bijker, T. Hughes, and T. Pinch, eds, *The Social Construction of Technical Systems: New Directions in the Sociology and History of Technology*, 111–34. Cambridge, Mass.: MIT

- 1991. 'Power, Discretion and Strategy.' In J. Law, ed., *A Sociology of Monsters: Essays on Power, Technology and Domination*, 165–91. London: Routledge
- 1992. 'Notes on the Theory of the Actor-Network.' *Systems Practice* 5: 379–93

Leadbeatter, A. 1996. 'Confession of Ignorance of Causation in Coroners' Necropsies – A Common Problem?' *Journal of Clinical Pathology* 49: 439–43

Longino, H. 1990. *Science as a Social Process*. Princeton: Princeton University Press

Luhmann, N. 1979. *Trust and Power*. Chichester: Wiley

- 1988. 'Familiarity, Confidence, Trust: Problems and Alternatives.' In D. Gambetta, ed., *Trust: Making and Breaking Co-operative Relations*, 41–63. Oxford: Basil Blackwell

Lundsgaarde, H. 1977. *Crime in Space City: A Cultural Analysis of Houston Homicide Patterns*. New York: Oxford University Press

Machiavelli, N. 1966. *The Prince*. Toronto: Bantam

MacKenzie, D. 1981. *Statistics in Britain, 1865–1930: The Social Construction of Scientific Knowledge*. Edinburgh: Edinburgh University Press

Maltz, M. 1977. 'Crime Statistics: A Historical Perspective.' *Crime and Delinquency* 23: 32–40

Manitoba. 1991. *Report of the Aboriginal Justice Inquiry of Manitoba*. Winnipeg: The Inquiry

Manning, P. 1992. 'Information Technologies and the Police.' In M. Tonry and N. Morris, eds, *Modern Policing*, 349–98. Chicago: University of Chicago Press

Martin, M., and L. Ogrodnik. 1996. 'Canadian Crime Trends.' In L. Kennedy and V. Sacco, eds, *Crime Counts: A Criminal Events Analysis*, 43–58. Toronto: Nelson

Mayhew, P., C. Mirrlees-Black, and N. Aye Maung. 1994. *Trends in Crime: Findings from the 1994 British Crime Survey*. Home Office Research Findings no. 14. London: HMSO

Medewar, P. 1963. 'Is the Scientific Paper a Fraud?' *The Listener*, 12 September: 377–8

Merton, R. 1973a. 'The Normative Structure of Science.' In *The Sociology of Science*, 267–78. Chicago: University of Chicago Press

– 1973b. 'The Matthew Effect in Science.' In *The Sociology of Science*, 439–59. Chicago: University of Chicago Press

Miles, I., and J. Irvine. 1979. 'The Critique of Official Statistics.' In J. Irvine, I. Miles, and J. Evans, eds, *Demystifying Social Statistics*, 113–29. London: Pluto

Miller, J. 1996. *Search and Destroy: African-American Males in the Criminal Justice System*. New York: Cambridge University Press

Miller, P. 1994. 'Accounting and Objectivity: The Invention of Calculating Selves and Calculable Spaces.' In A. Megill, ed., *Rethinking Objectivity*, 239–64. Durham: Duke University Press

Miller, P., and T. O'Leary. 1994. 'The Factory as Laboratory.' *Science in Context* 7: 469–96

Misztal, B. 1996. *Trust in Modern Societies*. Cambridge, Mass.: Polity

Murdoch, J. 1995. 'Actor-Networks and the Evolution of Economic Forms: Combining Description and Explanation in Theories of Regulation, Flexible Specialization, and Networks.' *Environment and Planning A* 27: 731–57

Nelkin, D., and S. Lindee. 1995. *The DNA Mystique: The Gene as a Cultural Icon*. New York: W.H. Freeman

Nettler, G. 1974. *Explaining Crime*. New York: McGraw-Hill

Nietzsche, F. 1974. *The Gay Science*. New York: Vintage

Nock, S. 1993. *The Costs of Privacy: Surveillance and Reputation in America*. New York: Aldine de Gruyter

NPRC. 1980. *The Future of National Justice Statistics and Information in Canada: Report of the National Project on Resource Coordination for Justice Statistics and Information, Volume 1*. Ottawa: Statistics Canada

O'Malley, P. 1992. 'Risk, Power and Crime Prevention.' *Economy and Society* 21: 252–75

– 1996. 'Risk and Responsibility.' In A. Barry, T. Osborne, and N. Rose, eds, *Foucault and Political Reason: Liberalism, Neo-Liberalism and Rationalities of Government*, 189–207. Chicago: University of Chicago Press

Orcutt, J., and J. Turner. 1993. 'Shocking Numbers and Graphic Accounts: Quantified Images of Drug Problems in the Print Media.' *Social Problems* 40: 190–206

Pasquino, P. 1991. 'Theatrum Politicum: The Genealogy of Capital – Police and the State of Prosperity.' In G. Burchell, C. Gordon, and P. Miller, eds,

The Foucault Effect: Studies in Governmentality, 105–18. Chicago: University of Chicago Press

Paulos, J. 1988. *Innumeracy: Mathematical Illiteracy and Its Consequences*. New York: Hill and Wang

– 1995. *A Mathematician Reads the Newspaper*. New York: Anchor

Perrow, C. 1984. *Normal Accidents: Living with High-Risk Technologies*. New York: Basic Books

Petersen, W. 1987. 'Politics and the Measurement of Ethnicity.' In W. Alonso and P. Starr, eds, *The Politics of Numbers*, 187–233. New York: Russell Sage

Porter, T. 1995. *Trust in Numbers: The Pursuit of Objectivity in Science and Public Life*. Princeton: Princeton University Press

Power, M. 1996. 'Making Things Auditable.' *Accounting, Organisations and Society* 21: 298–315

Quann, N., and S. Trevethan. 2000. *Police Reported Aboriginal Crime in Saskatchewan*. Ottawa: Canadian Centre for Justice Statistics

Reichman, N. 1986. 'Managing Crime Risks: Towards an Insurance Based Model of Social Control.' *Research in Law, Deviance and Social Control* 8: 151–72

Revised UCR Documentation. 1991. Ottawa: Canadian Centre for Justice Statistics

Ritzer, G. 1995. *Expressing America: A Critique of the Global Credit Card Society*. Thousand Oaks, Calif.: Pine Forge Press

Roberts, J. 1994. 'Crime and Race Statistics: Toward a Canadian Solution.' *Canadian Journal of Criminology* 36: 175–85

Roberts, J., and A. Doob. 1997. 'Race, Ethnicity, and Criminal Justice in Canada.' *Crime and Justice* 21: 469–522

Roberts, J., and T. Gabor. 1990. 'Lombrosian Wine in a New Bottle: Research on Crime and Race.' *Canadian Journal of Criminology* 32: 291–313

Rock, P. 1986. *A View from the Shadows: The Ministry of the Solicitor General of Canada and the Making of the Justice for Victims of Crime Initiative*. Oxford: Clarendon

Rorty, R. 1989. 'The Contingency of Language.' In *Contingency, Irony, and Solidarity*, 3–22. Cambridge: Cambridge University Press

– 1997. 'Philosophy as a Kind of Writing: An Essay on Derrida.' In L. Menand, ed., *Pragmatism: A Reader*, 304–28. New York: Vintage

Rose, N. 1991. 'Governing by Numbers: Figuring Out Democracy.' *Accounting, Organization and Society* 16: 673–92

– 1993. 'Government, Authority and Expertise in Advanced Liberalism.' *Economy and Society* 22: 283–99

– 1996. 'Governing "Advanced" Liberal Democracies.' In A. Barry, T. Osborne, and N. Rose, eds, *Foucault and Political Reason: Liberalism, Neo-Liberalism and Rationalities of Government*, 37–64. Chicago: University of Chicago Press

– 1999. *Powers of Freedom: Reframing Political Thought*. Cambridge: Cambridge University Press

Rose, N., and P. Miller. 1992. 'Political Power Beyond the State: Problematics of Government.' *British Journal of Sociology* 43: 173–205

Rouse, J. 1987. *Knowledge and Power: Toward a Political Philosophy of Science*. Ithaca: Cornell University Press

– 1993. 'Foucault and the Natural Sciences.' In J. Caputo and M. Yount, eds, *Foucault and the Critique of Institutions*, 137–62. Pennsylvania: Pennsylvania State University

Rueschemeyer, D. 1986. *Power and the Division of Labour*. Stanford: Stanford University Press

Rushton, P. 1988. 'Race Differences in Behaviour: A Review and Evolutionary Analysis.' *Personality and Individual Differences* 9: 1009–24

– 1990. 'Race and Crime: A Reply to Roberts and Gabor.' *Canadian Journal of Criminology* 32: 315–34

Rusnock, A. 1995. 'Quantification, Precision, and Accuracy: Determinations of Population in the Ancien Régime.' In N. Wise, ed., *The Values of Precision*, 17–38. Princeton: Princeton University Press

Sacco, V. 1998. 'Crime News That Counts: Newspaper Images of Crime Statistics.' Paper presented to the Annual Meetings of the American Society of Criminology, Washington, DC.

Said, E. 1978. *Orientalism*. New York: Vintage

Saskatchewan. 1992. *Report of the Saskatchewan Indian Justice Review Committee*. Canada: The Committee

Schlesinger, P., and H. Tumber 1994. *Reporting Crime: The Media Politics of Criminal Justice*. Oxford: Clarendon

Schlesinger, P., H. Tumber, and G. Murdock. 1991. 'The Media Politics of Crime and Criminal Justice.' *British Journal of Sociology* 42: 397–420

Schiller, H. 1996. *Information Inequality*. New York: Routledge

Selzer, J., ed. 1993. *Understanding Scientific Prose*. Wisconsin: University of Wisconsin Press

Shapin, S. 1994. *A Social History of Truth: Civility and Science in Seventeenth Century England*. Chicago: University of Chicago Press

– 1996. *The Scientific Revolution*. Chicago: University of Chicago Press

Shearing, C., and P. Stenning. 1983. 'Private Security: Implications for Social Control.' *Social Problems* 30: 493–506

Simmel, G. 1950. *The Sociology of Georg Simmel*. London: The Free Press

Simons, H., ed. 1989. *Rhetoric in the Human Sciences*. London: Sage

Smith, D. 1990. 'The Statistics on Women and Mental Illness.' In *The Conceptual Practices of Power: A Feminist Sociology of Knowledge*, 107–38. Toronto: University of Toronto Press

Smith, R. 1989. 'Forensic Pathology, Scientific Expertise and the Criminal Law.' In R. Smith and B. Wynne, eds, *Expert Evidence: Interpreting Science in the Law*, 56–92. London: Routledge

Soulé, M., and G. Lease, eds. 1995. *Reinventing Nature?* Washington: Island Press

South, N. 1987. 'The Security and Surveillance of the Environment.' In J. Lowman, R. Menzies, and T. Palys, eds, *Transcarceration: Essays in the Sociology of Social Control*, 139–52. Aldershot: Gower

– 1988. *Policing for Profit: The Private Security Sector*. London: Sage

Stamp, J. 1929. *Some Economic Factors in Modern Life*. London: P.S. King and Son

Starr, P. 1987. 'The Sociology of Official Statistics.' In W. Alonso and P. Starr, eds, *The Politics of Numbers*, 7–57. New York: Russell Sage Foundation

– 1992. 'Social Categories and Claims in the Liberal State.' *Social Research* 59: 263–95

Statistics Canada. 1993. *75 Years and Counting: A History of Statistics Canada*. Ottawa: Statistics Canada

Stehr, N. 1994. *Knowledge Societies*. London: Sage

Stenson, K. 1998. 'Beyond Histories of the Present.' *Economy and Society* 27: 333–52

Sudnow, D. 1964. 'Normal Crimes: Sociological Features of the Penal Code in a Public Defender Office.' *Social Problems* 12: 255–76

Sumner, C. 1994. *The Sociology of Deviance: An Obituary*. Buckingham, Eng.: Open University Press

Taylor, C. 1996. *Defining Science: A Rhetoric of Demarcation*. Wisconsin: University of Wisconsin Press

Taylor, R., and S. Gottfredson. 1986. 'Environmental Design, Crime, and Prevention: An Examination of Community Dynamics.' *Crime and Justice: A Review of Research* 8: 387–416

Thomson, W. 1889. *Popular Lectures and Addresses, Vol. 1*. London: Macmillan

Thrift, N. 1996. *Spatial Formations*. London: Sage

Tonry, M. 1995. *Malign Neglect: Race, Crime, and Criminal Punishment in America*. New York: Oxford University Press

Turow, J. 1997. *Breaking Up America: Advertisers and the New Media Order*. Chicago: University of Chicago Press

Valverde, M. 1998. *Diseases of the Will: Alcohol and the Dilemmas of Freedom.*
  Cambridge: Cambridge University Press
Verburg, P. 1995. 'Whatever Happened to Statscan?' *Alberta Report* 22(6): 6–9
Violence Against Women Survey. 1993. Ottawa: Statistics Canada
Weber, M. 1978. *Economy and Society.* Ed. G. Roth and C. Wittich. Berkeley:
  University of California Press
West, C. 1993. *Race Matters.* Boston: Beacon
Wright, C., and O. Fedorowycz. 1996. 'Homicide.' In L. Kennedy and
  V. Sacco, eds, *Crime Counts: A Criminal Events Analysis,* 63–84. Toronto:
  Nelson

Index

Abbott, A., 194
aboriginal crime data: as actor network, 113; classification of aboriginals for, 114–22; collection of, 11, 110–22; consultations, 112; as contingent, 121–2; need for, 112; politics of, 113–22; utility of, 119, 120
aboriginal data, proliferation of, 120
aboriginal groups: consultations with, 113, 116–22; diversity of opinion within, 117; Federation of Saskatchewan Indian Nations, 121; statistical training of, 113–14; study fatigue and, 120–1
academics and the CCJS, 173–4
academic studies in CCJS publications, 171–2
Ackroyd, S., 31, 67
actants, 60
actor networks: composed of other networks, 61–2; contingency of, 88; enrolment and, 61; interessement and, 60–1; intermediaries and, 61; race/crime data and, 108–10; studying, 62; translation and, 60–1
actor-network theory: agency and, 62–3; components of, 58–63;

explanatory phenomena and, 59; studies of governance and, 63, 88; truth and, 58–9; use of, 10
actuarial justice, 38, 51
adult corrections, resources, expenditures, and personnel survey, 20
adult corrections survey, 20
adult criminal-court survey, 20
adult and youth corrections key indicator report survey, 20
advisory committees, 21
agency, 62–3
agenda setting, 137–9
alcohol/drug variable, 78–80
alternative measures, 154–5
Anderson, B., 48, 115
Anderson, M., 86, 101
anonymous review, 163–4
Assembly of First Nations, 113–14
assignment, 101
Association of Canadian Court Administrators, 21
authorship: review process and, 163–5; statistical knowledge and, 162–86; of Statistics Canada's publications, 175–6. See also *Juristat* writing